Capital and Karma

The Institute
for Comparative Research
in Human Culture
Oslo

Instituttet for
sammenlignende
kulturforskning

Serie B: Skrifter
XCIX
Øyvind Jaer
Capital and Karma

Øyvind Jaer

Capital and Karma

Hinduism and Capitalism Compared

Orchid Press

The Institute for
Comparative Research
in Human Culture

Øyvind Jaer
CAPITAL AND KARMA
Hinduism and Kapitalism Compared
First published 1998

ISBN 974-8299-02-03

The Institute for Comparative Research in Human Culture
Address: Post office Box 2832 Solli, 0204 Oslo, Norway

Orchid Press
98/13 Soi Apha Phirom, Ratchada Road, Chatuchak,
Bangkok 10900, Thailand

British Library Cataloguing in Publication Data
Data available

Library of Congress Cataloguing in Publication Data
Data available

CONTENTS

PREFACE

Time has come to resume the old aspirations of civilizational studies in a comparative perspective. This was the enterprise of classical sociology, not least by Marx and Weber, who wanted to understand the modern epoch of Liberalism and Capitalism against the background of other civilizations, especially Hinduism. With a heavy debt to classical sociology, this work should be seen as a small contribution to that earlier enterprise, though with a rather opposite intent. The main focus of the comparison is not Capitalism against the background of other civilizations, but Hinduism against the 'inevitable' background of global Capitalism.

Some readers might object, and claim one cannot compare Hinduism with Capitalism, since the first is a system of beliefs and ritual practices, while the other is a socio-economic system. This, however, is only partly correct. Hinduism, though undoubtedly first and foremost a religion, is also the very key institution to organize Hindu society and economy. And Capitalism is not only an economic system, but indeed also a culture - a system of beliefs, ideas, values and practices which together inform the typical modern style of life. Hinduism and Capitalism can both be conceptualized as action systems: the first infused with a religious ethos, the other with pragmatism and economism.

Readers with a more philological orientation might object that the civilizational and comparative approaches of the present work require a level of generalization and abstraction improper to an 'empirical' science like anthropology. However, generalized forms and concepts which they find empty in their own context, might well prove to be rich in content, and provide fertile perspectives in a comparative light. I would in this regard like to endorse the view that the most fruitful feature of anthropological method is not its technique of participant observation, but rather its comparative, generalist approach.

The objective of the present work is to give an anthropological presentation of the Hindu Great Tradition and more specifically to present 'the cultural logic of Brahmanic Hinduism' - *the Logic of Karma* - within a comparative frame of reference - i.e., Classical Capitalism. The aim is to make a contribution to the comparative studies on human cultures. This approach will, hopefully, also prove useful for the field study of any Hindu community since the context of the Great Tradition is an indispensable variable for the description and interpretation of living Hinduism. The present book provides in this regard a framework for a more thorough understanding of my earlier monograph; *Karchana - Lifeworld Ethnography of an Indian Village* (Jaer 1995) which deals with a village community in Eastern Uttar Pradesh.

The source material of the present work is not data generated through anthropological field work, but rather texts of a religious, philosophical and political-economic character. Given the vast corpus of texts which make up the source materials of Hinduism and Capitalism, any given selection said to reflect the cognitive identity of its respective tradition will necessarily lend itself to argument. I have in the case of Hinduism restricted my presentation to Brahmanic Hinduism which represents the typical orthodox high caste view. I have followed famous Indian leaders and nationalists in selecting of the more important canonical texts. Capitalism has no corresponding canonical works. I follow Lukacs (1971), who regards Marx and Weber as the best theoretical entry points for obtaining a holistic and comparative understanding of Capitalism in its classical and 'pure' ideal type form.

I uphold the duality of action/structure as a necessary starting point for any theory of Man and Society. I claim, furthermore, that the conception of the duality of action/structure is a particularly fertile entry point for the understanding and presentation of Hinduism. The apperception of this duality is implicit in the *karma/Dharma* teachings which portray the essence of Hinduism. It is this shared reference point which makes translations and comparisons between Hinduism and Capitalism such a worthwhile endeavour.

ACKNOWLEDGEMENTS

My 'philosophical' fieldwork in India, on which this book is based, was sponsored by three institutions: The Norwegian Council for Science and the Humanities, the Government of India and the Hans Siewers scholarship fund, Oslo. I am grateful for their financial support.

Special thanks go to the renouncer Baba Kaushleshdass, whose guidance, hospitality and friendship were of utmost importance to my fieldwork in India. My Sanskrit Guru, Professor Misra, was a source of inspiration and knowledge. His private tuitions gave me a taste of the classical language. He was also a valuable informant into the world of Brahmanic Hinduism. I also thank my wife Kari Sommerseth Jacobsen, who was a close assistant and support during my field studies in India.

Thanks also go to Arne Martin Klausen, Eduardo Archetti, Olaf Smedal, Jens Braarvig and Pamela Price, all of whom read through the manuscript and offered valuable comments. Finally, a special note of thanks goes to my friend Marius Hauge who has worked his way through the manuscript to improve and correct my English.

ABBREVIATIONS

Brihad-Aranakya Upanishad	Br.Up.
Bhagavad-Gita	Gita
Chandogya Upanishad	Chand.Up.
Contributions to Indian Sociology	CIS
Isha Upanishad	Isha.Up.
Journal of Asian Studies	J.O.A.S.
Kaushitaki Upanishad	Kau.Up.
Katha Upanishad	Katha. Up.
Maitri Upanishad	Maitri.Up.
Mimamsa Sutra	M.S.
Mundaka Upanishad	Mund.Up.
Rig Veda	RV
Taittiriya Upanishad	Tait.Up.
Taittiriya Brahmana	T.B.
Samkhya Karika	Sam.Kar.
Shataphata Brahmana	S.B.
Svetashvatara Upanishad	Svet.Up.
Vedanta Sutra (Brahma Sutra)	Ved. Sutra

INTRODUCTION:
FOR AN ANTHROPOLOGY OF INDIA

THE QUESTION OF THE CULTURAL UNITY OF INDIA

If we compare India with Europe west of Ural and the Bosporus, India, although less than 1/3 in land area (3.3 mill. square kms) still have a much larger population (900 mill., 750 mill.). The Indian population is fare more complex than the European in racial and ethnic composition. India has more than 1000 languages belonging to four fundamentally different language families (Indo-European, Dravidian, Austro-Asiatic, Tibeto-Burman) while the overwhelming majority of the European languages are derived from the Indo-European branch only. The religious life in India, representing all the major world religions and tribal religions of different kinds, is also much more complex and diverse than its monolithic Christian counterpart. Finally, the socio-economic diversity of India ranges from extreme poverty through fast growing middle classes to those enjoying extreme wealth and power over people. In that perspective most Europeans appear as middled classed people only.

The striking diversity of India did not prevent scholars from postulating an underlying unity and continuity of that civilization (Raghavan 1955, Brown 1961, Singer 1955, 1961, 1964, Ingalls 1958, Staal 1963, Dumont & Pocock 1957, Dumont 1970).

In the vast subcontinent of India, where all levels of culture are represented and where the most diverse human types coexist, customs are of infinite variety. And yet at the moment that these peoples, the most disparate *inter se* in the world, proclaim themselves to be Hindus, they have all some point in common with Brahmanical orthodoxy. However low they may be in the social scale they are not barbarians, *mlecchas*. They participate at least to a humble degree in the maintenance of the eternal order, of *Dharma*. They have their functions and duties to perform. In performing them they expiate the faults of the past and prepare themselves for higher births. (Lingat 1973:205)

The founding fathers of the modern anthropology of India like Singer, Dumont, Srinivas and McKim Marriott were all, in one way or another, coping with the problem of the unity of India. This was a concern they shared with many other Indologists during the 1950s and 60s. The timing of this concern in the question of the unity of India was indeed not a random coincidence, but an implicit outcome of the process of nation building. India as a newly independent state brought forth a drive to search for a conception of a socio-cultural unity of the nation.

From an anthropological perspective, the concept of the unity of India has social as well as cultural roots. The social roots must still be said to be the caste system. Wherever one may be in India, even in the 1990s, one is in a universe where caste still has a major say. Caste even cuts across religious divisions. It is not only Hindus who are segmented into castes, but also Jains, Sikhs, Muslims and Christians.[1] The cultural basis - the cultural form or 'dress' of this unity - is the Hindu Great Tradition.

The Hindu Great Tradition

The concept of the Hindu Great Tradition developed by Singer (1955, 1964 and McKim Marriott (1955) was founded on the cultural anthropology of Redfield.

> In a civilization there is a Great Tradition of the reflective few, and there is a little tradition of the largely unreflective many. The Great Tradition is cultivated in schools or temples; the little tradition works itself out and keeps itself going in the lives of the unlettered in their village communities. (Redfield 1963:41-42)

The interdependence between the 'Great' and the 'little' aspects of Indian civilization gives rise to the processes of Sanskritization which is one of the moving historical forces of Hinduism. This process has been going on from the beginning of Indian history when the Indo-Aryans encountered the indigenous peoples of South Asia.[2] The Brahmins started their process of Sanskritization more than 2000 years ago when they became vegetarians under the influence of heterodox religions like Buddhism and Jainism. The Chamars - the traditional leather workers - only recently started their proper Sanskritization when they began to outlaw the eating of beef at the beginning of this century (see Cohn 1955:72).[3]

Independently of Singer and Marriott, Srinivas in his book *Religion and Society among the Coorgs of South India*, published in 1952, proposed another, but parallel approach to the study of Indian society and culture. Srinivas distinguished variations in Hinduism according to the degree of *horizontal* spread. 'All-India Hinduism' and 'Sanskritic Hinduism' have an all-India spread. 'Regional Hinduism' is restricted to the particular region and 'Local Hinduism' to the locality. Srinivas also introduced the notion of *vertical* spread which was founded on the degree of social distribution of different cultural forms within a given locality or region.

Obviously, there were many fertile points of convergence between the civilizational approach of American Cultural Anthropology and the perspectives of Srinivas. The Great Tradition was equated with All-India Hinduism. The concept of Sanskritization was broadened to include both the horizontal spread of the Great Tradition as well as its vertical spread in the locality.

The village perspective

Up to the beginning of the 1950s the anthropology of India was firmly founded on classical British social anthropology who conceived the fieldwork area as an isolate and a systemic whole. It seems clear that this stand suited the functionalism of Radcliffe-Brown, Malinowski and their students very well.[4] The classical Indian village studies of the 1950s did all, in one way or another, object to the conception of the 'primitive isolate' to question the sociological reality of the village.[5] The village, as a field of observation, was not considered to contain the useful unit of study since it was not a 'whole' - a complete system in itself. Anthropologists were forced to find another approach than the one offered by British social anthropology.[6]

> To try to understand a local Indian society as an anthropologist in the past approached a primitive society elsewhere in the world, or as Indian tribes have been approached, is to fail at the outset. (Dumont & Pocock 1957:25)

The new wave that entered the scene was the cultural anthropology of Redfield. Redfield conceived the peasant village as a combination of opposites (Redfield 1956) of '.. a Great Tradition of the reflective few, and.. a little tradition of the largely unreflective many.' (Redfield op.cit.). The question of the cultural unity of India formulated through terms like the Hindu Great Tradition and Sanskritic Hinduism came in the forefront on the anthropologist's agenda while, at the same time, the slogan unity in diversity became, as it were, a national anthem.

AN ANTHROPOLOGIST'S MODEL
OF THE HINDU GREAT TRADITION

> In our opinion, the first condition for a sound development of a Sociology of India is found in the establishment of the proper relation between it and classical Indology. (Dumont and Pocock 1957:7)

To construct an anthropologist's model of the Hindu Great Tradition through inductions from traditional anthropological field observation would be an enormous, if not an impossible task. I have therefore turned to the fertile textual tradition of Dumont who states that we have direct access to a society's values or ideology, its self-knowledge, through its literature, its encoded tradition (Dumont 1970:3, 263-264, Lynch 1977:241).

I shall in this book use texts as other anthropologists use informants, as source material, as data for reconstructing the indigenous system of ideas and values, in short what several anthropologists define as culture (see Keesing 1976). This cultural system of the orthodox ideas and values of Hinduism is regarded as the Hindu Great Tradition in this book. The Hindu Great Tradition is the cultural form - the dress - *encompassing* the caste system.

The source material of the Hindu Great Tradition

The corpus of holy texts which may be said to formulate the Hindu Great Tradition is vast. Criteria of selection are necessary. I propose the following two criteria: First, the texts should belong to orthodox Hinduism. Second, they should be of relevance not only for the formation of classical Hinduism, but also for modern India.

Mahatma Gandhi can be our first guide. He made the *Bhagavad-Gita* his personal bible from which the very influential ideas and practices of Gandhism arose. According to other leaders like Radhakrishnan, Rajagopalacharya, Bose and Dasgupta.

.., the essential ideas have continued for four or five millenniums. The germinal conceptions are contained in the Vedanta standard. The three *prasthanas*, or divisions of the Vedanta, the *Upanishads*, the *Vedanta Sutra* and the *Bhagavad-Gita*... They form together the Absolute standard for the Hindu religion.' (Radhakrishnan 1980:18, Rajagopalacharya 1959:18, Dasgupta 1957:11, Bose 1970:7)

But to rely on the Vedanta standard only would be to adopt a very exclusive view. I shall also utilize other parts of the holy scriptures, i.e., selections from the *Vedas*, the *Mimamsa*, *Yoga* and *Samkhya* philosophical systems, the *Laws of Manu* and the *Garuda Purana*.

The scriptures selected here can roughly be divided into three groups:

A) The Vedas which the Hindu tradition terms 'the part of actions' (*karmakanda*). I shall utilize selections from the *Rig Veda* and *Sataphata Brahmana*. The *Mimamsa* philosophical system, so important for Hindu jurisprudence, will also be taken into consideration as it elaborated and systematized the earlier ideas of the Vedas.

B) The Upanishads which the Hindu tradition terms 'the part of knowledge' (*jnanakanda*). I shall utilize the thirteen principle Upanishads (Hume 1975) and the three philosophical systems: The *Vedanta (Brahma) sutra*, the *Samkhya karika* and the *Yoga sutra* as source materials of this branch.

C) The *Bhagavad-Gita* and the *Laws of Manu* are often termed 'the part of the scriptures concerned with the combination of both knowledge and action' (*jnana-karma-samuchhaya vada*) (Mainkar 1969:51).[7] The Laws of Manu is the central scriptural authority on questions regarding Dharma (Lingat 1973:77) while the Gita is often esteemed as the gospel of the Hindus (Sharma 1965:266).

To facilitate the transmission of the holy scriptures into the living religion of society, I shall also make use of the interpretations of great philosophers and personalities within the Hindu tradition. The Vedic tradition will be represented by the orthodox philosopher Kumarila (600 A.D.). The Upanishadic tradition will be interpreted according to Shankara (800 A.D.) who reorganized the *sannyasi* (renouncer) orders and founded ten monasteries. The Manu-Gita tradition will be interpreted in the light of Ramanuja (1000 A.D.) who is a key figure in the development of *bhakti* religion.

Undoubtedly the holy scriptures of the Hindu Great Tradition selected here present a high caste view of society and cosmos. Thus *Brahmanic* Hinduism is an appropriate term for the cultural system being described in this book. Brahmanic ideas and values constitute, in a functional perspective, a dominant ideology in the legitimation of caste society.

The social carriers of Brahmanic Hinduism

Srinivas defined Sanskritization as follows:

> Sanskritization is the process by which a «low» caste Hindu, or tribal or other group, changes its customs ritual, ideology and way of life in the direction of a high, and frequently, «twice born» caste. (Srinivas 1972:6).

The higher castes, not least the Brahmins [8] and also other ritual specialists, are the local representatives of the All-India Hinduism' - the Great Tradition. It is through them, whether as role models in the villages or ritual specialists in ceremonies, temples and places of pilgrimage, that 'All-India Hinduism' diffuses throughout the population.[9] Brahmins and ritual specialists are the carriers of the unity of Hinduism. Indeed, a *Hindu* is, as the Hindus themselves perceive it, a person accepting the authority of the holy scriptures and the superiority of the Brahmins. The cultural unity of India formulated in terms like the Hindu Great Tradition, All India Hinduism or Sanskritic Hinduism was in more practical terms operationalized by Srinivas (1952) and anthropologists/Indologists following him into life style models seen to embody a complex of practices and values associated with the holy scriptures and their social carriers - the specialists that made them known to the 'largely unreflective many'.

The three parts of the holy scriptures referred to above are each attached to one type of specialists or role-occupiers in the social organization of the Hindu Great Tradition:

A) What I shall term the *magical* world view of the Vedic tradition is linked to the Brahmin ritualists - the priests of Hindu society.[10] In their capacity as teachers, temple priests, household priests or legislators, the Brahmin ritualists monopolized the occupational functions founded on the Vedas.[11]

B) What, furthermore, I shall term the *mystical* world view of the Upanishadic tradition is linked to the renouncer (*sadhu, sannyasi*). As specialists, models and cultural transmitters of the Hindu Great Tradition, the renouncers, like the Brahmin ritualists, also constitute a unique and indisputable All-India institution.[12] The Brahmin ritualist and the renouncer have both been the literati and the more articulate of the Hindus. They have been the main architects and social carriers of the Hindu Great Tradition. These two specialists shall be seen side by side and in relationship to the third type, the householder, the *lay* Hindu.

C) What I shall term the *religious* world view of the Gita-Manu is thus linked to the householder type of the Hindu Great Tradition. As an ideal type, the householder may be seen as a model for how lay Hindus should aspire to sanskritize themselves, in order to improve their caste rank.

The Logic of Karma

Most Indologists will agree that the main terms to be discovered in the holy texts of Brahmanic Hinduism can be reduced to the following: *karma* (action, merit/demerit), *kartri* (individual), *Dharma* (duty, moral law, structure), *jati* (caste group), *varna* (caste category), *varnashramadharma* (caste system), *samsara/maya/prakrti* (lifeworld), *Atman/Brahman/Purusha* (Self, Being, Absolute) and *Moksha* (emancipation). There is also agreement among most anthropologists working in the field that these terms are highly internalized among all strata of the Hindu population (Srinivas 1962, 1965, 1976, Lewis 1958, Mayer 1966, Babb 1975, Carstairs 1961, Campbell 1976, Karve 1961, Berreman 1963:197, Khare 1970, Jaer 1995).

Among these native terms I shall maintain the preeminence of karma.

There are several reasons for this selection.

In all these mutually opposite streams of thought, worship and culture, the cult of karma holds a very prominent position....., the entire structure of Indian culture from one end of the country to the other is dominated by the ideology associated with the doctrine of karma. Like recondite philosophers, most illiterate women and peasants of rural India have a strong belief in karma as well as in transmigration which is a necessary corollary of the doctrine of karma. (Walli 1977:277) (See also Edgerton 1942)

In the struggle between the father of the Indian constitution and the neo-Buddhist Dr Ambedkar and Mahatma Gandhi, karma is indeed in the forefront:

Hinduism upholds the law of karma, ..., so does Gandhism... All that Gandhism has done is to find a philosophic justification for Hinduism and its dogmas.... To the Untouchables, Hinduism is a veritable chamber of horrors. (Ambedkar 1946:307)

Naipaul, in his book *India: A Wounded Civilization*, has given a more popular endorsement of this statement:

In the country itself, the practice of slavery had attained (such) a sophistication that the victims themselves were made to feel a moral obligation to remain in slavery. Karma! (1979:48)

Finally, in *Vishnu Purana* chapter 3, section 2, it is claimed that India (*Bharatavarsha*) is the only place which should be considered *karma-bhumi*. This means India was regarded as the only place where men was of such a quality that they could act with a view to influencing their future destinies.

Thus, the importance of the concept of karma in Hinduism should be obvious. However, there are other points of view. Dumont has not accepted the importance of the concept of karma. He states that the idea of rebirth and of retributions for actions are not among the rare dogmatic beliefs of Hinduism as Weber formulated it.[13] Following Dumont, these concepts belong to the speculative plane (Dumont 1960:48). In a similar way, Dumont also rejects the sociological relevance of the concept of the individual in the context of caste society. Dumont regards caste society as a form of mechanical solidarity (Lynch 1977:257) and conceives the lay Hindu - 'the-man-inside-the-world' - as a reflection of the collective consciousness. 'I regard it as fundamental...., that on the level of life in the world the individual is *not*.' (Dumont 1960:42, my italics) A similar mode of thinking can be found in Touraine's 'Towards a sociology of action' (1975). In this work

Touraine restricts the validity of the concept of action to the industrial societies only (Op.cit.:87,94). Traditional man, according to Touraine, is not able to conceive of himself as a creator. But as the *Sataphata Brahmana* states. 'A man is born into the world *he has made.*' (VI.2.2.27, quoted from Panikkar 1972:28, my italics) Dumont's statements regarding the status of the concepts of action and individual are, as I shall argue in appendix 3, untenable. The conclusions he draws reflect his unidimensional structuralism and not the empirical facts.

It is the proposition of this book that the concepts of action and individual - *karma* and *kartri* - are fundamental to Hinduism. Karma and kartri, as well as the other Sanskrit terms mentioned above, constitute a chain of meaning, a cultural logic which I shall term the *Logic of Karma*. Karma presupposes Dharma as action presupposes structure. Together karma and Dharma make up the core concepts for an understanding of the fundamental values of Brahmanic Hinduism and the legitimation of caste society.

CULTURAL TRANSLATION AND COMPARISON

The objective of this work is, as stated in the Preface, to give an anthropological presentation of the cultural logic of Brahmanic Hinduism - the Logic of Karma - within a comparative frame of reference. The key concept selected as 'bridgehead' for cultural translation and medium for comparison is action - *karma*. I have selected this concept not because 'action' is a universal, but because most Indologists acknowledge the fundamental status of action (karma) in Hinduism and vice versa among important philosophical and sociological schools in the Western tradition. Both traditions have produced sophisticated concepts and theories of action and their relations to the concepts of individual and structure.[14]

The classical Sanskrit grammarians derived the Sanskrit noun karma from the verbal root *kri* = to do, make, cause, effect (Monier Williams 1979). Following most Indologists, the primary meaning of karma is *action*. In the Western context 'action' is a concept which, since the time of Aristotle, has been at the forefront of discussion since action, morality and free will are closely interrelated and belong to the *differentia specificia* of Man - i.e. the ability to act are among those criteria which differentiate Man from animals. The problem of 'action' runs straight to the heart of the social sciences. The debate centred around positivism has its basis in the question of a satisfactory concept of action (Giddens 1976, 1979). On the behavioral level, the problem of action is also intrusive. Are we observing actions or events?

The rationality behind the ideology of the caste system requires the *idea* of an ultimately free actor with personal responsibility for his present situation. The Sanskrit language reflects this rationality through its discrimination between what we can properly call an action = *karma*, an activity = *kriya*, movement = *pravrti* and play = *lila*. The concept of action presupposes the concept of the individual as the agent of action. Without accepting the relevance of action (karma) and the individual agent (kartri) in the Hindu context, we shall not be able to account for the problem of meaning nor the ideological legitimation of caste society. In short, we shall not be able to give any presentation of those Hindu institutions, which, like Azande witchcraft (Evans-Pritchard 1980), supply individuals and groups with answers to questions like 'why me', 'why us'?' (Obeyesekere 1981:106). Nor shall we be able to account for Man as a moral being who is responsible for his doings.

Action and agent presuppose the concept of structure. I furthermore uphold, as earlier stated, that the duality of action/structure is a necessary starting point for any theory of Man and Society and that the apperception of this duality is implicit in the karma/Dharma teachings of Hinduism. It is, as I shall try to show throughout this work, these common reference points which make translations and comparisons between Hinduism and Capitalism a fertile one.

Philosophy and social science

Most of the important concepts of the social sciences have their roots in philosophy. The anthropologist Marvin Harris states that the empiricism of Hume is the archetype of modern day positivism. Parsons somewhere says that his concept of action is not understandable without a previous knowledge of Kant's concept of action. The phenomenology of Schutz is more or less a direct translation of the philosophy of Husserl. And Giddens emphasizes that Marx still represents the most significant single fund of ideas that can be drawn upon in seeking to illuminate problems of action and structure (Giddens 1979:53).

Hegel's definition of philosophy as 'a conceptualization of one's own present historical epoch in thoughts' (Hegel 1930:15 - 1820) provides a philosophical justification for the textual approach in the anthropological study of the Hindu Great Tradition. The textual approach assumes that philosophical and religious texts like those selected in the present work, will prove fertile in the anthropological reconstruction of culture.

Given the focus on concepts like 'action' , 'individual' and 'structure', the character of the source material and Hegel's definition of philosophy endorsed here, it is only natural that the present work will have a philosophical flavour in spite of its anthropological objective.[15]

NOTES TO INTRODUCTION

1. The debate on the problem of the uniqueness of the Hindu caste system is extensive. See Dumont 1978: 'Caste, racism and «stratification»: reflections of a social anthropologist'.

2. Shiva, with his contradictory qualities (cf. O'Flaherty 1973), is an example of Sanskritization. Archaeological evidence support the hypothesis that Shiva has his roots in the 'Yogi' of the Indus valley civilization.

3. Following Radhakrishnan, the epics may be seen as narrations of the processes of Sanskritization (1980:29-30).

4. Dumont & Pocock describe the approach of traditional British social anthropology as follows '... the field worker approaches his area untied by questions of a historical and cultural nature and that he be concerned with social wholes in themselves,.... But the Indian sociologist dare not isolate the area of his inquiry from neighbouring areas or from history.' (Dumont & Pocock 1957:24) In his book *Social Anthropology (1982)*, Edmund Leach gives us a presentation of the conflict inherent in social as opposed to cultural anthropology.

5. See Dumont & Pocock 1957: 'Village studies' in *Contributions to Indian Sociology*, 1 pp. 23-41.

6. It is with an awareness of the problem of demarcating cultural/social wholes in the field, and also with some irony, that Leach in his monograph *Political Systems of Highland Burma* (1954) wrote as follows: 'For the time being I will follow Radcliffe-Brown's unsatisfactory advice and interpret "a society" as meaning "any convenient locality"'. (Leach 1977:5).

7. The Gita refers, most probably, directly to the Laws of Manu in several verses: 'So let the *Shastra* be thy authority in ascertaining what ought to be done and what ought not to be done. Having known what is said in the ordinance in the *Shastra*, thou should act here.' (Gita 16.24) The Laws of Manu is the most authoritative among the *Dharmashastras* and, following Zaehner, the term *Shastra* in this verse refers to the Laws of Manu. (Zaehner 1969:374) This is also indicated in an earlier verse where the Laws of Manu is explicitly mentioned. (Gita 4.1) Furthermore, according to the Sanskritist Bühler (1979:LXXIV-XC III), about one-tenth of Manu's verses can be found in the *Mahabharata* where the Gita composes a small part. This underscores at least a close relationship between the two texts even if the identities in ideas are not always striking.

8. Srinivas and others following him are certainly aware that the culture of the Brahmins is not always highly Sanskritized (see Srinivas 1972:20) But as Marriott (1955:211) notes, 'Brahmans are, by their position in the caste hierarchy, and by their association with priesthood, the best potential local agents of the Great Tradition.', and Srinivas: 'In short, it [the Sanskritizing group ØJ] took over, as far as possible, the customs, rites and beliefs of the Brahmins,...' (Srinivas 1965:30).

9. As proposed by Redfield, a civilization can be conceived of as '..an organization of specialists, of kinds of roleoccupiers in characteristic functions concerned with the transmission of tradition.' (Redfield 1963:58)

10. The Laws of Manu even conceived the Vedas as attributes of the Brahmin ritualist (Manu 1.98).

11. As noted by Singer, the Brahmin ritualists are mostly recruited from the *Smarta* "orthopraxis" tradition (Singer 1955:26).

12. Philip Singer (1970) has suggested that the terms Sanskritization and Westernization need a third - i.e., *Sadhuization* - to form a more complete heuristic nomenclature of what is happening in present day India (see Bharati 1969:277).

13. 'All Hindus accept two basic principles. The samsara belief in the transmigration of souls and the related karman doctrine of compensation. These alone are the truly dogmatic doctrines of all Hinduism and in their very interrelatedness, they represent the unique Hindu theodicy of the existing social, that is to say caste system.' (Weber 1967:118)

14. My focus on the concept of action should not be confused with the approach of the anthropological formalists (Leclair, Burling, Herskovits, Salisbury, Schneider etc.). Their concern for action is not on the conceptual level. They have selected one type of action - i.e., economic action - as their principle starting point for explaining all kinds of social actions. The Formalists inherited their theoretical framework from marginalist economic theory (Godelier 1975).

15. 'For any worthwhile study of society must be philosophical in character and any worthwhile philosophy must be concerned with the nature of human society.' (Winch 1958:3)

PART I

THE CONTEXT FOR TRANSLATION AND COMPARISON

THE PHILOSOPHICAL ROOTS OF THE CONCEPT OF ACTION

EMPIRICISM

In his book *Cultural Materialism*, Harris states that his approach shares the same epistemological foundation as socio-biology (1980:141). He further states that both cultural materialism and socio-biology have derived their position from the empiricism of David Hume which Harris elevates as the archetype of modern day positivism (op.cit.:9). A presentation of the basics of Hume's empiricism is a useful starting point for a broader understanding of the concept of action.

The axiomatic starting point in the epistemology of Hume is sense impression. Hume, as Locke before him, considered the human mind as a *tabula rasa* and rejected the possibility of any kind of *a priori* knowledge. Ideas, relations and concepts are derived from simple impressions.[1] Next we have the concept of causality. Hume argued that the concept of causality was based on a 'psychological inclination' arrived at through repeated experiences.[2] Hume further asks what kind of status we can ascribe to the subject (the I, the individual) and the object (substance). From which impression could the subject or the object be derived. Hume has an illuminating passage on the nature of the subject. 'I may venture to affirm of the rest of mankind, that they are nothing but a bundle or collection of different perceptions, which succeed each other with an inconceivable rapidity, and are in a perpetual flux and movement.' (Hume 1975:252) The subject and the object are seen to be imaginary identities constructed through habit. They have no substance, no being, to use the language of Dumont. The concept of Man as a rational being seems to have little relevance in the philosophy of David Hume when he states that 'Reason is, and ought to be the slave of the passions, and can never pretend to any other office than to serve and obey them.' (op.cit.:415)

The empiricism of Hume and his successors constitutes a form of philosophy where action and structure are epiphenomena of nature with a derived, non-independent status. Hume's empiricism makes it difficult to account for concepts and terms in use. How, for instance, should Hume be able to distinguish 'Man' from 'animal'? From which impression could this difference be derived?[3]

Rationalism, the other important philosophical trend of the

Enlightenment, reveals common characteristics with the empiricism of Hume, though in reverse.[4] While impressions constitute the axiomatic starting point for empiricism, innate ideas is the starting point for rationalism. Empiricism induces human mind from nature. Rationalism deduces nature from the pregiven ideas of the human mind. Both empiricism and rationalism are based on a *unidimensional* epistemology.

The battle between empiricism and rationalism has been a part of the modern anthropological discourse (Leach 1977) as exemplified in the debate which went on between the so-called formalists and substantivists.[5] To overcome this battle, it is necessary to seek another epistemological foundation.

THE ANTHROPOCENTRIC REVOLUTION

In the sphere of epistemology and morals, Kant (1724 - 1804) is the precursor of the anthropocentric revolution. Kant states in the introduction to the *Critique of Pure Reason*:

> For, on the contrary, it is quite possible that our empirical knowledge is a compound of that which we receive through impressions, and that which the faculty of cognition supplies from itself.... (Kant 1934:25 - 1783)

The object of knowledge in Kant's terminology - the phenomenon - is a product of two sources; a) the impressions and b) their synthetic a priori structuration and objectivation by an act of the cognitive faculties. Where Hume was forced to introduce the notion of habit to account for unperceivable categories like substance, self and causality, Kant turned to the a priori action of the cognitive faculties as the constituting factor (Kant 1934:92-93 - 1783). Through the encounter between 'passive' sensuality and 'active' cognition, the object given to consciousness is produced.[6]

After presenting his arguments for the necessary application of cognitive structures, Kant proceeds to state the transcendental reality of the I - the individual. There must be an 'I think' - an active I - which accompanies all conscious content, which is pure active form and never itself able to be reduced to the contents thereof.[7] In contrast to Hume, Kant has ascribed transcendental status to the I. The I is the formal unity of the cognitive faculties, an a priori condition for any rationality whatsoever.

As can be expected from his epistemology, Kant cannot accept the position of Hume with regards to the determination of morality. Once again 'action' is in the forefront of analysis. The I is conceived as the prime mover in the chain of causality initiated to realize the intended aim. That is, Kant's moral philosophy emphasizes the I - the individual - as an agent of action (see Kant 1922:224 - 1794). The freedom of the will is of basic importance to the moral philosophy of Kant. It should not be understood as a metaphysical postulate. It is an a priori principle discovered from what Kant cites as transcendental argumentation. If we say that Man acts and has responsibility, in short if we assume that action and morality are constitutive qualities of human existence, then we must by implication regard freedom of the will as an a priori principle (see Kant 1915:125 - 1788).

As the spontaneous act of the I was 'constrained' through the application of the cognitive structures, so the freedom of the will is informed/governed/structured in Kant's moral philosophy through the application of the moral law (Kant 1923:47). The more the autonomous individual agent is able to structure and form his subjective intensions after the prescriptions of the moral law, the higher is his moral character.

We learn from Kant that there is no such thing as an unmediated impression which passively reflects itself in the human mind. The so called facts of the phenomenal world are always constituted through the application of the a priori structures. Second, we learn that all actions are mediated through what we will call structures which inform and structure actions. And third, we learn that these structures not only structure the phenomenal world into an ordered whole, they also objectify and unify the impression into things - material or ideal. Kant, in short, establishes a philosophical fundament for the interrelated perspective on 'action-structure'.

FROM PHILOSOPHY TO SOCIAL SCIENCE

Marx rejects the 'passive' epistemological empiricism of the materialist (Feuerbach) and empiricist (Hume) schools. He acknowledges his inheritance from the German idealists (Kant, Hegel). Marx found that the German idealists had developed the 'active side' of the epistemological process (Marx 1975:421) which Marx endorsed. Marx furthermore affirms the relationship between his concept of labour and Hegel's notion of action.[8] In the philosophy of Marx, 'action' is no longer restricted to the transcendental sphere of Kant or the ideational sphere of Hegel. Action/Praxis is Marx's main concept for understanding all levels of reality (Schmidt 1971, Poggi 1972, Livergood 1967, Bernstein 1972).[9] From Kant via Hegel to Marx, 'action' has been made 'concrete' to become the theoretical key concept for the understanding of social life.

A similar process of concretization can also be observed with respect to the concept of the individual.[10] Marx rejects the concept of the 'abstract individual' in the philosophy of Kant. Marx conceives the individual in a concrete way as a socially and historically mediated being.

Individual and society.

Parallel to the concretization process of the concepts of action and individual which we have seen in the transmission from Kant via Hegel to Marx is a development in the conception of the social. The relationship between individual and society/action and structure is the key element in the concept of the social.

Hegel observed that there was a growing antagonism between the individual and society. He conceived this antagonism as a *social fall* peculiar to the modern period as the religious fall was peculiar to an earlier epoch. Hegel's perspectives on the social fall of the modern period reflects the growth of individualism as an ideology. Hegel's 'weapon' against individualism was the sociological apperception. Hegel defined the sociological apperception as follows: 'Ego that is 'we'... and 'we' that is a single Ego.' (Hegel 1971:227 - 1807) Hegel's aim with his theory of the sociological apperception was not solely to combat the growth of individualism, but to restore the knowledge that human beings are only selfconscious - aware of themselves as individuals - in and through social life.

Marx inherits Hegel's ideas on the relationship between the individual and society. Marx assumes, as did Hegel before him, the priority of society over the individual.[11] But this priority is dialectical. It is a priority within the mediation of the two which does not reduce the one to the other.

Absolutism versus relativism

As the classical Evolutionists coming after him, Hegel's conception of history involves an idea of a process which starts in the simple and ends in the complex. History is conceived as the growth of a plant from seed to fruit. There are no qualitative 'jumps'. The historical process reflects in a progressive way the 'eternal, dialectical thoughts of God'. Hegel thus assumes a system of reason or a meta-logic which is valid *sui generis*. At the end of the historical process, Man is finally in such a position that he is able to understand this eternal meta-logic. The meta-logic has become manifest for what it is.[12]

When Marx turns to historical analyses of the prehistory of Capitalism, he seems to conceive traditional societies as more or less unmediated, naturally or spontaneously arisen (Marx 1973:485, 492 -1857-58). Commenting on India, Marx's naturalist perspectives seems obvious. '..this undignified, stagnatory and vegetative life, that this passive sort of existence, evoked...' (Marx 1853: New York Daily Tribune, June 25th - quoted from

Thorner 1966)[13] This, certainly, is nothing but a vulgar example of ethnocentrism, an ethnocentrism which is an outcome of the shortcomings of Historical materialism which always accords causal priority to socio-material variables irrespective of society or historical epoch analyzed (Marx 1970:20 - 1859).

Historical materialism should not be used as a meta theory valid *sui generis* and for all kind of societies. Lukacs argues that Historical materialism must be applied with great caution on pre-capitalist societies (Lukacs 1971:57). He claims that much more subtle and complex analyses are needed in order to determine the role of 'materiality' (Lukacs 1971:238).

Notes to Chapter 1

1. 'One general position, *That all our simple ideas...are derived from simple impressions, which are correspondent to them, and which they exactly represent.*' (Hume 1975:4)

2. 'For after we have observ'd the resemblance in a sufficient number of instances, we immediately feel a determination of the mind to pass from one object to its usual attendant,... Necessity, then, is the effect of this observation. (Hume 1975:165)

3. Let us recall the definition of Man made in the academy of Plato. 'Man, the being with two legs without feathers.'

4. Hume underscores this point.'We have establish'd it as a principle, that as all ideas are deriv'd from impressions....,'tis impossible we can have any idea of power and efficacy, unless some instances can be produc'd wherein this power is *perciev'd* to exert itself. Now as these instances can never be discovered in body, the *Cartesians*, proceeding upon their principle of *innate* ideas, have had recourse to a supreme spirit or deity whom they consider as the only active being in the universe, and as immediate cause of every alteration in matter.' (Hume 1975:160)

5. 'The laws of the one (rationalism) are those of the mind, the laws of the other are those of nature (empiricism).' (Polyani 1958)

6. The activity of the cognitive faculties which produced the object as it appears to us is at this basic level an unconscious process. In this process, the cognitive faculties draw upon the representation of time and space, the twelve categories of understanding and the paradigms of reason. The process of objectivation presents to us an object in time and space where its various qualities are unified into a single object - the thing with its many qualities. The process of structuration relates objects to each other. We combine events as causes and effects and we maintain an identifiable substance in objects which maintain their identity during the process of change. Through this dual *action* of the cognitive faculties, the phenomenal world appears as an ordered system of elements.

7. 'The *I think* must accompany all my representations, for otherwise something would be represented in me which could not be thought; in other words, the representation would either be impossible, or at least be, in relation to me, nothing..., *I think* is an *act of my spontaneity*; that is to say, it cannot be regarded as belonging to mere sensibility.' (Kant 1934:94 - 1783)

8. 'Hegel grasps the nature of labour and conceives objective man - true,..' But; 'The only labour Hegel knows and recognizes is abstract mental labour.' (Marx 1975:386)

9. Aristotle introduced the differentiation between theory and praxis and gives praxis a quasi-technical meaning (Bernstein 1972:ix) which was inherited by Marx. 'Praxis', as used by Marx, involves the idea of practical reason (Sahlins 1976).

10 'But the human essence is no abstraction inherent in each individual. In its reality, it is the ensemble of the social relations. Feuerbach, who does not enter upon a criticism of this real essence, is consequently compelled to abstract from the historical process and fix the religious sentiment as something by itself and to presuppose and abstract - isolated - human individual.' (Marx 1975:423 - 1845)

11. 'In a sort of way, it is with man as with commodities. Since he comes into the world neither with a looking glass in his hand, nor as a Fichtean philosopher, to whom "I am I" is sufficient, man first sees and recognizes himself in other men. Peter only establishes his own identity as a man by comparing himself with Paul as a being of like kind.' (Marx 1887:59)

12. Hegel had not, according to Marx, discovered that the movement from the abstract and simple to the concrete and complex, was a method to comprehend the present and not the historical process itself. Hegel, as Marx saw him, confused the historical process with the method used to understand it (Marx 1973:101 - 1857-58).

13. In the same manner, Marx also calls the Middle Ages the 'animal history', the 'zoology' of mankind (Poggi 1972).

2

THE ACTION SYSTEM

I shall now proceed to elaborate a model of the action system which shall serve as a frame of reference for the translation and comparison of Hinduism. The model consists of two levels: The action level (the lifeworld) and the structural level.

THE ACTION LEVEL

The key characteristic of an activity which deserves to be defined as an action is *consciousness*. Consciousness is the ability of Man to work out in his mind an intention, purpose, aim, plan of what he wants to do before he realizes it in the objective world where it can be shared by others. It is the intentional acts of consciousness which differentiate action from mere reactive behaviour. Actions so conceived are always mapped out in the 'future perfect tense' (Schutz 1967:63). The individual agent assumes that his intervention in the chain of events will cause certain specific effects to appear - effects which were the aim and goal of the action anticipated in advance.

We discover next that consciousness is not only empty form. It is always consciousness of something - it is *knowledge* (Giddens 1979:5). The actor needs knowledge about the means appropriate for his enterprise. He needs to know his own abilities, whether he has sufficient transformative capacity - resources to accomplish his aim. The actor ought furthermore to know whether his aim is legally and morally acceptable to society, and thus whether he will meet with sanctions from his fellow beings.

No actor is almighty. His knowledge is always restricted. He can never have complete insight, either of prevailing conditions or of the consequences of actions. I shall follow Gidden's stratified model of personality and distinguish between discourse, practical consciousness and the unconscious (Giddens 1979).

Intentions, purposes, plans and aims belong to that level of consciousness on which the individual is able to argue and rationalize in discourse. The *discourse* level refers to what the individual is able to 'talk about'. *Practical consciousness* is knowledge embodied in what actors know about how to do things. And the *unconscious* level is out of reach for the individual. But during the process of life, as we are growing older together, the individual can make explicit what was implicit before. He can discover antecedent causes which were unconscious to him at the time of performance.[1]

Action is objectivation. Action brings forth the effects of the purpose - the intention of the actor - into the intersubjective world where the subjective meanings of actors can be shared by others. Action is also structuration. Structuration orders the world into a structured cosmos. The process of objectivation produces the elements of structures while structuration organizes the elements into an ordered whole. Through objectivation and structuration, actions are 'frozen' in the intersubjective world. They become evidence of earlier actions.

A valid concept of action requires that we maintain a degree of freedom and autonomy on the part of the individual as a necessary a priori presupposition (Weber 1974, Schutz 1967:66-69). We find the best example of the social relevance of the 'freedom of the will postulate' in the moral and legal codes and practices of societies. Actors are held responsible for their doings. It is for society to judge whether their actions are good or bad, whether they are responsible or not and whether they could have acted otherwise. Without assuming a certain degree of freedom and autonomy, we shall not be able to account for concepts like action and morality at all.[2]

Social action

Action is social in so far as, by virtue of the subjective meaning attached to it by the acting individual (or individuals), it takes account of the behaviour of others and is thereby oriented in its course. (Weber 1947:88)

When analyzing social action, we are forced to leave a given behaviour in front of us - leave the 'here and now' of behavioral theories - and instead look at those acts in the past which commenced the causal chain of the action process.

How should we proceed when these acts, as Schutz says, are constituted within the unique stream of consciousness of each individual and as such are essentially inaccessible to others (Schutz 1967:99)? We have to identify and interpret the intentions, purposes and aims of the actors observed by employing knowledge derived from previous experiences. 'This is that everything I know about your conscious life is really based on my knowledge of my own lived experiences.' (Schutz 1967:106) The receiver understands the sender by employing an *interpretative scheme* which is a configuration of his own past experiences. Thus social action is a *hermeneutical process* - a process of interpretation of meanings (Gadamer 1967, Steiner 1975, Schutz 1967:220, Giddens 1979:245-253).[3]

Subjective and objective meaning

Both Weber and Shutz discriminate between subjective and objective meaning. Subjective meaning is meaning which can be referred to an individual or a group of individuals acting or treated as one subject (for example an organization). Objective meaning is anonymous in relation to its producer. It is meaning which relates to finished products like things, relations, persons, signs, symbols and rules abstracted from their historical genesis (Schutz 1967: 35,36). Objective meaning is, however, itself an object of interpretation and thus given a subjective imprint. Let us take an example from jurisprudence. Lawyers interpret the law differently. But as long as the laws appear legitimate, the lawyers agree that they are interpreting the same context of objective meaning.

Objective meaning has three forms which are manifestations of the ideational, social and material aspects of the system. These forms can be equated with modalities in the social theory of Giddens (1079:82). I shall build on Giddens terminology. I shall term the ideational form of objective meaning *interpretative schemes* or *world views* depending on the scale of the perspective. I shall term the social form *norms* and *rules* depending on whether it has legislative force or not. And finally, I shall term the material form of objective meaning *facilities*. These three forms of objective meaning are utilized, drawn upon and presupposed by individuals and groups engaged in social action.

Individuals *inherit* facilities and resources which equip them with more or less transformative capacity of actions. They internalize interpretative schemes and norms and thereby acquire the mutual knowledge necessary to participate in social life as competent members of the society. Thus individuals are socialized into the world of objective meaning.

Power and ideology

Power refers to the transformative capacity of actions and can be defined as the capabilities of actors or groups to realize their intended goals of actions (Giddens 1979:88). An actor or group who wield power could have acted otherwise, and the actor or group over whom power is wielded, would have acted otherwise if power had not been exercised (Lukes 1977:6-7). Actors can utilize various facilities and force their fellow beings to accept their intended course of action. These facilities can either be of an ideational kind, for example magic, or they can be of a social kind, i.e., the many forcing the few or they can be of a material kind like guns and money.

If, because of status, age, charisma or wisdom, means and ends of a process of action appear legitimate and thus acceptable to society, then an actor has authority.[4] *Legitimate* power - what Weber defined as authority (Weber 1947:328) - leads us to the concept of ideology. The function of ideologies is to make the institutions of society appear to the members as a legitimate order. The concept of ideology shows how objective meaning can be transmuted to serve sectional interests. This can happen in three ways:

i) Sectional interests of dominant groups can be pictured as universal interests. An example; it appears necessary that the Brahmin stands supreme in the Hindu world, because, according to Karmic ideology, he is the only person pure enough to function as a mediator between men and the Gods.

ii) Through reification; The social order is transmuted to appear as an eternal, divine arrangement instituted by God or pictured as an aspect of nature. Social change appears irrational and impossible.

iii) Through concealment: The main function of ideological concealment is to deny or at least transmute systemic contradictions (Giddens 1979:194).

THE STRUCTURAL LEVEL

'How is society possible?' This famous dictum of Simmel emphasizes his inheritance from Kant who asked an analogous question 'How is knowledge possible?'. Simmel's dictum leads us to discover the *a priori* structures that operate behind the back of the actors in order to inform and structure the social world and the actors participating there so that they may understand each other.

The grammar of language is an example of what is meant by the concept of structure. The grammar operates without any conscious effort by the actor. The grammar structures the speech of the senders. Ungrammatical speech will simply not be understood by other members of the language community.

I shall speak about three kinds of structures: ideational structures, social structures and material structures. These structures make the interpretative schemes, norms and facilities - the modalities of the lifeworld - possible.

Ideational structure

Following Gadamer, ideational structures can be viewed as 'the language' of the system which Gadamer defines as 'the all embracing form of the constitution of the world' (Gadamer 1966:3). From this perspective, ideational structures are seen to *constitute* the culturally specific formal knowledge which persons have of their lifeworld, that is the 'grammar', categories, codes and forms of perception (time and space) of the lifeworld.[5]

The grammar, syntax and structure of language - all those elements which linguistic science makes thematic - are factors of which we are not necessarily conscious when we speak. Every competent member of the speech community must have acquired and internalized these elements of ideational structure for meaningful communication to be possible. They must be intersubjectively shared as a common cognitive *set Up*.

Social structure

Ideational structures are constitutive, social structures on the other hand, are *regulative*. They contribute to the structuration of the continuing arrangements of persons in relationships defined by socially established norms. Social structure so conceived is that objective reality which makes normative regulation possible.

Material structure

Material structure is a product of man's cultivation of nature. As historically established structures, they *act back* (Poggi 1972:97) on the subjects and thereby contribute to the reproduction of the action system as a whole. An important function of material structures is the reproductive *allocation* of resources/facilities through which the owner can acquire authorization over persons.

The paradigms of the system

I shall now take a more concrete stand and ask: How is this *specific* society possible? That question leads us to inquire into the form of relationship which exists between the social structure on the one hand and the ideational and material structure on the other. I shall call the specific arrangements of interconnection between structures the *paradigms* of the action system in focus. The paradigms of the system appear, on the objective side, as highly valued models for action and, on the intersubjective side, as need dispositions. An illustration might indicate my point.

The paradigms of Capitalism structure social life towards 'economic actions' guided by the desire and need for profit and accumulation of economic wealth. To the extent the capitalists are in conformity with the socio-economic paradigms and invest their profit for further accumulation, they do not only reproduce that form itself. They also contribute to the reproduction of the Capitalist action system as a whole.

The paradigms of Hinduism structure social life towards 'religious actions' guided by the value and personal desire for religious liberation. The road which is supposed to lead there, is different from caste to caste. By seeking religious liberation and acting in conformity with one's ascribed duties, the Hindu society is reproduced.

Summary

The action level - the lifeworld - is the phenomenological level of the action system made up by interacting individuals and groups. The lifeworld is the world of action, knowledge and experience - the world as it appears to the participants of the system. A lifeworld is limited in time and space - coextensive, as it were, with the horizons of actions, knowledge and experience of its members.

The study of the lifeworld is a form of analysis which intends to present its subject matter in terms of indigenous theoretical categories and terms. It is a kind of method which tries to picture the world from the point of view of the participants - *their* model of *their* world.

Social life implies a continuous process of hermeneutical activity. This hermeneutical activity assumes as well as produces a common medium and denominator - a framework of objective meaning. What money is for commodities, objective meaning is for communication and interpretation. In addition to the subjective meaning of actors, we thus also have the objective meaning of the system as such.

The analytical tools for analyzing and describing the lifeworld are the ideal types of interpretative sociology (Weber, Schutz). The Brahmin ritualist, renouncer and householder represent ideal types each with their respective set of interpretative schemes, norms and facilities. The causal and meaning adequacy (Weber, Schutz) of ideal types are in principle open for statistical verification by comparing the predictable course of action with the real course of events.

One problem facing the science of the lifeworld is what Giddens calls the lay critique of sociology (Giddens 1979:249). By presenting ideal type constructions, sociology is only formulating what is already well known and familiar. However, without knowing what people think, believe and do, we can neither describe them nor explain why they are as they are.

The method to discover the characteristics of the structural level is different from the ideal type 'inductions' of the lifeworld.[6] The structural level contains elements which may be a priori to the participants. A form of structural analysis which makes explicit the structural presupposition for communication, social integration and reproduction is the method needed. Inference and deduction, and not inductions, are crucial elements of this method. The study of the structural level of the action system is, in the terminology used here, anthropology in the *etic* mode. The study of the lifeworld is anthropology in its *emic* mode.[7]

As with the lifeworld, the structural level also has its subjective and objective 'viewpoints'. The subjective viewpoint refers to the *intersubjective* structures - the prereflexive, a priori mental set up which must be shared by all the competent members of the system.[8] The objective viewpoint refers to the structures of social being itself, the social and material structures which are external to the individuals.

The methodological position advocated here is thus as follows. We should first try to form a picture of the specific formulations of a culture. For this task interpretative and hermeneutical methods must be used. Then we should inquire why the cultural order is like it is. For this purpose we must draw upon the specific paradigms of the socio-cultural system as explanatory variables.

NOTES TO CHAPTER 2

1. The problem of the freedom of the will should also be reflected from the perspective of time. Seen from the point of view of the agent gazing into the future, choice and decisions are always a matter of fact. Conceived retrospectively, either by the agent himself or as a reconstruction done by the observer, an action looses its free character by discovering antecedent causes.

2. The problem of freedom of the will also strikes at the heart of the methodology of the social sciences. A Durkheimian conception based on objective explanations from social facts reduces the agent to social determinism. And methodological individualists like Weber and Schutz overemphasize subjectivity and freedom of the will at the expense of structure.

3. 'Meaning is a certain way of directing ones gaze at an item of ones experience. This item is thus selected out and rendered discrete by a reflexive act.' (Schutz 1967:42) Meaning is, to use the words of Barthes: '...an order with chaos on each side...' (Barthes 1969), an order created by Man.

4. Status, as Weber notes, is a quality of social honour or a lack of it, and is in the main conditioned as well as expressed through a specific form of life (Weber 1967.39).

5. The concept of the 'ideational structure' as used here, converges to a large extent with the following definition of culture: 'We will use "culture" to refer to systems of shared ideas, to the conceptual designs, the shared systems of meaning, that underlie the ways in which a people live.' (Keesing 1976:139)

6. The methodological individualism of Schutz does not suffice outside the horizons of the lifeworld. The problem of intersubjectivity/objectivity and deep structures remains intractable and seems to haunt the phenomenological movement (Giddens 1976:26, Gadamer 1969:186). In the end, Schutz always falls back on the same unambiguous solution; only from the standpoint of transcendental solipsism can one legitimate the concept of 'we' (Gadamer op.cit.). That is, Schutz postulates a kind of abstract individual; '...the unchangeable unity of the human mind ....as the essence of human experience.' Schutz' unchangeable unity of the human mind resembles Levi-Strauss's structures of the brain. Both positions involve a kind of higher naturalism which attempts to formulate 'the laws of the human mind'.

7. As a mode of analyses, we shall equate emics with 'understanding' and etics with 'explanation'. Emics reflects the point of view of the participants - etics the point of view of the anthropologist. As a mode of description, emics intends to present the subject matter in terms of indigenous theoretical categories. An etic description utilizes scientific concepts (cf. Pelto & Pelto 1972).

8. It is important to note that intersubjectivity must not be confused with 'consensus' or common meanings in general. Consensus means convergence of subjective meaning on certain basic matters. And common meaning is shared aspirations and evaluations of objects.

3

ANTHROPOLOGICAL TRANSLATION

Anthropological translation can be pictured as a kind of dialogue - a kind of *semantic transference* between cultures - where understanding is reached through the 'fusion' of horizons. 'His (the anthropologist's - ØJ) specific task, indeed, is that of mediating the one in terms of the other.' (Giddens 1976:149)

Giddens suggests that the problem of semantic transference within cultures and between cultures can be handled with reference to a distinction between meta-language and lay-language (Giddens 1976:148, 1979:246-253).[1]

The classical example on the relationship between meta-language and lay-language is to be found in Hegel's *Phenomenology of Mind*. In the dialectics between meta-language (Absolute knowledge) and lay-language (natural consciousness), Hegel establishes what we may see as the three steps of anthropological translation: the 'in itself', the 'for itself' and the 'for us'.

When anthropologists, from the standpoint of meta-language, study lay-language as it is *'in itself'*, we translate the structural level of the action system which is not necessarily conscious to lay actors. When we study lay-language as it is *'for itself'*, we translate the conscious sphere of the social world, that is the lifeworld. *'For us'* indicates that we, as observers, have withdrawn from the 'immersion' in our subject matter, withdrawn from description, understanding and translation, to explanatory reflections, from field research to presentation. 'For us' indicates that we are somehow always thrown back upon ourselves. It is we - the anthropologists or other students of cultures - who translate, describe, interpret and explain.

The relationship between us and them is asymmetrical (Gellner 1975:156). Hegel furnishes a kind of ideology for this asymmetrical relationship by conceiving the relation between us and them, between 'Absolute knowledge' and 'natural consciousness', as a kind of 'Jacob's ladder' (Gellner 1970:29). This kind of thinking involving the superiority of Western culture and the imperative of 'educating' other peoples 'up to our level of knowledge and refinement' was inherited by the evolutionist of the Victorian era as a functional ideology in the period of colonialism.

Theories of translation and comparison of cultures like the one advocated in this work take their point of departure from the philosophical-anthropological concept of the 'unity of mankind'. The concept of the 'unity of mankind' was formulated already by Aristotle when he defined Man as the living being who has *logos*.[2] Man, following Aristotle, is distinguished from all other creatures by his capacity for thought, language and action.[3] But as Geertz notes, to take the giant step away from 'the basic unity of mankind' is, so far as the social sciences are concerned, to leave the Garden (Geertz 1973:34,36). The anthropological starting point is thus not Man as he is given by nature - Man as an abstract individual (Lukes 1973:73) - but Man as a social and historical being.

Gellner, in his critique of the relativism of Winch and Wittgenstein (Gellner 1975), concludes that it is the rapid, global diffusion of industrial civilization which provides us with a solution to cultural relativism. In abstracto, Gellner says, relativism has no solution. I agree with Gellner. I hold that the problem of anthropological translation can be solved if it is regarded as a historical process of acculturation whose social carriers are entrepreneurs, brokers, foreign aid workers, missionaries, Gurus, anthropologists, tourists etc. In this 'exchange praxis' between different cultures, a common medium is established through which semantic transference is made possible.

TRANSITION TO THE LOGIC OF KARMA

What follows is an attempt to translate and organize certain key native terms of Brahmanic Hinduism into the anthropological meta-language of the action system presented above. It might appear rather 'crude' to translate imposing religious concepts into an anthropological meta-language. But as social scientists this is the only way to proceed since we must handle religion as a sociological phenomenon.[4] This does not mean that social scientists necessarily reject the existential reality of mystical, religious and magical experiences. We only maintain it falls outside our task to give any other kind of ontological status to these phenomena than those which can be explained through social being.

The lifeworld

There are two native categories which signify the Hindu conception of the lifeworld: *maya* and *samsara*.

Maya is derived from the verbal root *ma* = 'to measure, creating illusions'. The term variously denotes art and supernatural power in the Vedic period, while the connotations change to illusion and unreality during the Upanishadic period. Maya signifies the created world having the ontological status of an appearance.

Samsara is derived from the verbal root *sam sri* = 'to wander or walk through'. The term refers to the 'process of transmigrations, the world and secular life'. Thus, maya/samsara refer to an extended form of a lifeworld; the Hindu lifeworld.

The concept of karma was discussed in the introduction. We shall therefore proceed with the concept of kartri. *Kartri* is one Sanskrit term for 'individual agent'. Kartri refers to a subject who acts on his own accord. Kartri is derived from the verbal root *kri* = to do. As actions cannot be conceived without an agent, karma cannot be conceived without a kartri.

I should also like to add the distinction between agent and actor. The agent was translated as kartri. A possible term for the actor would be *kara* = the doer. Another term is the more general *manushya* meaning man, human being etc. Manushya is derived from *man* = to think and connotes a meaning reflecting our initial definition of Man as a rational, thinking being who has a meaning with his doings.

Long before psychoanalysis, Hinduism showed the importance of the subconscious (Eliade 1969:45). The native term is *vasana* derived from *vas*, bearing the connotation to perfume. *Vasana* signifies impressions - unconscious categories in the mind.

The native term which can be compared with the level of the practical consciousness is *samskara*. *Samskara* is a compositum consisting of the prefix *sam* = coming together, making complete and the verbal noun *kara* derived from the important root *kri* = to do, signifying making, doing and also the observable actor. The meaning of the compositum is the faculty of memory, recollection, mental impression of acts done in a previous existence. It is difficult to draw a sharp line between the two native terms, but the above considerations will do for our purpose. I should also stress that both terms are products of previous karma, deeds done in an earlier life and further conditioning language, perception and knowledge in this life. *Vasana* can be compared with our idea of a priori knowledge and *samskara* with memory.

Manas is the term selected to denote the level of discourse. *Manas* is derived from *man* = to think and signifies the mind, the intellect, intelligence and understanding.

The indigenous term for norm in Hinduism is *svadharma*. The term is a compositum of the reflexive pronoun *sva* meaning 'one's own' and *Dharma* having a wide range of connotations which I shall discuss below. The meaning of the compositum is 'one's own duty' - in short those ascribed duties defining the various Hindus in relation to their *jati* (caste group).

Shakti is one Sanskrit term for power. It signifies both power, ability, strength and might. In the Hindu pantheon, *Shakti* is personalized as the consort of Shiva. She is often pictured with terrible attributes - a symbol of power. It is also symptomatic that the religious cult of Shakti is of special relevance to the *Kshatriya varna* - the warriors and rulers in Hinduism.[5]

'Facilities' in the Hindu context refers to authorizations and allocations inherent in the status position of actors.[6] A Brahmin controls the sacred knowledge through which he obtains and controls magical forces, i.e., the power of *Brahman*. The Kshatriya on the other hand, is the ruler of the land ('Kshatriya' means literally 'the people of empire'). They embody the *kshatra* which means 'might and secular force'. By submitting to the supremacy of the Brahmins and Brahman, the Kshatriya varna is invested with legitimate force - the *kshatra*.

Then we have the Sanskrit terms connoting sanction. I have selected two: *danda* and *prayaschitta* (Dumont 1970:168). *Danda* signifies a 'stick, a club' and is the term which symbolizes punishment, judicial authority. In the Hindu pantheon, danda is often personified as Dharma = justice.

Punishment is the 'strong' version of sanctions. Therefore I have also included prayaschitta as another kind of sanction. *Prayaschitta* means atonement, expiation. It signifies actions of penance and self torture undertaken to remove sins - accumulated bad karma. The relationship between danda and prayaschitta might be very close. When actions have violated rules and demand punishment, punishment is also conceived as a necessary torture to remove bad karma. Danda involves legal sanctions, prayaschittas not necessarily so.

The structural level

There are two religious terms in Hinduism which may be said to reflect the structural level; Atman/Brahman. In Indian thinking these terms refers to the Absolute - the Reality behind appearances.

Following Radhakrishnan, *Atman* is the principle of Man's life, the Soul that pervades his being (1953:73). Atman is the subjective viewpoint of the Absolute (Sharma 1972:14). In our anthropological meta-language, Atman is a religious extension of the intersubjective ideational structure of the action system. *Brahman* is derived from the root *brh* = 'to swell, to expand'. The general meaning of Brahman is impersonal God - the Absolute. Brahman signifies the objective viewpoint of the Absolute (Sharma 1972). Brahman is a religious extension of the 'objective' social and material structures of the action system.

The distinction between reality and appearance, Brahman/Atman on the one side and samsara/maya on the other, has its counterpart in native epistemological concepts.[7] The knowledge which discloses reality is called *para-vidya* = the higher knowledge. The knowledge which remains ingrained within appearance - the lifeworld - is called *apara-vidya*, the lower knowledge. By obtaining higher knowledge, the devoted Hindu attains the state of *Moksha*, identity with the Absolute.

The socalled '*law of karma*' is one essential representation of the ideational structure of Hinduism. The law of karma consist of the following components:

i) A belief in a universal causality, not only within the domain of nature, but also within the moral world. All acts (karma) will sooner or later produce their respective effects.

ii) A belief in rebirth. All beings which have a store of accumulated karma, must be reborn in order to experience the fruits of previous actions.

iii) The idea of ethicization (O'Flaherty 1980:XI). Good acts produce pleasant results, bad acts produce unfavourable results.

iv) The law of karma also has a soteriological aspect which can be linked to the karmic problem.

Against the background of these four components of the law of karma and the problems they raise for the devoted Hindu, the three interpretative schemes of ritualist, renouncer and householder appear as parts of a unifying whole.

The relevant term for 'social structure' in Hinduism is *varnashramadharma*. Varnashramadharma is a compositum of three terms. *Varna* means outward appearance and colour and signify the classical four caste categories of Hinduism. *Ashrama* means a hermitage, an abode of renouncers. Ashrama also signifies the four stages of life incumbent upon all devoted twiceborns (the three higher castes) of Hindu society. *Dharma* is derived from the root *dhr* = the action of maintaining, supporting (Lingat 1973:3) and its primary meaning would be duty, eternal law, cosmic order, religion etc. The meaning of the whole compositum would be the prescribed actions immanent in caste and life stage, contributing to the reproduction of the social order as a whole and to the religious freedom of the individual.

As I shall argue in Part Three, material structures have a secondary significance in Hinduism. Material objects - wealth, land etc. - enter the picture as a kind of residual categories (Dumont 1970:38). For example, caste groups utilize material resources in their strategic encounters in the lifeworld, seeking to obtain higher social recognition in the hierarchy. Material resources are the means, higher religious recognition is the aim.

The dualistic terminology of Gita/Manu

The reader should be aware that the Gita/Manu inherit a terminology from the dualistic system of *Samkhya* philosophy. In this system, Atman/Brahman is termed *Purusha*, literally meaning 'human being, mankind' etc. We shall translate Purusha as spirit. Maya/samsara is termed *prakrti* which we can translate as matter or nature. The important difference between the Upanishads and the Gita/Manu is the Absolute dualism of the latter. Gita/Manu do not accept that the lifeworld (maya/samsara/prakrti) only has the ontological status of an appearance. Both levels of being are real.

Ahamkara is another term of importance in the Gita/Manu. The meaning of *ahamkara* is the 'I-doer'. *Aham* means 'I' and *kara*, as noted before, means the 'doer'. In the dualistic system of Gita/Manu, ahamkara is the term which denotes the individual agent. I shall therefore use kartri and ahamkara as synonymous terms throughout the book.

NOTES TO CHAPTER 3

1. Semantic transference is intrinsic to communication itself (Steiner 1975:256).

2. 'Logos' is a Greek word with various meanings; language, reason, word, etc.

3. 'Life seems to be common even to plants, but we are seeking what is *peculiar* to Man. Let us exclude, therefore, the life of nutrition and growth. Next there would be a life of perception, but it also seems to be common even to the horse, the ox, and every animal. There remains then, an active life of the element that has a *rational* principle." (Aristotle *N. Ethics* - 1.7. 1098)

4. 'If religion has given birth to all that is essential in society, it is because the idea of society is the soul of religion. Religious forces are therefore human forces, moral forces.' (Durkheim 1976:419)

5. On the problem of power in Hindu ideology, see Wadley 1977

6. The Sanskrit term *karana* meaning the instruments of action, may in some contexts be translated as 'facilities'.

7. Sanskrit grammarians, on their part, utilized a distinction coming close to the *langue/ parole* of Saussure (1916). In their grammatical model, Brahman is regarded as being of the nature of the word (*sabdatattva*). As such, Brahman is pictured as the source and structure of words (*pada*) and sentences (*vakya*), through the application of which the whole cosmos is constituted.

PART II

THE LOGIC OF KARMA

4

THE THREE WORLD VIEWS OF BRAHMANIC HINDUISM

In his book *Indian Sadhus*, Ghurye emphasizes India's unique contribution to social thought and practice by upholding two kinds of life as ideal types, the disinterested householder and the renouncer (Ghurye 1953:1). Dumont also makes these two types one of his fundamental starting points. Dumont distinguishes between the-man-in-the-world - the householder - and the-man-outside-the-world - the renouncer (Dumont 1960).

Following Weber, there are not two, but four *possible* types (Weber 1964:166-183). Weber arrived at his scheme as follows: In the sphere of ideas, he distinguished between the path of mastery, which he called asceticism, and that of resignedness or 'adjustment', which he called mysticism. In the realm of social structure he distinguished between inner-worldly and other-worldly. Thus we get inner-worldly and other-worldly ascetics in addition to inner-worldly and other-worldly mystics.

I have selected the 'middle way'. I hold that Hinduism offers three life models; ritualist, renouncer and householder. These can each be presented as having their historical roots in three successive periods; the Vedic period, the Upanishadic period and the Hindu period. Each of them is, as we already know, connected with one of the three holy books of Brahmanic Hinduism; the Vedas, the Upanishads and the Manu/Gita.

The *ritualist* who is influenced by a system of ideas having its origin in the Vedic period and who upholds the Vedas as his holy book, follows the path of activity (*pravrtikarmamarga*),[1] performs the sacrificial karma-type (action type) and upholds Dharma (duty, reproduction of world order) as his main aim of life. In the terminology of Weber, the ritualist is an inner-worldly ascetic, a man of the world with an attitude of mastery. I shall argue that this mode of consciousness closely resembles magical thinking in general.

The *renouncer* who is influenced by a system of ideas having its origin in the Upanishadic period and who upholds the Upanishads as his holy book, follows the path of renunciation of actions (*nivrtikarmamarga*), performs the meditative karma-type and upholds the spiritual value of *Moksha* as his main aim of life. In a general scheme of religious classification, the renouncer may be subsumed under the mystical type. In Weber's terminology, the renouncer is an other-worldly mystic who has lost all interest in the power and pleasure of this world and seeks mystical illumination through the ideal of *inactivity* (Weber 1958:222, 1964:171). From the perspective of the other-worldly mystic, the ascetic is always immersing himself into the burden of the created world. The *householder* who is influenced by a system of ideas having its origin in the Hindu period and who upholds the Manu/Gita as his holy books, follows the path of action without desire (*nishkamakarmamarga*), performs the holistic karma-type and believes in the ethic/spiritual value of reaching Moksha through Dharma. The path of the householder of Gita/Manu is, in the terminology of Weber, inner-worldly mysticism (1958:189). The householder seeks liberation by understanding himself as a servant, slave or instrument in the hands of God. He adapts himself to the duty to which he is born (Gita 18.48). In the general scheme of religious classification, the householder is the religious type proper.

I have thus not followed Dumont and others (see Dumont 1982) by selecting the king as an independent type. The king, along with the other-worldly ascetic - the magical 'mastery' renouncer - are in the perspective of the present work to be regarded as secondary lifestyle models. Undoubtedly they have great importance in the Hindu scheme of things, but they are not the main carriers of the ideas and values of Brahmanic Hinduism. For example, the king does not necessarily accept values like vegetarianism and teetotalism which are fundamental to Brahmanic Hinduism as well as the process of Sanskritization (Srinivas 1965). In the Brahmanic scheme of ideas, the king is also secondary in relation to the ritualist who makes kingship legitimate. With regard to Sanskritization, Cohn's description of the *Chamars* (leather workers) in an Eastern Uttar Pradesh village presents us with an example of relevance for the issue of lifestyle models. In their effort to try to raise their status, the Chamars seem to be completely indifferent to those very aspects of social life which are favoured by the dominant caste - the kingly model represented by the *Thakurs*. It is above all the Brahmin ritualists who constitute the reference group for the Chamars (Cohn 1955, Dumont & Pocock 1957:34).

History and culture lags

For the modern scholar, each of the above mentioned texts constitutes a unique piece of information determined by its place in history and its rela-tions to other texts. Such historical and atomistic perspectives run counter to the apprehensions of the Hindus themselves who regard the holy scriptures as one coexisting complete whole - the eternal order in the form of words.[2] 'The *Shruti* texts give rise to a wrong view if they are not studied as one connected whole.' (*Brahma Sutra*:xv) Consequently, the Hindus study their holy scriptures *sub specie aeternitatis*. They believe that the different texts carry similar meanings (Van Buitenen 1968:29).

But, the Hindus accept an interior segmentation of the scriptures with regard to different ethic-spiritual paths. They admit that these paths have special relevance for different groups of the people. The indigenous explanation for this interior differentiation is the idea that individuals belong to diverse levels of ethic-spiritual perfection. Hence, they are in need of various paths and formulations of the one single truth.

An anthropological approach can combine the diachronic perspective of the philologist with the synchronic perspectives of the Hindus themselves. This means that we can read the presentation in the following chapter both as a kind of cultural history and as a presentation of the interrelated culture lags of Brahmanic Hinduism.[3]

THE MAGICAL WORLD VIEW OF THE VEDAS AND THE RITUALIST

Brahmanism, the first chapter of Hinduism proper, is an Indian creation on Indian soil born out of a clash between the Indo-Aryan, Munda and Dravidian speaking peoples. As there are few primary sources from the non-Aryan element of the population, we shall have to focus our attention on the Indo-Aryans, undoubtedly the dominant people in the acculturation process (Gonda 1965:21).

In the Vedic period (1200-800 B.C.), society was still on the tribal level (Kosambi 1965:120) organized according to a system of patriarchal kinship. There is much evidence in the early Vedic material in support of Dumezil's theories of Indo-European tripartite division.[4] Vedic society was tribal chiefdoms with ranked lineages performing specialized social functions.

The Indo-Aryans were still a pastoral, warrior people after they had settled in their first main homeland, the Punjab. The horse and the cattle which later became the holy Indian cows must have been some of the factors for their success.

Later in this first period, the myth of the four varnas appear (Rig Veda X 90), probably because of the encounter between the Aryans and the original inhabitants of India, the Dravidians and the Munda speaking people. The early Vedic people were still living in the bronze age (Kosambi 1965:85) and did not know the art of writing.

It is fertile to consider the Vedas in light of the division of labour among the ritualists of the Brahmin varna.[5] The Vedas consist of four collections the *Rig- Yajur- Sama-* and *Atharva-Veda*. They contained the necessary words, prayers and instructions for the four main categories of priests in the sacrificial performance.

The *Hotri* priest belonged to the Rig Veda. His function was to recite the different prayers as clearly and precisely as possible. The *Udgatri* priest belonged to the Sama Veda. His function was to sing melodious in the background. The function of the *Adhvarya* priest was primarily to attend to the manual work of the ritual, the preparation of the sacrificial area and the instruments of sacrifice and the slaughtering of the animal. The Adhvaryu priest belonged to the Yajur Veda which gives a thorough description of the ritual action as it is performed by this priest. The *Brahmin* priest was the chief supervisor of the whole ritual. He was expected to know the three other Vedas and should, by taking recourse to the magical formulas of the Atharva Veda, counteract the mistakes that might have been done during the sacrificial performance. Any mistake, whether in the pronunciation of words and grammar or in the physical performance of the sacrifice could, according to the ratio of the ritualists, have disastrous consequences. Therefore, alongside the four Vedas one saw the development of the six *Vedangas* meaning the auxiliary sciences to secure the right understanding, performance, phonetics, grammar etc. of the ritual.[6]

The Vedas were later systematized in the *Mimamsa* philosophical system of Jaimini, the origin of which is dated to some centuries before Christ. The most famous interpreter of the Mimamsa philosophy was the ritualist Kumarila, a South Indian living in the seventh century A.D. Kumarila is rightly called by Radhakrishnan as '.. the vigorous exponent of Brahmanical orthodoxy which assumes the authorativeness of the Vedas and the supremacy of the priest,..' (Radhakrishnan op.cit.:377) Through these sources, the ritualists are influenced by a system of ideas which can be traced back to the Vedic period. Belonging to this oldest culture lag, they are definitely the most orthodox strata of Hindu-society.

The ritualist and sacrifice

All that is, (all being and) all the Gods, have a single life principle, the sacrifice. (S.B. 14.3.2.1).

In the Vedic scriptures it is stated that 'The sacrifice is the greatest of all actions' ((S.B. 1.7.1.-5, and T.B. 3.2.1.4, see Basu 1969:140) For this reason Aguilar calls the Vedic Indians the people of sacrifice, just as the Bible calls the tribes of Jacob the people of Yahweh (Aguilar 1976:57). The importance of sacrifice was carried so far that to lie, in the Vedic context, simply meant *not* to sacrifice (Aguilar 1976:26). Undoubtedly, this signifies that sacrifice was an important mark of ethnic identity for the Indo-Aryans confronting the aboriginal peoples.[7]

The Vedic people thought that sacrifice was the essence of life and Being. Sacrifice is often identified with the cosmic order - *Rta* (Aguilar 1976:45) - and symbolized as the navel of the world.[8] The etymology of *Rta* is 'what sets in motion' (op.cit.: 25) and the essence of this motion is the act of sacrifice. As the highest principle of the cosmic order, sacrifice was incumbent upon men and Gods. The Gods were themselves sacrificers who reached their exalted position through accumulation of sacrificial merit (S.B. 3.1.4.3).

Through sacrifice, Gods and men were weaving the threads that kept the three regions together in harmony and abundance (op.cit.:66, 91). The earthly sacrifice ascends with *Agni* - the fire - to the heavenly regions of the Gods. There it is consumed and transformed into water which descends as rain for prosperity of the earthly region. The entire economy of the cosmos is thus dependent on the proper performance of the sacrifice.

The Sanskrit term *yajna* is derived from the root *yaj* which has a double meaning; i) to eat, to destroy,[9] which refer to the destructive element of the sacrifice and ii) to create, to cause to be, (op.cit.:39, 148) which refer to the belief in the function and efficacy of the sacrificial act. The prototype of the sacrifice can be found in the *Purusha Shukta* of the Rig Veda, where the Gods are the agents and the primeval giant, *Purusha*, the victim of sacrifice.[10]

From the sacrifice of the primeval person, Purusha, the heavenly prototypes of the four *varnas* were produced.

His mouth was the Brahman, his two arms were made the warrior, his two thighs the Vaishya, from his two feet the Sudra was born. (Rig Veda 10.90.12)

In spite of the differences between the varnas caused by their origin from different parts of Purusha, there is an underlying identity between the four varnas. They are all a product of one victim - Purusha - and one sacrificial action - the first heavenly sacrifice. The verse dispels an important aspect of caste ideology, namely the idea of a *functional organism*.

From his navel was produced the air, from his head the sky was evolved, from his two feet the earth, from his ear the quarters; thus they fashioned the worlds. (op.cit.:14)

The three regions evolved from different parts of Purusha. We can see the typical identification between the macro- and the micro-cosmos as the Brahmin varna is identified with the upper-region, the Shudra with earth. The whole orderly cosmos was brought into being through this primordial act of cultural action (Aguilar 1976:18). And as the Gods did in the beginning, so should men proceed and follow the prototype of the heavenly liturgy (see Rig Veda 10.130.6). By doing what the Gods did in the beginning, by repeating the eternal archetype, the sacrificers reproduce the universe. They contribute to world maintenance (Berger 1974).

Magical creativity and the causal chain

When the Vedic rulers wanted to proclaim sovereignty over new conquered land, they performed the greatest of all Vedic sacrifices, the *Ashvamedha* - the horse sacrifice. For one year a horse was let loose to roam about freely in the new country. From certain marks the enemies could easily recognize it to be a sacrificial horse. If anyone seized the horse, it was an act of opposition to the claim to the land and a signal of war. But if the horse was not captured during the year, the owner could proclaim himself a ruler and perform the Ashvamedha.

A new sacrificial altar (*vedi*) was built and the act of its construction was seen as a symbolic cosmogony. The sacrificial post was consecrated as the new centre of the world (Aguilar 1976:130) and as the *axis mundi* through which direct communication was possible between Gods and men (Hubert & Mauss 1964:27). Thus the new land was made holy and fit for the Vedic Indians. For these warrior-people, the expansion of territory was like a magical creation.

> One who performs the *Ashvamedha* conquers all the quarters, conquers the world, the priest make him a ruler and upholder.' (S.B. 13.1.2.3. translated by Basu 1969:95)

The most important component of the sacrificial ritual was undoubtedly the slaying of the victim. The transmission from life to death of the victim released a strong, ambiguous power which had to be tamed and manipulated by the priests, to the benefit of the sacrificer (Hubert & Mauss 1964:41-52). This power could either transform the sacrificer into a heavenly state beyond life and death or it could remove his sins by absorbing the demerit of his person.

No sacrificial ritual was properly constituted without the structuring power of speech. Certain castes were specialized to perform the physical operations of sacrifice and others to utter the correct words (*mantra*). The language through which these words were expressed was Sanskrit, meaning 'well formed'. The words of Sanskrit were considered the reproduction in sound of the structures of reality (Hopkins 1971:20).

The patron of the Ashvamedha sacrifice was the king - the Kshatriya. The officiants were the ritualists, the Brahmin priests. According to the laws of Manu, the Brahmin priests were the only persons authorized to take recourse to magic (Manu 9.314, 11,32-33). The Brahmins represented the only varna seen to have the knowledge and power to manipulate Brahman, the holy magical power. Through ritual action, the Brahmins, that is, men who possess Brahman, could manipulate the magical power to desired ends (Mauss 1972:5, 116-117).[11]

One Sanskrit term for magic is *maya* which, as we know, has several connotations like art, wisdom, illusion, lifeworld, witchcraft and magic (Reyna 1962:5, Mauss 1972:61-63). It is often stated in the Vedas that Indra triumphs over the demons through his maya (Rig Veda 1.2.7). The importance of maya is twofold. When the power of Brahman is put into creative activity, or, in epistemological language, when Brahman is made manifest, - the act of creation and constitution is called maya. Brahman signifies the cosmic power, and maya signifies the personified ability to put this power into operation. The second meaning refers to the effect - the product - of this activity.

That which coming into being, was covered with the void, that One arose through the power of heat (*tapas*). Desire (*kama*) in the beginning came upon that (desire), that was the first seed of mind.' (Rig Veda 10.129.3-4)

Two notions are of importance for understanding the magical power of maya:

i) *Tapas* which in the hymn is conceived as an integral part of the Absolute. Through the activity of tapas, the infinite manifested itself as *that One*.[12]

ii) *Kama* meaning desire/will, which in the hymn is seen as the first seed of mind. Kama was not an integral part of the Absolute. It arose as a result of the productive activity of tapas.[13] Through maya a causal chain is seen to be activated - a chain which denotes a belief in the efficacy of the ritual and a mechanical relationship between the sacrificial action and its effect.

The Mimamsa philosophy of the ritualists explains the relationship between cause and effect, action and result, through the theory of *apurva* (meaning 'what was not before, not earlier'). Apurva is perceived as a metaphysical entity which attaches itself to the soul of the performer and clings to him until it ripens and bears fruit. Apurva then, is important for understanding the idea of the *efficacy* of the ritual. Whatever acts a man has performed, the *apurva* will never be lost, it will mature in due course.[14]

As far as magical elements can be identified in the Vedic sacrifice, we can conclude with Marcel Mauss that it gives 'every outward appearance of being a gigantic variation on the principle of causality' (Mauss 1972:63).[15] The belief in the efficacy of the rite developed so far that the ritual was conceived more or less as a kind of *mechanical* system. The success of the ritual became completely dependent on the correct performance. Any mistakes and abbreviations from the prescribed mode could, according to the belief of the ritualists, have disastrous consequences. It was not the feelings, the attitude or intentions that were important for the success of the ritual. It was the correct exterior movements, the correct pronunciation and grammar, the correctness of timing etc. (Macdonald 1979:46). In this *mechanical world view*, Gods were of secondary importance. They were conceived to be the personifications of the cosmical power of Brahman. In the Mimamsa philosophy of the ritualists, the Gods are supposed to be nothing more than a name inflected in the dative case (Radhakrishnan 1966 v.2:429). We can conclude with Radhakrishnan that the sacrificial ritualism of the Vedic period was a mechanical ceremonialism (op.cit.:420) based on a mechanical ethic (op.cit.:429). We shall see, when reaching the Upanishadic period, that karma develops into moral action proper (Dasgupta 1957:317).

Sacrifice, magic and primitive science

There are various opinions on the question of the similarity between Vedic sacrifice and magic. Aguilar, for example, in his *The sacrifice of the Rig Veda* (1976:101) wants to warn against reducing the Vedic liturgy to some sort of magic. The Indologist Keith reached the opposite conclusion. 'Scarcely any rite can be so adapted as to produce magic ends.' (Keith 1925 v.2:379) Weber, likewise, seems to regard the Vedic sacrifice as a form of magical instrumentality (Weber 1964:26). And Marcel Mauss concludes in his *A general Theory of Magic* (1972:52) that sacrifice and magic may be associated together.

Mauss and Durkheim defined magic as '...any private rite which does not play a part in organized cult.' (Mauss 1972:24 - Durkheim 1976:44).[16] 'There is no church of magic', while 'Religion on the other hand, is inseparable from the idea of a church.' (Durkheim loc.cit.) Seen in connection with the fact that there did not exist any public cult in Vedic sacrificial ritualism (Heestermann 1978:87, Lingat 1973:10), we have one criteria for identifying Vedic sacrifice as magic.

However, there is one problem with Durkheim and Mauss' sociological definition of magic. One can hardly say that Hinduism has any church at all, if by 'church' we should mean as Weber, a universalistic establishment, (1958:6), a centralized authority.

Van der Leeuw (1937) found the difference between magic and religion in the attitude of actors. Magical man approach the power -the Gods - with a superior attitude. He commands and manipulates. Van der Leeuw's definition is significant as it brings us back to the 'inner-worldly asceticism' - the path of mastery - with which I earlier described the ritualist. Seen in context with the statement of the Mimamsa philosophy of the ritualist which describes the Gods as nothing more than a name inflected in the dative case (Radhakrishnan op.cit.), we have another criterion for identifying Vedic sacrifice with magic.

Religious man according to the phenomenological school of religion, has another attitude. He subordinates himself in the service of God. He regards himself as an instrument in the hands of the higher power. He kneels, prays and feels himself as nothing in relation to the *mysterium tremendum* - the complete otherness of the holy.

The pragmatic and utilitarian theory of magic advanced by Malinowski (Nadel:1970:195) underscores the individualistic traits in magic. According to Malinowski, magic is above all action - the power of creating desired ends (Malinowski 1948:56-59). Magic and religion are opposed, according to Malinowski, by this very instrumental and utilitarian character of magic (op.cit.:20). Compared with the usually accepted fact that sacrificial ritualism has a strong individualistic flavour in the way it only promises the benefits from sacrifice to the single sacrificer, we have yet another criterion for defining sacrifice as magic.[17] Religion, on the other hand, 'is an affair of the all.' (Nadel 1970:199,204).

As a sub category of religious phenomena in general, the ritualist and his sacrificial karma represent an example of magic. My conclusion will appear more well founded after the reader has been presented with the mystical world view of the renouncer and the religious world view of the householder.

To what extent can magic be identified as a primitive science?[18]

We have seen that the principle of causality was one of the main ideas behind the sacrificial ritualism. We have also seen the importance attached to correct performance and the growth of the six *Vedangas* - the auxiliary 'sciences' to be used as manuals in this regard. These aspects make it reasonable to identify Vedic ritualism as a primitive science. But there are other and more important criteria defining science as a specific form of knowledge which are not to be found in Vedic ritualism.

First, there is no such thing as an institutionalized critical attitude in Vedic ritualism and thus no practise of experiment.[19] Failure in reaching the desired aim of a ritual is explained with reference to wrong procedures and mistakes in performance.

Second, Vedic ritualism (and magic in general) was not based on knowledge accumulation. The knowledge of sacrifice was, as we have seen, instituted by the Gods. There is nothing that man can contribute except repeating the archetype.

Third, science is based on a fundamental demarcation between subject and object, spirit and nature, metaphysics and the realm of empirical investigation. The magical world view of the Vedic period is on the contrary, based on a monistic perception of the world, as I shall later argue. What modern science would call metaphysics was a sphere open to 'empirical' experience for the Hindus. The ancient Vedic *Rishis*, the culture heroes of the Hindus, did not just believe the truth. They *saw* it.[20] They experienced it.

A well known example in this regard is the claim of Hinduism that those who have spiritual powers can remember previous lives and see what kind of karmas caused the characteristics of present life (*Yoga Sutra*: 3.18). Through certain practices and disciplines, the Yoga Sutra says, the adept will reach a mode of being which enables him to utilize certain faculties of the human psyche which otherwise would lie dormant. In this manner the Hindus claim to have verified their belief in reincarnation. And how can we disregard them if we have not undergone the prescribed procedure?

Similarly, in Vedic society as in primitive societies in general, sickness usually has a spiritual explanation. Any cure, whether of a shamanistic, magical or sacrificial type, implies a manipulation of spiritual forces. Any removal of spiritual causes is believed to heal the sickness, however natural the causes might appear to us. And because the metaphysical ideas are believed, they exist; 'They exist objectively, as social facts.' (Hubert & Mauss op.cit.:101)[21]

Tylor and Frazer's idea of magic as based on a faulty manipulation of ideas is grounded in an epistemological confusion; a confusion, as noted by Levi-Strauss, between form and content (1966:65). Both Vedic ritualism and modern science presuppose the principle of causality. But which causes can be connected with which effects is a question of *empirical* investigation and experiment.

For example, parapsychological research is working with many hypotheses which at the present level of modern science can neither be verified nor falsified. One interesting case is the research made by I. Stevenson with people who claim to have lived a previous life. In this manner he is inquiring into the validity of the belief in reincarnation (Stevenson 1974). We cannot overlook the possibility that future research might produce other scientific paradigms where our ideas of the borders of experience will be broadened. As Weber noted, any judgement of magic as correct or fallacious, is a perspective derived from the context of modern science (Weber 1964:2).

Although magic has some similarities with modern science, for example its pragmatic attitude, I prefer to call it a rational system rather than a primitive science (Jarvie, Agassie op.cit.). It is rational because it is based on the principle of causality and purposive instrumental action. It is unscientific because it does not share some fundamental presuppositions of modern science. It is not based on experiment and knowledge accumulation. Magical knowledge is believed to be instituted by the Gods.

The ritualist and his understanding of the law of karma
'by sacrifice he shall effect heaven.' (Staal 1969:511)

Sacrifices performed the correct way produce merit on the part of the
sacrificer - merit which will influence his after worldly existence.

Now truly this man is composed of sacrifice. So many sacrifices as he
has performed when he departs from this world, with so many is he
born in the other world after his death. (S.B. 10.6.3.1)

In the next world they place his good and evil deeds in a balance.
(S.B. 11.2.7.3)

Due to differences in sacrificial merit, the sacrificers reached different heav-
ens (see Rig Veda X 60.6, X.88.15). This path of 'merit accumulation' is in
Sanskrit called *pravrti marga* (lit. the path of activity) and is of great
importance in practical Hinduism. The renouncer, on the other hand,
follows the *nivrti marga*, the path of 'blowing out' and cessation of all activities (Manu 12.88).

The notion of suffering is not to be found in the Vedas (Kunhan Raja
1963:250). Life was consummated through the fulfilment of desires (*kama*);
'...may we see for a hundred years and live for a hundred years.' (Rig Veda
7.66.16) Heavenly life is conceived in a sensual way like the Vedic life
affirming attitude in general; '...he retains in heaven all his functions, even
to that of sexual intercourse.' (S.B. 10.4.4.4) The ritualists seek happiness
through action and active participation in the duties and regard
actionlessness as a lapse into the unconsciousness of pure materiality. The
ritualist Kumarila pictures the ideal of freedom of competing schools
following the *nivrti marga* as the condition of a stone (Keith 1921:75).

The ritualists do not accept the devaluation of the world and karma
(Radhakrishnan 1966 2:415). They do not accept Shankara's doctrine of
maya whose aim the ritualist Kumarila interpreted as the 'instilling of the
feeling of disgust in the worldly affairs..' (Quoted from Devaraja 1972:196).
It is doubtful whether the Vedas distinguish between reality and appearance,
a distinction so important in the Upanishads.

The sacrificial ritualism of the Vedas belonged to what Bellah has
classified as archaic religion, a stage in religious evolution characterized by
a monistic world view (Bellah 1969). 'The dualism between matter and
spirit is a later accretion in Indian thought, when the idea of salvation,
final release became a powerful factor in the Indian mind.' (Raja 1963:230)

The Vedic world view was indeed monistic. Gods and men were seen to inhabit the same cosmos, just like the old Gods of the Greek or the Nordic people who lived on the top of the mountains. The various spheres of creation, from the Gods in heaven to those of animals and plants, were conceived as attributes or personifications of the powers of sacrifice, that is the power of Brahman.

The principle difference between the ritualist and the householder, both of them men-inside-the-world, is that *desire* is an important normative element in the actions of the ritualist, whereas to the householder it is not. In many verses of the Gita (see 2.41-46) the *pravrti marga* of the ritualist, is alluded to in rather denunciatory terms. The Vedic path of karma is called the lower path because the ritualists were perceived always to have some selfish end in view.

The ritualist as he exists in traditional Hindu society is certainly not a pure survival from the Vedic period. The force of history has naturally made its impact on him. For example, in the Vedas we do not find any theory of rebirth.[22] But during the course of history, the ritualist accepted the classical rebirth doctrine as it was developed in the Upanishads. The Vedic ritualist, who was originally a cow slaughterer and meat eater (cf. Dumont 1970:146-151), also accepted vegetarianism and *ahimsa* from the renouncers.

The rise of the doctrine of karmic transfer

The historical roots of the doctrine of karmic transfer[23] are to be found in the Vedic rites for the 'living dead',[24] the *sapindikarana* and *shraddha* rituals for the departed forefathers.

A short etymological analysis will be of value for a more refined understanding. *Sapindikarana* is a compositum consisting of the prefix *sa* signifying conjunction and *pinda* referring to the sacrificial substance of a ball of cooked rice. *Sapinda* then, means 'having the same pinda' which means the same maternal and paternal kinship relations through seven generations from ego's great grandfather to ego's son's grandson or daughter's grandson. The crucial term in the compositum is *karana*. *Karana* is related to karma and is also derived from the verbal root *kri* = to do. The meaning of the term is effecting, causing, and 'the means or instrument by which an action is effected'. *Sapindikarana* is a ritual which is seen to effect the entry of the deceased into the world of ancestors through a series of bodily constructions and dissolutions which the deceased undergoes by the instrumentality of the ritual (Knipe 1977:11).

The soul of the dead person does not reach the world of ancestors at once. It remains separate from them for a time as a *preta* = ghost or disembodied spirit. This is a very vulnerable period both for the deceased and the descendants. Relatives observe *sutaka*, the state of ritual impurity which results from death, usually for a period of twelve days. The twelfth day after death is normally the time for the ritual of sapindikarana (Pandey 1969:267). Through the instrumentality of this rite, the *preta* receives a new body necessary for enjoying the pleasures of immortal life in heaven. 'This sacrificer is born with his whole body in the next world.' (S.B. 4.6.1.1) Thereafter he is moved 'up' and out of limbo to the first heaven of the fathers and united with his ancestors.[25]

Through the offerings of *pinda* - cooked rice balls - the ritual performers *transfer* merit and ritual food (karmic transfer) which enable the *preta* to enter the next stage of existence. And in exchange, the descendants are not haunted any longer by the preta.

It is important to note the crucial value attached to the body in the Vedic conception of after worldly existence. Without body and regular ritual nourishment, heavenly life was not possible (Knipe 1977:114). Compared to the degradation of all kinds of bodily existence in the Upanishads, we have before us another manifestation of the Brahmanical opposition.

Then we have the *shraddha* ritual. *Shraddha* means to put trust in, to be loyal, to credit, and signifies a ceremony in honour of and for the benefit of father, grandfather and great grandfather both on the paternal and maternal side. Following the Laws of Manu, shraddha should be performed each month on the new-moon day by all Brahmins keeping the sacred fire (Manu 3.123). The shraddha ritual is a monthly ceremony to the ancestors involving the exchange of ritual food and merit flowing in both directions. The ancestors are secured a better destiny. The descendants receive in return progeny and fertility, sons for the security of one's own after worldly existence. We can read in Carstair's book *The twice born* that one of his informants defined a son as one who saves his father from hell.

> Because when he has no son, after his death there is no one to perform the funeral rites and for lack of these rites he can't get Nirvana. (Carstairs 1961:122)

The ritual activity directed towards the departed, the sapindikarana and shraddha rites, includes several representations which are understandable within a general theory of transaction. Sacrificial substances and merit are believed to be transferred from the living to the dead in exchange for security, peace, fertility etc. The Vedic relationship between the living and the departed is transactional.

The otherworldly ascetic

In the tenth book of the Rig Veda we come across a small section of society which does not seem to seek the delights of this world. The reference is to the *munis*. His chief characteristics are his long hair and yellow robes. He seems to have obtained many magical powers through the practice of *tapas* (Rig Veda 10.136.1-7). The practice of tapas involves hard ascetic methods, sexual abstinence and breathing exercises. The result of the practice was the creation of magical heat or spiritual soul force. Through tapas the *muni* could, as it is stated, achieve all his desires. He could manipulate the cosmical order and he could even create the worlds. The muni also seeks ecstasy and he can fly through the air and visit the Gods (Rig Veda 10.136.1-7). All these ideas seem to indicate that the muni resembled shamans and had close affinities with magical thinking (Eliade 1958:101-111).

Although we find many of these characteristics with the renouncer of the later ages, I agree with Eliade that the muni only vaguely resembles the *yogin* - the renouncer of the Upanishadic period (Eliade 1958:102). The muni had a strong desire to obtain magical powers to seek mastery over himself and the world.

But the other-worldly ascetic, the fourth type of Weber, is not seen as a normative model in Brahmanic Hinduism. We learn from Patanjali's *Yoga Sutra* that the attainment of powers should not be regarded as an end in itself (Yoga Sutra chap. 3). The muni as an other-worldly ascetic is similarly not contributing anything new to the development of Hinduism, as this type is a survival from shamanism (Eliade 1958:102). It was the renouncer as a normative model which became the main mover towards world fleeing mysticism so peculiar to Hinduism.

THE MYSTICAL WORLD-VIEW OF THE UPANISHADS AND THE RENOUNCERS

One of the most important changes from the Vedic to the Upanishadic period (800 - 600 B.C.) was the transformation from a pastoral to an agrarian economy. This transformation involved clearing vast areas of forests. We can read about this struggle with nature in the *Mahabharata* when the Pandavas burnt down the forest of Indraprashtha, located close to modern Delhi. Afterwards they cultivated the area with plough farming in much the same way as the peasants do in contemporary India.

The early scriptures give evidence of movements towards the east (Muir 1880, vol. 2:358 - 444). The centre of Upanishadic society is in the Ganges valley and the first cities after the ruin of Mohenjodaro and Harappa are to be found here. The first states, Kosala and Magadha, so often mentioned in the early Buddhist Sutras, conquered and assembled the earlier 16 tribes and instituted absolute monarchies (Kosambi 1965:120). Magadha was the germ for the later famous Mauryan dynasty.

The caste system of the Upanishadic period is more advanced than its rudimentary forms in early Vedic society. But the growth of new ideas and the challenge of heterodox religions which the Upanishadic period experienced resulted in a setback of Brahmanical power. The sacrificial formalism of the Vedic period was widely questioned and the priestly functions did not command the same prestige and power as earlier.

There are many indications from this period of busy trade and well developed caravan routes. Archaeologists have discovered coins from this period and iron seems to have been widely used.

The *Brahmi* alphabet, the mother of *Devanagari* - the official alphabet of modern India - was probably known from around 700 B.C. (Kosambi 1965:88, see also Basham 1967:400). It must have been used for mercantile purposes in the beginning. Later it also became important in political administration. But as I shall explain later, the holy scriptures were persistently kept within the oral tradition of the Brahmin caste.

These changes in socio-material conditions run parallel to a new development in the evolution of the holy scriptures of India. The first Upanishads are to be found among the *Aranyakas* which means 'the scriptures produced in the forest'.[26] The term '*Aranyaka*' seems to emphasize that the Upanishads indeed belong to the sannyasi - the renouncer outside the world. The literal meaning of the term sannyasi is he who no longer recites mantras and performs sacrificial karma. Similarly, the Upanishads do not attach any value to the outward ritualism of the previous period.

> Unsafe boats however are these sacrificial forms...in which is expressed the lower work.... (Mund.Up. 1.2.7.)

The three philosophical systems, the *Vedanta-*, *Yoga-*, and *Samkhya-Sutras*, systematized and preserved the main ideas of the Upanishads.[27] These Sutras are all particularly relevant for the renouncer. Through these sources the renouncer is influenced by a system of ideas having its genesis in the Upanishadic period. The greatest philosopher and religious personality of the Hindus is considered to be Shankara (800 A.D.). He regarded himself as a follower of the Upanishads (Devaraja 1972:44) and the Vedanta Sutras.

The interiorization of sacrifice
and the genesis of the concept of 'man'

He indeed who knows this is an ascetic.... and a performer of the sacrifice to the soul (*Atman*) Maitri Up. 6.10

The Sanskrit term for the inner sacrifice is *Atmayajna*. *Yajna* is the term for sacrifice and *Atman* signifies the Self. The interiorization of sacrifice is best exemplified in the way the outer sacrificial formalism of the Vedic period is reinterpreted into symbolic forms of meditation. Thus we find in the beginning of the *Brihadaranyaka Upanishad* that the old horse sacrifice is transformed into an act of meditation where the horse symbolizes the visible cosmos and the sacrifice the act of creation. Meditation as thought-activity is replacing the external ritual (Dasgupta v. 1 1957:35). The spoken words that used to accompany the external rite are transformed into objects of meditation without loosing their spiritual power.

It is the conception of the interiorized sacrifice involving a differentiation between the inner and outer - subjective and objective - which establishes a starting point for a proper conception of Man in Hinduism.

Man in the Upanishads is first of all conceived of as a moral agent capable of producing new karma for improving his future destiny (Walli 1977:153, 164). Man as the Hindus perceive him has unlimited powers and potentialities. That is probably why Eliade called the other-worldly ascetic the man-God (1958:88). The man-God, as we remember, could manipulate the cosmic order and conquer even the Gods. But the successful renouncer of the Upanishadic period is regarded as being even greater than the man-God. He is the Absolute, the *unio mystica* of subject and object - the Atman/ Brahman.

When compared with the conception of Man in classical Greek and Semitic culture, the Hindu ideas of the man-God and the perfect renouncer seem to be unique. The omnipotence of the God of Abraham and Job as well as the many myths of hubris in Greek mythology (as, for example, in the story of Sisyphus and Prometheus), clearly point to a clear line of demarcation between God and men. Not so according to Hinduism. Both men and Gods were subject to the law of karma. Man was even greater than the Gods in some respects because it was the privilege of man - the man born in *Bharatavarsha* (ancient name for India) to be more specific - to be able to produce karma for future release.

The concept of action

The notion that 'action' is a *differentia specificia* of Man, was shared by the ancient Hindus also: 'Verily a person is sacrifice.' (Chand. 3.16.1) And sacrifice as we have earlier stated is *karma* - action in its pristine state. Thus, the concept of action exhibits a similar development as the concept of Man. 'Action' undergoes a transformation from a mechanistic to a moral concept. Volition, intention and motive are emerging as the defining criteria of 'action' during the Upanishadic period. An interior differentiation of karma into its constitutive parts is emerging during the Upanishadic period.

A person is made of desires (*kama*) only. As is his desire, such is his resolve (*kratu*), as is his resolve, such the action (*karma*) he performs, into that does he become changed. (Br. Up. 4.4.5, my italics)

Kama, kratu and *karma* are the three terms of importance in this verse. One could interpret kama as the volition and kratu as the intention, purpose, aim of karma. So conceived, kama and kratu would be the causes of karma. But there are no indications in the above verse that such an interpretation is reasonable. In case kama and kratu were conceived as causes of karma, they would probably have been inflected in the ablative case which expresses causal relations in Sanskrit. But all three terms are in nominative indicating there is not yet any clear structural differentiation between them.

The Upanishadic concept of karma is often identified with purpose or volition.

> Now verily, a person consists of purpose (*kratumaya*). According to the purpose which a person has in this world, thus does he become on departing hence. (Chand. Up. 3.14.1)

The Buddha, undoubtedly the most subtle outcome of Upanishadic speculation, is even more explicit: 'Volition, O bhikkhus, I call karma. A person having had the thoughts in his mind, performs bodily, verbal and mental action. (Anguttara-Nikaya Chakkanipata 22.334. 463.-464. Quoted from Sunthorn Na-Rangsi 1976:49) Volition, intention, purpose, motive and will are the new terms which clearly differentiate the Upanishadic concept of karma from its Vedic predecessor. The Upanishads also stress the need for self consciousness: 'My mind was elsewhere, one says, I did not cognize that action.' (Kau. Up. 3.7) Consciousness (knowledge) and volition, intention etc. are, as argued in the first part, basic elements of the concept of action. Together they constitute the presuppositions for moral responsibility.

Certain verses in the *Vedanta Sutra* underscore the problem of purposeful action: '(Brahman is) not (the creator of the world) on account of (every activity) having a motive.' (Brahma Sutra 2.1.32) But if we do not ascribe such a motive to him (i.e. Brahman), creation seems to loose its meaning. The answer to the problem is that the creative activity of Brahma is just a mere play for fun and pastime (Brahma Sutra 2.1.33). Motives and intentions are, as the renouncers perceive it, manifestations of an imperfect mode of being which should not be attributed to Brahman.

The renouncer and his understanding of the law of karma

The various perceptions, ideas and beliefs which constitute the so-called law of karma were not properly developed before the time of the Upanishads (Radhakrishnan 1966 VI:116).[28] Thus the *Brihadaranyaka* and *Chandogya Upanishads* state as follows:

Arthabhaga, my dear, take my hand. We two only will know of this. This is not for us two (to speak of) in public. The two went away and deliberated. What they said was karma, what they praised was karma. Verily, one becomes good by good action, bad by bad action. (Br.Up. 3.2.13, also Br.Up. 6.2.8)

O Gautama, this knowledge has never yet come to Brahmans before you, and therefore in all the worlds has the rule belonged to Kshatriya only. (Chand.Up. 5.3.7)

The first novelty of the Upanishadic period is the idea of rebirth and the wheel of existence, the *samsara* doctrine. The set of ideas pertaining to samsara and rebirth is developed in the famous doctrine of the five fires (Br.Up. 6.2, Chand.Up. 5.3.10) which goes as follows: The young Brahmin Svetaketu attended an assembly of the famous Kshatriya Jaibali of the Panchalas tribe. The Kshatriya asked:

Do you know unto what creatures go forth hence? No sir. Do you know how they return again? No sir. Do you know the parting of the two ways, one leading to the Gods (*devayana*) and one leading to the fathers? No sir. Do you know how (it is that) yonder world is not filled up? No sir. Do you know how in the fifth oblation water comes to have a human voice? No indeed sir. (Chand.Up. 5.2-3)

As answers to these questions it is said that the passage of the soul is like a sacrificial transformation through five fires. Heaven itself is a sacrificial fire and in this fire the Gods offer faith (*shraddha*).[29]

From shraddha arises King Soma which was the intoxicating drug of the Indo-Aryans and the material for the *soma* sacrifice (Hubert & Mauss 1964:90). *Soma* symbolizes the waxing and waning moon and is a cosmic symbol for the ever returning cycle.

The rain cloud is a sacrificial fire. In this fire the Gods offer King Soma. Rain is produced, the third sacrificial fire. From the offering of rain to earth, food is produced. Food is eaten by man, the fourth fire. From the oblation of food in man, semen is produced.

Woman, verily O Gautama, is a sacrificial fire. In this case the sexual organ is the fuel, when one invites, the smoke, the vulva, the flame, when one inserts, the coals, the sexual pleasure, the sparks. In this fire the Gods offer semen. From this oblation arises the fetus. Thus indeed in the fifth oblation water comes to have a human voice... When deceased, they carry him hence to the appointed place for the fire from whence indeed he came, from whence he arose. (Chand.Up. 5.8, 5.9)

The passage of the soul is symbolized in macro-cosmic perspectives. The cyclic return of the seasons is pictured as the return of the soul due to karma. The wheel of *samsara* reflects the cyclic conception of time prevalent in agrarian societies where the seasons of nature and the work of man is intimately connected.

The next verse contains the important Upanishadic dictum: '*Ya evam veda*' 'So those who know this.' (Chand.Up. 5.10) Those persons successfully following the Upanishadic way of knowledge will, after death, proceed on the *devayana*, the path of the Gods, during the six months when the sun moves northward, to the world of Brahma (Chand.Up. 5.10. 1-2). 'Of these there is no return.' (Br.Up. 6.2.15) Having reached *mystical* knowledge, the renouncer has seen the constitution of the world and therefore withdrawn into solitude (Chand.Up. 5.10.1 and Br.Up. 6.2.15).

The ritualists, on the other hand, follow the southern path of the fathers (*pitryana*) and reach the moon where they, according to their past karma, become the sacrificial food of the Gods. When their merit is exhausted, they return again to this world of action[30] and enter a womb according to their past karma:

> Accordingly, those who are of pleasant conduct here - the prospect is, indeed, that they will enter a pleasant womb, either the womb of a Brahman, or ... Kshatriya, or ... Vaisya. But those who are of stinking conduct here - the prospect is indeed, that they will enter a stinking womb, either the womb of a dog, or ... swine, or ... an outcast.' (Chand.Up. 5.10.7)

As long as there is any accumulated karma left, either good or bad, the soul proceeds by necessity its voyage in the wheel of samsara.

The karmic problem

> Sir, in this ill-smelling, unsubstantial body, which is a conglomerate of bone, skin, muscle, marrow, flesh, semen, ... afflicted with desire, anger, covetousness, delusion and fear, ... what is the good of enjoyment of desires? .... With a crowd of relatives looking on, they *renounced* great wealth and went forth from this world into that.' (Maitri Up. 1.3.4)

Existence *is* suffering. Not only as a feeling, but as an inherent quality in the very ontological structure of man and the world (Mishra 1971:164). This is the karmic problem.

Shankara is one of the great champions of the Hindu tradition. He is known to have reorganized the sannyasi (type of renouncer) orders and to have built ten different monasteries throughout India. For the sannyasi school among the renouncers Shankara is still the first Guru and founder. For all Hindus Shankara is a prototype of a renouncer. Of other prototypes of renouncers the great philosopher Yajnavalkya of the Brihadaranyaka Upanishad is a good example: 'Maitreyi! said Yajnavalkya, lo verily, I am about to wander forth from this state.' (Br.Up. 4.5.2)

What shall we do with offspring, we whose is this Soul, this world? They verily, rising above the desire for sons and the desire for wealth and the desire for worlds, lived the life of a mendicant. (Br.Up. 4.4.22)

Maitreyi is one of Yajnavalkya's two wives. From the first verse we can understand that Yajnavalkya had not taken the vow of lifelong celibacy. He is one of the earliest scriptural examples following a kind of *ashrama* system (the four life periods). Another famous example is the Buddha. He was, as the legend has it, kept inside his castle where he lived a life of luxury and pleasure. The Buddha was to be protected against the reality of the world, as it was forecasted that he would become a renouncer. But he managed one day to leave the castle and what he observed was as follows:

I see everywhere the impression of change! Therefore my heart is heavy. Men grow old, sicken and die. That is enough to take away the zest of life. (Carus 1975:13)

And the succeeding night, the Buddha decided to leave his young wife, his newborn baby and the life of an aristocrat to become a renouncer.

How was this extreme devaluation of social life possible? The answer lies in the emerging dualistic world view of the Upanishadic period which surpasses the monism of the Vedas.[31] There are two worlds, the world of *Atman/Brahman* on the one hand and the world of *samsara/maya* on the other - the real world of the Absolute and the apparent world of becoming, change and action. There are two types of knowledge, *paravidya* and *aparavidya* - the higher and lower knowledge. In short, the Upanishadic period perceives the world as a duality through the categories of reality and appearance.[32]

Thinking this [i.e., the samsara/maya] is the world! There is no other! - Again and again he comes under my control. (Katha Up. 2.6)

For those who are not able to discriminate between the Absolute world and the world of maya, the samsaric/karmic world, there is no release from rebirth and suffering.

Following the Upanishads as interpreted by Shankara, there is a close relation between ignorance (*avidya*) and the dualistic world view. It is ignorance which, as it were, constitutes the two worlds and hides the Absolute behind the veil of appearances, the *maya*. It is ignorance which 'individualizes' the agent of action and constitutes the world of samsara and karma and thus the karmic problem.

The renouncer

The Upanishads reverse the life affirming attitude of the Vedic world view. Maya, which signifies the world, is only meaningful due to ignorance. Maya is an appearance, a *relative* mode of being; '... (apparently)... a doer in the unreal - ...(Maitri 2.7) Accordingly, Shankara's doctrine of maya implies a *devaluation* of society and action. This indeed is what the ritualist Kumarila is emphasising in the following quotation.

> The main aim of the Advaita doctrine [Shankara's doctrine] of the unreality of the world is .. the instilling of the feeling of disgust in the worldly affairs,... (Quoted from Devaraja 1972.:196)

The search for the real world requires that the seeker becomes a renouncer.

Two important ideas, characteristic of Hinduism in general, were closely related to the spiritual quest of the renouncers, *ahimsa* - not injuring any living being - and vegetarianism. The ideal of ahimsa was developed by the renouncers against the background of the Vedic tradition of animal sacrifices. Thus the renouncers came to undermine the Brahmanic power holders (Lodrick 1981:55). Ahimsa is the first of the ten ethical vows which must be adopted before embarking on the path of renunciation. It was also the renouncer who carried the notion of ahimsa through to its practical consequences for diet - vegetarianism (Dumont 1970:149).

In the Vedas and Upanishads, people are meat eaters. Still in Manu animal sacrifice and meat diet are defended (Manu 5.30-39). Yet in a later verse (Manu 5.53) vegetarianism is praised to be equivalent in merit to a hundred horse sacrifices. In the Gita we also find several verses speaking about the different qualities of food and how people of diverse castes need different kind of foods (Gita 17.7-10). But vegetarianism as such is not explicitly mentioned in the Gita. Ahimsa and vegetarianism were developed by the heterodox renouncer religions of the Upanishadic period. In the course of history, ahimsa and vegetarianism came to be cultural values of relevance to all Hindus.

Of other requirements incumbent upon the renouncer, the Upanishads particularly mention *yoga*.

If a man practices Yoga for six months, And is constantly freed (from the senses), the infinite, supreme, mysterious Yoga is perfectly produced. (Maitri Up. 6.28)

Six months' training for spiritual liberation might be a form of classical advertisement practice. The point, however, is that mystical knowledge can be reached through yoga and meditation which are believed to produce *Moksha*.

Moksha - 'freedom from'

The Sanskrit term *Moksha* (see Svet.Up. 6.16 and Maitri Up. 6.30.34) expresses the new eschatological ideas of the Upanishadic period. The primary meaning of the term is freedom from, emancipation and release. Freedom from what?

Freedom from the causal chain of karma which links the soul to the wheel of samsara. The aim of the Upanishadic renouncer is therefore to suppress all karma-producing factors and conquer rebirth and suffering.

They who being without desire,....., pass beyond the seed (of rebirth) here. (Mund.Up. 3.2.1)

As fire of fuel destitute, Becomes extinct in its own source, So thought by loss of activeness, Becomes extinct in its own source. (Maitri Up. 6.34)

By analogy, we could compare the concept of karma, as expressed in these verses, with the driving of a car. Desire is like the fuel. Thought activity steering the desire into purposive action is like the driver. When the fuel is empty, there is no more exterior movement. But the thinking faculty of the driver does not stop. It keeps on making its own plans and fancies.

By making mind all motionless, From sloth and from distraction freed, When unto mindlessness one comes. Then that is the supreme estate.' (Maitri Up. 6.34)[33]

One is here reminded of the tripartite classification of karma based on the medium - mind, speech or body (cf. Gita 18.15) - through which karma is produced. Mental acts are seen to be very subtle (*sattvik*), speech acts somewhere in between (*rajasik*) and bodily acts are gross (*tamasik*). The renouncer attempts to reach Moksha by making his karma more and more subtle. So he withdraws from the 'gross' transactional karma of caste society and reduces his verbal and bodily karma as much as possible. (i.e., the 'muni' - he who never speaks.) He purifies his diet (more subtle, more sattvik) and seeks finally to live on 'the sun and the air, the products of the

cow and the fruits of the forest' as many present day renouncers formulate it.
Thus two requisites were necessary for obtaining the spiritual freedom of Moksha. First, it was necessary to become a renouncer and physically leave the social world of caste and duty. And second, it was necessary to reach knowledge to dissolve *maya* and break the chain of karma.
The knowledge in question should not be confused with intellectual comprehension. Mystical knowledge signifies a kind of illumination (*gnosis*) at once knowledge, being and bliss - an absorption or extinction of the individuality into the Absolute of the Atman/Brahman.

The seer sees not death, Nor sickness, Nor any distress. The seer sees only the All, Obtains the All entirely. (Chand.Up. 7.26.2)

Through this kind of experience and knowledge, his karma comes to naught because he has seen through his relative, illusory existence as an individual. The others who have not seen through the veil of maya remain in the grip of karmic bondage: 'In thinking This is I and That is mine, he binds himself with his self, as does a bird with a snare.' (Maitri 3.2) What then can be stated about the Absolute, the *Atman/Brahman* of the Upanishads?
Following the mystical tradition of the Upanishads, the Absolute is a state of being which language cannot define. The Absolute can only be defined in negative terms (*neti - neti*), as a negation of duality and manifoldness, as a negation of the samsaric world, as a negation of the individual and action and, finally, as a negation of suffering.

Where knowledge is not of dual nature, being devoid of action, cause or effect, unspeakable, incomparable, indescribable - what is that? It is impossible to say! (Maitri Up.6.7)

There is a positive statement, however, which is found in the famous Upanishadic dictum of identity between Atman and Brahman - the mystical union between the subjective and objective parts of the Absolute (Sharma 1972:14):

I am Brahman. (Br.Up. 1.4.10)

It is the nature of the experience itself which, according to Shankara, gives the renouncer the certainty that he has reached Moksha while alive. The liberated person does not produce any new karma (*kriyamana*karma). He will die when the karmic causes of his present life (*prarabdha*karma) are exhausted. His self will then be absorbed and dissolved in Brahman in eternal unity (Deussen 1972:418-435).[34]

There is a striking similarity between the Upanishadic conception of yoga (Maitri Up. 6.34. See also Katha 3,13, Svet.2.8-15, Maitri 6.20-21) and the later definition of the classical Yoga text of Patanjali: 'Yoga means suppression of mental modifications.' (Yoga Sutra 1.2) The meaning of the Sutra is that yoga aims at the annihilation of all karma through the suppression of mental activity. When karmic activity has stopped, the embodied soul reflects the Absolute in a direct way.

> Even as a mirror stained by dust shines brilliantly when it has been cleansed, so the embodied one, on seeing the nature of the Soul (*Atman*), becomes unitary, his end attained, from sorrow freed. (Svet. Up.2.14)

Epistemological perspectives

In the philosophical debate between ritualists and renouncers, the problem of an 'active' and 'passive' epistemology was a matter of great concern. The ritualist maintained a theory of the process of knowledge as activity, while for the renouncer knowledge was pure 'passive' immediacy, 'passive' reflections of the objects of knowledge.

The line of argument in this debate has its starting point from the relation between *jnana* (knowledge) and karma (action). For the ritualist: 'Knowledge is a movement brought about by the activity of the self' (Radhakrishnan 1966 v.2: 399) - an active cognition belonging to the substance called the soul (Op.cit. 408). The outcome of the epistemology of the ritualists was a denial of the theory of mystical intuition (Op.cit.:385).

For the renouncer, on the other hand, the activity of knowledge involves an unacceptable dualism. Shankara's solution, '...is that the self is the knower, not by virtue of any activity in it, but by its mere existence. The self is merely the principle of relation in experience,...' (ibid).[35] By regarding knowledge as a kind of karma, the ritualist will, according to the philosophy of the renouncer, be forever enmeshed in the world of maya.

Mysticism

> Die *Subjekt-Objekt Spaltung*, von der wir ausgegangen, besteht nicht mehr auf den höchsten Stufen der Mystik. Da schrumpft die Distanz zwischen Subjekt und Objekt zu einem Nichts zusammen (Jaspers); Gott und Mensch, hernach Mensch und Welt, fliessen in eins zusammen. (Van der Leeuw 1925:138)

The *differentia specificia* of mysticism, as opposed to magic and religion, is found in its spiritual aim. The spiritual aim of mysticism is to transcend duality, difference and diversity, whether this difference is formulated as a

'Subject-Object Spaltung', as an appearance/reality discrimination, as the one and the many or as unity/diversity. The magical world-view of the ritualist based on the metaphysical position of diversity as karma, indeed, presupposes the perception of diversity. In the Absolute unity, there can be no perception of change, movement or karma (Sharma 1965:240).

Now, Atman is infinite, universal, inactive. (Svet.Up. 1.9)
That is the full, the Non-active. (Chand.Up. 3.12.7)

Shankara's interpretations of the Upanishads and the Vedanta Sutras are labelled the *Advaita Vedanta* school. The meaning of the term *advaita* is 'no-duality'. Shankara often refers to certain verses in the Upanishads to prove his viewpoint.

By the mind alone is it to be perceived. There is on earth no diversity.
He gets death after death, who perceives here seeming diversity.
(Br.Up. 4.4.19)

While the activist ethic of the ritualist is based on the conception of 'diversity' as the essence of being, Advaita Vedanta, on the contrary, upholds the conception of 'unity' as its basic reality. Following Shankara, there can be no reconciliation between the ritualist's path of action and the renouncer's path of knowledge. The opposition between the ritualists and renouncers is in this field as elsewhere 'irremovable like a mountain' (Shankara Bhasya - Isa Up. 1.2).

The renouncer, as Staahl states, is the Hindu mystic par excellence (Staahl 1975:100). His highest aim is the unity of the Atman/Brahman. The Upanishads are, as the Sanskrit term 'Upanishad' itself indicates (mystical doctrine), the classical mystical scriptures of the Hindus.

The problem of rationality and irrationality in mysticism (Staahl 1975) can, as I shall argue, be solved by differentiating between the mystical *path* and the mystical *state*. The mystical path as well as the spiritual aim of mysticism can be communicated in a rational language. The systematic and seemingly 'scientific' exposition of yoga in Patanjali's Yoga Sutra is held by the renouncers to be based on experience. Hindu mysticism, they say, can be 'tested' by undergoing the prescribed procedures of the various mystical doctrines (Staahl 1975:31, 124). The way to the mystical state is certainly open for an intellectual, rational debate. But the mystical state itself is beyond the reach of a rational language: '(Brahman is that) from which words return - having failed to reach it with the mind.' (Tait.Up. 2.9, quoted from Staahl 1975:45) It is best pictured in a poetic or erotic language. Staahl argues that mysticism need not necessarily be regarded as a part of religion (1975:4). 'The view that mysticism has nothing to do with Gods is not as revolutionary as it may sound, at least if we remember ...that ...Buddhism and Jainism, though replete with mysticism and 'divine' personages, are atheistic... The attitude of Advaita Vedanta...are in many respects similar. (Staahl 1975:196)'

Theism is not necessarily a component part of mystical thinking. Often, as in the Upanishads, an impersonal Absolute is the spiritual aim of mystical absorption. The mysticism of the renouncers in Hinduism is, in principle, chiefly a kind of privatism with little or no concern for the welfare of the whole.[36]

THE RELIGIOUS WORLD-VIEW
OF THE GITA/MANU AND THE HOUSEHOLDERS

The Upanishadic period was succeeded by the emergence of the Magadha state and the coming of the Mauryan dynasty which subdued the greater part of modern India and Pakistan. Many Greek sources are available from this period due to the campaign of Alexander. We know, for instance, that Chandragupta Maurya had a standing army, paid in silver coins, of about 500 000 men (Kosambi 1965). One can well understand that such an empire must have had deep influences on the masses of the people. Under Ashoka Buddhism was made the state religion in India and his son exported Buddhism to Sri Lanka. The Mauryan dynasty was succeeded by the Sungas who claimed Brahmin status and tried to revive the sacrificial ritualism of the Vedas. They did not succeed in this effort (Kosambi 1965:187), but the Sunga dynasty is usually equated with the beginning of Hinduism proper. The period from 200 B.C. to 200 A.D. produced the Gita and the Laws of Manu which, with regard to ideology and normative social organization, are the best sources for understanding traditional Hindu society.

After the Upanishadic period the heterodox religions of Buddhism and Jainism arose as major cultural forces. The greatest religious value was renunciation, which involved an extreme devaluation of worldly life (Gombrich 1975, Conze 1962:31). In the *MahapariNirvana Sutta* (1.24.5), we read that there was an intense outcry against the preaching missions of Buddha because he intended to make women widows, families sonless and to cut off the line of succession.

A spirit of Sannyasa dominated the entire society and this is *how every one tried to avoid Karman and its disastrous effects*. The consequence was that members of society neglected their duties. (Mainkar 1969:62, my italics)

It is against this anti-social tendency, which threatened to disrupt the social order, that the Gita and Manu become sociologically intelligible (Bhagat 1976:58, Mainkar 1969:64, Lingat 1973:51). The Gita/Manu is the main textual corpus which belong to the Hindu householder. Hindu interpreters regard the Gita/Manu as that part of the holy scriptures concerned with the combination of knowledge and action (*jnana-karma-samucchayavada*) (Mainkar 1969:51). I have chosen Ramanuja (A.D. 1027) as the most representative interpreter of the Gita. Through the teaching of Ramanuja the householder was influenced by a system of ideas having its origin in the early Hindu period.

The absolute dualism of the Gita/Manu

The Gita/Manu inherited the absolute dualism of the Samkhya/Yoga philosophy which replace the idea of the world as *maya* with the idea of the world as *prakrti*. In the new perspective of the Gita/Manu, the lifeworld was no longer viewed as an illusion. The world of change and becoming was as real as the passive eternity of spirit. It is this absolute dualism which provides the theoretical foundation upon which the Gita/Manu could raise their attack against the anti-social tendencies of the renouncer and develop the holistic karma-type.

The absolute dualism is based on two fundamental realities, *Purusha* and *prakrti* - spirit and matter (Zaehner 1969).

Know thou that Prakrti and Purusha are both beginningless and know thou also that all modifications and Gunas are born of Prakrti. (Gita 13.19)

Purusha is the passive spirit, pure consciousness - the unchanging, eternal witness of the transformations and activities of prakrti. Prakrti is the ever changing and active matter without any consciousness in itself. 'In the production of the body and the senses, prakrti is said to be the cause, in the experience of pleasure and pain, Purusha is said to be the cause.' (Gita 13.20)

Purusha and prakrti should be understood both in macro- and micro-cosmical terms (Beidler 1975:30,168). The Purusha of the individual person - the soul - is called the *kshetrajna* and the prakrti of the individual - the body - is called the kshetra.[37] *Kshetrajna* means lit. the knower of the field. And the body itself is called the field because it is in the body that the seed of karma is sown and it is through it that the fruits are experienced.

The relationship between the soul and body is well expressed in the Samkhya philosophy by the metaphor of a lame and a blind man (Sam.Kar.21). The soul is the conscious principle of man, the body the principle of activity. So the soul is lame, but contributes sight, and the body is blind and needs a guide in its movements through the world. Together they experience and produce karma which ties the soul to the wheel of *samsara*.

The soul is the eternal part of man. In the wandering from life to life it is the soul which retains the identity of the person.

> Even as a man casts off worn-out clothes, and puts on others which are new, so the embodied casts off worn-out bodies, and enters into others which are new. (Gita 2.22)

It is the soul that carries the accumulated karma which, by necessity, compels it to take up a new body according to merit.

The householders' interpretation of the law of karma

What transforms the activity of *prakrti* into karma-producing actions?

> The Gunas of Prakrti perform all action. With the understanding deluded by egoism (*ahamkara*), man thinks I am the doer. (Gita 3.27)

The answer is egoism and ignorance. Ignorance, in this context, means not differentiating between the passive Purusha and the active prakrti. It means not recognizing the absolute dualism of the Gita/ Manu. The outcome is a confusion between the empirical self and the soul resulting in the conception that the eternal and real part of man is affected by the change and becoming of the lifeworld.

The Sanskrit term for ego is *ahamkara* meaning the 'I doer'. In the Gita, ahamkara is considered one of the three internal organs of the human psyche. Ahamkara has several meanings. First, ahamkara is the principle of self consciousness which makes being reflect itself as an 'I'. In this act the constitution of the individual is effected (see Gita 2.71). Second,

> Thy right is to work only, but never to the fruits thereof. Be thou not the *producer of the fruits of (thy) actions*, (*karma-phala-hetur*), neither let thy attachment be towards inaction.' (Gita 2.47, my italics)

The important key term in this verse is the compositum *karma-phala-hetur*. *Karma-phala* means the fruit of action and *hetur* the cause. How can ahamkara be the cause - the producer of the fruits of actions? When the activity of prakrti is experienced as mine - 'I am the doer' - and stamped with a selfish, egoistic motive, then ahamkara becomes the producer of the fruits of actions. The activity of prakrti is given an individual imprint through intentionality towards the expected fruits, the aimed at objects of action. The activity of prakrti is thereby transformed into karmic actions proper.

The Upanishads did not clearly differentiate between karma and its constitutive factors, *kama* and *kratu*, subjective will and purpose. In the Gita/Manu, on the other hand, there is a clear differentiation between karma and its constitutive factors:

> Whose undertakings are all *devoid of plan and desire for results*, (*kama-samkalpa-varjitah*) and whose actions are burnt by the fire of knowledge, him the sages call wise. (Gita 4.19, my italics)[38]

The Gita/Manu perceives the factors of karma as the cause of karmic actions. And by annihilating the causes, the effect which ties the person to the world of maya and suffering will disappear.[39]

> *Forsaking the clinging to fruits of action* (...) ever satisfied, depending on nothing, though engaged in action, he does not do anything. (Gita 4.20, my italics)

It is the clinging to the fruits expected from the performance of actions that transform the activity of prakrti into actions with karmic consequences. On the other hand, activities devoid of selfishness, plans and desire for results will not tie the agent to the wheel of samsara.

From the standpoint of absolute dualism and the new conception of karma, the Gita/Manu attacks other schools which uphold the ideal of renunciation, actionlessness and immobility.

> He who restraining the organs of action, sits revolving in the mind... he of deluded understanding is called a hypocrite. (Gita 3.6, cf. 3,4,18,3)

The verse indicates that there were people who believed even bodily movements produced karmic consequences. This is also emphasized in one Buddhist Sutra where the Buddha is reported to have discussed the effects of different karmas with another famous heretic of those days - Mahavira, the founder of Jainism (*Upalivada Sutra, Majjhima - Nikaya*, 13. 62. 54).

Following Jainism, which has an archaic understanding of the law of karma, even bodily movements are supposed to have karmic consequences. Consequently, Jainism developed an extreme ideal of immobility where ritual suicide through starvation was considered the better path.[40] The mechanical outlook of the Jainas is a survival from the Vedic period into the Upanishadic context of karma negation. The Buddha, who defined karma as intention (*cetana*), could certainly not accept the archaic views of the Jainas. The implication of a Jainistic understanding is:

> O King, if man could obtain perfection by renunciation, then even
> the mountains and the trees should very soon attain salvation. It is
> true that a person staying in the forest can stay peacefully...., but their
> life is like that of animals. (*Mahabharata* 12.10.18.24.25 and 12.10.22,
> quoted from Bhagat 1976)

The Gita refutes any view which upholds the possibility of reaching
actionlessness of the archaic kind, whether in thought, speech or body.
The renunciation of karma demanded by Shankara's interpretation of the
Upanishads is also not accepted by the Gita. In the dualistic perspective of
the Gita, pure actionlessness is an impossibility: 'Verily none can ever rest
for even an instant, without performing action, for all are made to act,
helplessly indeed by .... Prakrti.' (Gita 3.5)

The *new* solution to the karmic problem is a synthesis of the two earlier
paths of karma, the *pravrtimarga* and the *nivrtimarga*.

> He who sees inaction in action, and action in inaction is intelligent
> among men, he is a Yogi and a doer of all action. (Gita 4.18)

Tilak has called Gita's solution to the karmic problem the
nishkamakarmamarga (Tilak 1935:1.xxv), lit., the disinterested, unselfish
path of karma. On the one hand, the *nishkamakarmamarga* negates the
egocentric approach of the Vedic ritualist, but preserves its social
implications of life in the world. On the other hand, the path of
nishkamakarma negates the need that exists in the Upanishadic context of
becoming a renouncer, but preserves the Upanishadic idea of freedom from
karma for attaining liberation.[41]

The Gita's path of nishkamakarmamarga consists of three sub paths;
jnanayoga (the path of knowledge), *karmayoga* (the path of action) and
bhaktiyoga (the path of devotion).[42] Great nationalist leaders such as Tilak
and Gandhi have strongly supported an integrated perspective on the three
sub paths (see Gandhi 1926:304). The term *yoga* itself - jnanayoga,
karmayoga, bhaktiyoga - indicates an integrated perspective. The basic
meaning of the root *yuj* is 'to yoke or join' and 'to make efforts for' (Zaehner
1969:24). The derived meaning is 'union and integration'. Following the
Gita, it is through perfection in yoga that the karmic problem is solved,
not through knowledge, action or devotion independently. The point is
not what one does, but how one does it: 'Yoga is skill in the performance of
karma.' (Gita 2.50 - my translation) Thus, the Gita maintains that the karmic
problem can be solved while performing the duties of a householder.

The Gita upholds the intimate relationship between theory and practice.[43] Through an improved practise, the adept is ritually and existentially cleaned to reach a deeper understanding which again will result in a more perfect practice. 'The Yogi,..., gradually gaining perfection through many births, then reaches the highest goal.' (Gita 6.45) This doctrine of gradual liberation is, as we shall see, important for understanding the ideology of the caste system.

There is a tendency in Ramanuja's interpretations of the Gita to overemphasize the path of *bhakti* on account of the two others (Mainkar 1969:14). This attitude reflects the development of theism from the time of the Gita onwards to the establishment of Vaishnavism as a major sectarian system (Hopkins 1971:122). Furthermore, bhakti receives a broad meaning in the teaching of Ramanuja which includes both the performance of caste duty, the training of the will and the intellect, knowledge and devotion (Radhakrishnan 1966 v.2:704-705). Ramanuja preached equality in worship. He even admitted the pariahs to the temple at Melkote (Op.cit.:709). But he accepted the *varnashramadharma* system and took upon himself the task of transforming Vaishnava devotion (ibid.) into a part of orthodoxy. In opposition to Shankara, Ramanuja preserved the main spirit of the Gita by accepting philosophical ideas which render possible the attainment of liberation while performing the duties of a householder.

Ramanuja preserved the organic outlook of the Gita which can be traced back to the hymn of Purusha in Rig Veda 10.90. This outlook regards reality not as a pure unity, but as a determinate whole, which maintains its identity in and through the differences.[44] The doctrine of maya was not accepted. The lifeworld was real, being the product of the Lord's creative power. According to Ramanuja, the absolute unity of Shankara leads him to a blank, lifeless void with no link to living humanity (Radhakrishnan op.cit.: 683 and 716).

The holistic karma type

Following the Vedas and the Upanishads, only the twice born were entitled to Vedic studies and rituals and only the twice born could embrace asceticism (*Brahma Sutra* 1.3.33). By implication this meant that women and other people of low status were not entitled to the saving knowledge or techniques believed to lead to freedom (Deussen 1972:64). The Gita proclaims a more egalitarian view:

> For taking refuge in Me, they also, O son of Prtha, who might be of inferior birth - women, *Vaisyas*, as well as *Sudras* - even they attain to the Supreme Goal. (Gita 9.32)[45]

The religious liberalization witnessed in the Gita/Manu is based on a new ideology of the caste system which reinterprets sacrifice as *altruistic action*.

Gandhi is to the point when he interpreted the new meaning of *yajna*, sacrifice, in the Gita as 'public good' (Gandhi 1926:124). The Sanskrit term for 'altruistic action' is *lokasamgraha*.[46] In the language of the Gita *lokasamgraha* means maintenance of the world order. By doing one's duty (*svadharma*) without selfinterest, one is reproducing the world order to the benefit of the whole creation. Furthermore, one is acting in a manner which can serve as a guideline for others (Gita 3.21,3.25).

A dharmic action (good action) in the context of Gita/Manu is an action which supports and maintains the creation. By performing one's duty according to caste and stage of life, as a sacrifice to the collectivity (Gita 3.21, 3.21) or as a sacrifice to God (Gita 9.27), the production of new karma ceases and the past karma is exhausted.

The ambiguity which has evolved in the concept of karma during the course of the Hindu period, can best be phrased in a dialectical manner. Karma signifies both destiny and action depending on the time perspective. 'Past karma' explains the person's present destiny. 'Present karma' refers to present action as such, an action which produces karma which will influence the future destiny of the person. 'Future karma' refers to the fruits, the self produced destiny, which the person will experience in a later incarnation.

Holism, theism and religion

The absolute dualism of the Gita/Manu provides the metaphysical starting point for the development of Hindu theism, bhakti. Bhakti is derived from the root *bhaj* meaning to divide, to participate in. In the Gita, bhakti means devotion and loyalty to Krishna, the personal God, trust in him, love of him. In the eleventh chapter, where Krishna reveals his real attributes, the theistic difference between God and Man is the essential topic displayed. Krishna is 'Das Ganz Andere', that complete otherness in front of which Arjuna can only exclaim:

> You are the father of the world of moving and unmoving things, You their venerable teacher, most highly prized; none is there like You, - how could there be another greater? - in the three worlds, Oh, match-less is your power. And so I bow to You, prostrate my body, crave grace of You, (my) Lord adorable: bear with me, I beg You as father (bears) with son, or friend with friend, or lover with the one he loves, O God! (Gita 11.43-44, Zaehner edition)

These verses exemplify the definition of religion made by the religious phenomenologist Rudolf Otto as the fear and trembling rousing experience of 'Das Ganz Andere'.

In Puranic theism and among the great bhakti poets of the Hindu middle ages, the bhakti theme of distinction between devotee and personal God is further developed. In the words of Pandey and Zide in the book *Krishna: Myths, Rites and Attitudes* (1971): 'Bhakti is nothing but the feelings of sorrow in separation from God and the effort toward union with him.' (Op.cit.:191)

We need not only rely on the paradigms of Durkheimian sociology to understand the relation between holism and religion.[47] The Gita itself stresses the identification between Krishna and the *varna* system (4.13). As a part of the cosmos, as created and instituted by Krishna, Hindu caste society appears to its members as an eternal and holy arrangement. The caste society appears as a holy organism, as the different organs and parts of the primeval giant Purusha (Rig Veda X 90).[48] The religious sentiment of the householder is not mastery, but subordination. The devotee conceives his ascribed caste duties as the expression of God's will. By being God's obedient servant, slave or instrument, the devotee has *e'o ipso* subordinated himself to the 'needs of the whole, the social system' (see Gita 18.46).

In opposition to the theism of Gita/Manu, Hindu magical thinking is founded on the Vedic monistic world view with no clear line of demarcation between Gods and men. Accordingly, the Gods do not receive any exalted position as witnessed in the Mimamsa ritualist philosophy, where the Gods are nothing but names inflected in the dative case. The magical sentiment is directed towards mastery and there are few holistic/altruistic traits to be discovered.

Epistemological implications

Being a part of the epic literature and not a systematical philosophical treatise, the Gita does not easily explicate its epistemological presuppositions. Furthermore, the Gita is a blending of the two earlier parts of the holy scriptures; it integrates jnana and karma into its new development of the *nishkamakarmamarga*.

In one important verse, the Gita states: 'These are the five causes of whatever work a man undertakes - of body, speech, or mind, no matter whether right or wrong.' (18.15) The point to be noted here is the conception of the activity of speech and mind as karma. Mental activity is, according to the activist epistemology, a necessary feature of the constitution of knowledge. Knowledge is regarded as a form of karma. Accordingly, the Manu/Gita upholds an activist epistemology.

But the Gita also seems to rely upon orthodox Samkhya teaching where the Self is regarded as the witness (*sakshin*); the sentient onlooker detached from all forms of activity (Sam.Kar. 19). The concept of the Self as a passive witness undoubtedly upholds a passivist epistemology. The Gita, as a *synthesis* of the earlier Brahmanical contradiction, is itself a scripture with many contradictory statements.

Contradiction and synthesis in the Brahmanic lifeworld

The sacrificial karma of the ritualists seems to require an activist and realist stand. Without stretching the point too far, this position may, from the perspective of the sociology of knowledge, be seen as an outcome of the privileged position of the ritualists in the hierarchy of castes. The renouncer, on the other hand, is an otherworldly mystic whose interpretative schemes are centred around passivism, the dualization of the world into reality and appearance, and a mystical intuition of pure unity as the essence of being. This philosophical outlook may be explainable by his overt release from caste society. As a man-outside-the-world, the renouncer is as a *value* a negator, a negator of the metaphysical notion of diversity in favour of pure unity, a negator of karma, indeed, a negator of everything related to the lifeworld of the ritualist and householder.

The householder neither accepts the *pravrtimarga* (activism) of the ritualist nor the *nivrtimarga* of the renouncer. The householder should perceive *action in inaction and inaction in action* (Gita 4.18). In addition, the householder is usually a *bheda-bheda vadin*, that is one who conceives the essence of being as unity in difference. In short, the householder is a synthesis of the ritualist and the renouncer.[49] As a man-inside-the-world, the householder performs his social duties. He accepts hierarchy as the order of things. But he has also accepted the spiritual ideal of the renouncers (Moksha) with its stress on karma annihilation and the ultimate release from the spatio-temporal world (samsara/maya). The householder is *in* the world, but not of it.[50] Being the lay hindu, he subordinates himself to the whole; to the ritualist in caste matters, to the renouncer in sectarian matters.

NOTES TO CHAPTER 4

1. *Pravrti* is derived from the verbal root *pra-vrit* meaning 'to roll, go onwards, originate etc.'

2. The indigenous term is *Shabda Brahman*, the Absolute of the Hindu grammarians. *Shabda Brahman* is manifested in the Vedas which is the first scripture to be breathed forth by the creator God Brahma at the beginning of each new cosmic cycle (Br.Up. 2.4.10).

3. 'Culture lag' here means the tendency of social groups to be influenced by a system of ideas having its genesis in different periods in the evolution of their culture (Goody & Watt 1968:57).

4. For an introduction to the works of Dumezil, see Littleton 1966.

5. 'Or *Katha* as a class (of Brahmins) is held by us to be eternal; and it is this class (as denoted by Katha) which appears in the name *Kathaka* which (means that the particular section of

the Veda belongs to the particular class of *Brahmins* called *Katha* and) serves to distinguish that particular section from other sections of the Veda.' (Mimamsa philosophy quoted from Radhakrishnan & Moore 1973:505)

6. The *Vedangas* undoubtedly gave rise to the advanced science of language in Hinduism (see Staal 1969).

7. 'Let not the phallus worshippers penetrate into our *rta.*' was stated by the Vedic people. (Quoted from Aguilar 1976:109) Is this an indication of Shiva worshippers?

8. Following Eliade, the navel symbolizes the centre of the world. As the *yupa* = the sacrificial pole symbolizes *axis mundi.*

9. 'The sacrifice is the eater of everything.' (Keith 1925:460) See also Br.Up. 1.4.6. and Tait.Up. 3.10.6.

10. In a comparative perspective, the hymn of *Purusha* exhibits several similarities with important mythical patterns as the dema Gods and the dying and rising vegetation Gods like the Egyptian Osiris. It also belongs, according to Hubert & Mauss, to the pattern of 'The sacrifice of the God' (Hubert & Mauss 1964:92).

11. 'That ..... priest who knows this - whatever desire he desires either for himself or for the sacrificer, that he obtains by singing. This indeed is world - conquering.' (Br.Up.1.3.28)

12. *Tapas* is derived from the root *tapa* meaning heat. Tapas signify religious austerities creating 'heath'.

13. *Kama* in this context is better translated with 'will' than the more physiologically conceived 'desire' (Kunhan Raja 1963: 226).

14. The Mimamsa philosophy adopts two arguments for the acceptance of the reality of *apurva*. First, the theory of apurva is what gives all the Vedic injunctions their meaning. 'If there were no such thing as *apurva* - such an injunction would be meaningless, as the act of the sacrifice itself is perishable..., then the cause having ceased to exist, the result (in the shape of heaven) could never come about.' (Mimamsa Sutra 2.1.5, commentary) The second argument for accepting the reality of apurva is: 'Also because *such is the common notion* (of people).' (M.S.4.3.16) The important statement of Durkheim that people base their conduct upon their beliefs (Durkheim 1976) is here expressed clearly.

15. Following Durkheim the principle of causality had its genesis in magical thinking paramount under certain social conditions in the evolution of mankind (Durkheim 1976:303).

16. The nature of a definition is problematical. If we follow Spinoza's famous dictum '*Definatio est negatio*" - 'To define is to negate' - it follows that a definition is dependent both on the level of abstraction intended and the other relevant phenomena in opposition to which our defined item seeks to distinguish itself. Thus, the distinctions between magic, mysticism and religion must be understood as sub-categories within the meta-category of religious phenomena in general.

17. Even in the imperial sacrifices like the *Ashvameda* and the *Rajasuya*, no concern for the general well being is evinced (Heesterman 1978:86).

18. The ideas put forward by the classical evolutionists, Tylor and Frazer, are still in the forefront of the discussion (Jarvie, Agassi 1979).

19. If alchemy is also considered, this argument is not valid. The alchemist used experiment in his practice.

20. The Sanskrit term for philosophy, *darshana*, may stress the point. *Darshana* is derived from *drs* 'to see' and means lit. seeing.

21. Regarding the problem of the effectiveness of magic, see Levi-Strauss 1977: 'The effectiveness of symbols'.

22. But we do find a theory of re-death (*punarmrtyu*) and its woes (O'Flaherty 1980:3). 'Redeath' and 'rebirth' is another example of the opposition between ritualist and renouncer.

23. O'Flaherty defines karmic transfer (merit transfer) as the process by which one living creature willingly or accidentally gives to another a non-physical quality of his own, such as virtue, credit for a religious achievement, a talent, or a power - often in exchange for a negative quality given by the recipient (O'Flaherty 1980:3).

24. This term is borrowed from Kopytoff's article: 'Ancestors as elders in Africa' (1969).

25. For an ethnographic presentation of the Hindu mortuary ritual, see Jaer 1995.

26. The meaning of *Upanishad* is mystical doctrine or sitting down at the feet of a teacher to listen.

27. They are even called *Bhikshu Sutras* - i.e., philosophy for the monks (Vireswarananda 1978:VII).

28. Dasgupta observed that the law of karma had its origin in the belief in the magical efficacy of the sacrificial action (Dasgupta v.1 1957:22).

29. *Shraddha* is the ritual transfer of karma in the form of merit and food which prevents dissolution and recreated the departed in their new life in heaven. It is in line with the Vedic idea of *shraddha* that it generates and reproduces the life to come.

30. 'But they who by sacrificial offering, charity and austerity (*tapas*) *conquer* the worlds, ... cycle round again thus.' (Br.Up. 6.2.16, my italics)

31. I shall call the Upanishadic outlook *apparent* dualism to distinguish it from the absolute dualism of the Gita/Manu.

32. Bellah, in his article on religious evolution (1969), describes the characteristics of the second stage (represented by the Upanishadic period in the present case) as follows: 'The first of these facts is the emergence in the first millennium B.C. all across the old world, at least in centres of high culture, of the phenomenon of *religious rejection* of the world characterized by an extremely negative evaluation of man and society and the exaltation of another realm of reality as alone true and infinitely valuable.' (Bellah 1969)

33. A Buddhist statement: 'To be thinking at all is the inferior state.', stresses the point (Eliade 1969:173).

34. The difference between 'liberated while alive' and 'complete liberation' at death is important. The Buddhist iconography reflects this by distinguishing between the merely sleeping Buddha and the liberated Buddha. Buddhist philosophy also distinguishes between *Nirvana* with or without substratum, i.e., body (Na-Rangsi 1976:249).

35. Shankara has two important terms for denoting mystical knowledge, *anubhava* and *shakshijnana* (Op.cit.: 68, 95). Anubhava means direct apprehension, shakshijnana means the witness of knowledge. Both terms connote the relation between passivity and knowledge.

36. Cf. the quotation above from the ritualist philosopher Kumarila who stated that Shankara's doctrine of maya was nothing but a kind of antisocial philosophy.

37. 'This body, ..., is called *Kshetra*, and he who knows it is called *Kshetrajna*...' (Gita 3.1)

38. *Kama* is no longer the first seed of mind as in Rig Veda 10.129. Kama has got much clearer physiological connotations in the Hindu period. *Samkalpa*, which replaces the earlier *kratu*, definitely belongs to the faculty of thinking. The meaning of the noun samkalpa is; conception, idea, plan, purpose, intention, fancy, etc. - in many ways the same as kratu.

39. We should note that the Gita/Manu inherits the axiomatic ideas of suffering, samsara and Moksha: '...; reflection on the evils of birth, death, old age and pain...' (Gita 13.8)

40. See von Glasenapp's book *The doctrine of Karman in Jain philosophy*. (1942)

41. The Gita is explicit in indicating the integrated path of *niskamakarmamarga*: 'Children, not the wise, speak of knowledge and performance of action, as distinct.' (Gita 5.4)

42. In addition to the synthesis of the two earlier paths, the Gita introduces the new doctrine of *bhakti* - devotion and surrender. Though not entirely unknown to the Upanishads, it is almost a new note in Hindu religious speculation (Edgerton 1944:70-71).

43. 'This wisdom has (now) been revealed to you in theory; (*samkhye*) listen now to how it should be practised (*yoge*).' (Gita 2.39, Zaehner edition)

44. Ramanuja called his philosophy *Vishishtadvaita*, which can be translated as 'qualified non dualism'. Ramanuja interprets the Gita as a *Bhedabheda-vadin*, that is, one who upholds the doctrine of identity in difference and difference in identity. By rejecting the philosophy of pure unity and accepting a modified version of absolute dualism in the form of identity in difference, unity in diversity, Ramanuja maintains a metaphysical perspective which secures karma as a part of reality.

45. The Sanskrit term for inferior birth is *papayonyah*, which literally means 'sinful wombs' as a deserved birthplace for past karma.

46. The literal meaning of the term is "holding the worlds together".

47. Following Durkheim (1976:419), God is the symbolic expression of the collectivity, the whole.

48. 'The regulations enjoined by the religion are therefore regarded, like the arrangements of the cosmos as a whole, as eternally valid-susceptible of interpretation, but not of alteration, unless the God himself reveals a new commandment.' (Weber 1964:207)

49. Dumont and Raja have also suggested that the metaphysical terms of Gita/Manu, the passive Purusha and the active prakrti, should be seen against the background of an opposition between passive renunciation and active householder life (Dumont 1960:56, Raja 1963 b:23). Compared with Western tradition the point is interesting. In the occidental dualisms, spirit is conceived as the active principle. The attribution of activity to matter was an absurdity in a tradition where God was regarded as the prime mover. However, one should not generalize too far the idea of a relationship between Purusha/prakrti and renouncers/householders. In Tantric Buddhism, which inherits the absolute dualism of the Samkhya/Yoga philosophy, the 'male' Purusha is the active and the 'female' prakrti the passive principle (Bharati 1965:31).

50. The ideal of renunciation has filtered into caste society through the idea of giving up the fruits of actions (*tyaga*), the reduction of sensual appetites, vegetarianism and in the form of the four *ashramas*, the four stages of life. According to Manu, nobody should become a renouncer before his hair turns white and he sees the sons of his sons (Manu 6.2). There are good reasons to believe that the emergence of the prescriptions in the *Dharma* and *Artha* literature formulating the institution of the four ashramas was a reaction against the great drive towards renunciation after the Upanishadic period (see Bhagat 1976).

5

THE SOCIAL ORGANIZATION OF TRADITION

The ritualist and the king

The Brahmin ritualist who possesses *Brahman* (the spiritual/magical power) should execute the sacred legislative authority: 'What they interpret as the law (*Dharma*) shall undoubtedly have legal force.' (Manu 12.108) The king who possesses the *kshatra* (imperium) and thus has secular power executes judicial authority (Dumont 1970:168). He judges according to the precepts given. Together the ritualists and the king sustain the divine order of the world, the ritualists by their counsels, the king by punishment (Manu 9.322). They should sanction individuals and groups who break away from the prescribed norms. Ritualist and king thereby secure the reproduction of the status quo by making the people follow their duties.

It is not only in the administration of justice that the advice of Brahmin ritualists is required, but in all important state affairs. Thus the king is bound to choose among the learned Brahmins a *purohita* (literally he who stands in front) who will be his chief counsellor (Lingat 1973:217).

The hierarchical relationship between Brahmin ritualist and Kshatriya king is clearly stated in a passage in the *Sataphata Brahmana* (4.1.4.1): Brahma is 'he who conceives' (*abhigantr*) and *kshatra* 'he who does' (*kartr*) or, again, the *purohita* is to the king as thought is to will, as Mitra is to Varuna (Dumont 1971:65). The superiority of spiritual authority over temporal authority is affirmed by Manu when he derives the latter from the former (Manu 9.320). In order to maintain their superior position, the Brahmins are seen to represent the only varna that has recourse to magical spells and prayers through which they are believed able to destroy their enemies (Manu 9.314, 11.33).

The ritualists are always recruited from the Brahmin varna. Their status is ascribed. The king, on the other hand, need not originally be a Kshatriya. Kingship belongs to him who possesses the *kshatra*. The king's position was often achieved through secular power or military campaigns. To become legitimate, however, the king had to accept his secondary position in the hierarchy. He had to acknowledge that his power was derived from the Brahmins; '..., the priest makes him a ruler and upholder.' (S.B. 13.1.2.3)

The close relationship between ritualist and king in the organization of caste society tends to emphasize that there is an indistinct line of demarcation between rules of a juridical character and moral exhortations (Lingat 1973:93). The point is strengthened when we look at the sanctioning function of ritualist and king respectively. The Brahmin ritualists prescribe penances (*prayaschittas*) while the king gives punishment (*danda*). It is true that penance, as distinguished from punishment, is voluntary. But the threat of exclusion from caste is an indirect means of constraint to make the culprit perform the prescribed penances (op.cit.:63). Expiation and punishment are correlative conceptions (ibid). They do not only contribute to social control, they also have the object of cleaning the sinner from his sins.

The social organization of the Brahmin varna spells out an interesting and close connection between the holy texts of Hinduism and society. The Brahmin ritualist *is* the Veda (lit. knowledge) (Heesterman 1978) because the sacred knowledge was not written in books. It was *orally* transmitted through the various ritual schools, *gotras* (Madan 1962:70) of the Brahmin varna. From history we learn that as the sacred knowledge grew in extent and ritual performances became more elaborate, many new recensions and schools developed. The *Rig Veda* was organized in 21 recensions, *Yajur Veda* 101, *Sama Veda* 1000 and *Atharva Veda* in 9 recensions (Müller 1860:123). This suggests that Brahmin families with equal status and function - the same *jati* - settled in a common locality and founded ritual schools (*gotra*) for memorizing certain recensions of the sacred knowledge (Op.cit.:368-388, Madan 1962:70).

The importance of genealogical charters for the Brahmins also underscores the probable relation between oral transmission and the internal differentiation of the Brahmin varna. A Brahmin who keeps the holy fire should know which of the 49 original clans (*pravara*) he belongs to. Each of these clans was supposed to have connections with certain parts of the sacred knowledge and to occupy a certain function in the Vedic ritual. These 49 clans were further supposed to descend from the seven *Rishis* who, at the beginning of time, saw the eternal and sacred knowledge through direct revelation. In this manner the whole Brahmin varna was assumed to be related through genealogical charters.

The tradition of oral transmission is also reflected in the classification of the holy texts. The Vedas and the Upanishads belong to *Shruti*. *Shruti* is a noun derived from the verbal root *shru* = to hear, and connotes; 'that which has been heard or communicated from the beginning.'[1]

What has been heard? According to the orthodox Hindus, it is the eternal thoughts and forms of God, those sounds and sentences (*mantra*) which embody the fundamental reality and power of *Brahman* in the form of speech. These *mantras* were revealed to the seven Rishis, the culture heroes of the Hindus, at the beginning of time. But unlike Moses at Sinai, who received the laws of God written on stone tables, the sacred knowledge of the Rishis was not written down before the 13th - 14th century A.D.

(Kosambi op.cit.:78). It is stated in the *Mahabharata*: 'Those who sell the Vedas, and even those who write them...shall go to hell.' (Quoted from Max Müller 1860:502) Words and sounds (*mantra*) were believed to contain a power which, through repetition, could produce magical or mystical effects. To write a mantra in the old India was to freeze the holy power of Brahman in a profane sphere where it did not belong. From an ideological perspective the picture is somewhat different. The holy knowledge was the resource of the Brahmin varna, the only varna that could instruct and teach in Hindu society. Following the ideology the Brahmins formed the only varna pure enough to manipulate the power revealed by the sacred knowledge. By monopolizing this sacred knowledge, the Brahmins could sustain their exalted position.

The term *shruti* is an integral part of the native definition of a Hindu: *A Hindu is a person who accepts the Shruti as his highest authority*. To deny the authority of Shruti was accordingly a denial of the authority and holy character (Manu 1.93-101) of its social carriers, the Brahmin ritualists.[2]

The ritualists as they exist in Hindu society today are the supervisors of the Sanskritic temples and deities (cf. Babb 1975:191). They are the 'managers' of the Great Tradition in its Great Community centres and in the villages (Berreman 1964). They are ritual technicians and priests who are expected to be well versed in the Veda and Dharma literature. The Brahmin priests perform the life cycle rites (*samskaras*). They are also necessary religious functionaries in a variety of periodic and special observances at family, lineage and village level. In short, the ritualist is the main religious authority in the realm of caste duty and social relations and for the important rituals of the life cycle and the annual festivals.

The renouncers[3]

About the ideal renouncer the Gita states:

> The knowers of the self look with an equal eye on a Brahmana endowed with learning and humility, a cow, an elephant, a dog and a pariah. (Gita 5.18)

The ideal renouncer should perceive equality and *not* hierarchy. He should be free from the preoccupation with purity/impurity and thus be able to perform religious functions which were closed to orthodox ritualists. The sect *Gurus* were recruited from among the renouncers. Originally the Guru was a learned Brahmin of the Vedas privileged to teach the twice born the sacred teaching on Dharma. Low caste people were not entitled to this teaching (Manu 2.16 - Vedanta Sutra 1.3.34-38). Through the renouncer, however, the universal extension of the Guru-conception became a reality for members of all castes. Practically all the sects have been founded by renouncers who, apart from the worldly adherents, constitute the nucleus of the sects (Dumont 1960:59). Through the sect, the renouncer functions as a spiritual teacher, Guru, for householders.

The religious functions of the sect Guru are restricted to the personal realm of Hinduism governed by the personal choice of the believers such as sect affiliation, choice of personal God etc. Often heads of families are initiated by a Guru and given a personal mantra for prayers and meditation. A Guru might hold considerable power. He is often regarded as a God by his followers. Weber compares the leading Guru of a region with a bishop of a Western church (Weber 1958:319). The rise of the institution of the sect Guru symbolized the restoration of Hinduism (Weber 1958:319). The Gita also contributed to this restoration by, among other things, promising the possibility of religious liberation to members of all castes (Gita 9.32). The door was opened for a dialogue between the householder and the renouncer.

> ...the sannyasi although dead to society not merely has the right to speak but also is a sought after spiritual teacher; his thought, which is a negation of caste, in this way filters back into the caste. (Dumont and Pocock 1957:17)

The householder

The householder, with his attitude of service and subordination, is the *layman* of Brahmanic Hinduism. He accepts the ritualist as his spiritual authority in caste matters. He also accepts the king (or the dominant caste) as his authority in secular matters. And finally, the householder accepts the authority of the sect and the Guru in matters concerning his personal religion.

Householder life should be organized with due respect to the four fundamental human values (*purusharthas*). These are the following: *Kama*, meaning desire, pleasure and love (sexual love); *artha*, meaning interest, utility, similar to our economic interest; *Dharma*, meaning living in harmony with - in accordance with - the law and order of the cosmos. These three aims are hierarchically arranged and of specific importance to the householder. The fourth aim is *Moksha*, spiritual liberation. Following Weber and Parsons, we may classify actions motivated by kama as affective, by artha as instrumental, by Dharma as moral and by Moksha as ultimate (Marriott 1976:129-130). The four fundamental values of human life correspond to the four aspects of individual and society (viz. body, mind, intellect and soul = the four varnas). The four values also correspond to an elaborate fourfold scheme of life known as *ashrama Dharmas*, or four stages of life.

Sharma (1965:78) has suggested that the theory of the four varnas could be connected with the theory of the four human values. A Shudra who is believed to be on a low stage of religious self realization is dominated by affective actions, a Brahmin by ultimate actions. However, by the time of Gita/Manu, and because of its more religious liberal outlook, all four human ends may be theoretically relevant to analyzing any behaviour of any actor (Marriott 1976:130). Let us now have a closer look at the four ashramas in the light of the four human values.

The first stage, *Brahmacharya ashrama*, commences with the ceremony of initiation (*upanayana*) at the age of eight for a Brahmin and three or four years later for a Kshatriya and a Vaishya. According to the orthodox, this ceremony is closed to the Shudras because it makes the neophyte a *dvija* - a twice born. This first stage of life may last for 25 years and is meant for the acquisition of learning. The student must learn to master his senses, to keep himself from all impure contacts, to learn the sacred *Gayatri mantra* and, finally, to practice the virtues appropriate to his status. The dominant human value in this first stage of life is Dharma, moral education. The preceptor (Guru) is considered the student's spiritual father.

The second stage is *Grihashta ashrama*. During this stage the individual commences his family life. Marriage is a social and religious duty for every pious Hindu, bound as he is to continue the family and to secure the perpetuation of the domestic cult. As the productive period of life, the Grihashta ashrama is considered by the *Dharma Shastra* texts to be the most important, upon which the three others are dependent (Manu 3.77-78). The Grihashta ashrama is the period dominated by *kama* and *artha*.

The third stage, *Vanaprashtha ashrama* (lit. forest dweller), commences when the householder sees his skin wrinkled, his hair white, and the sons of his sons; then he may resort to the forest (Manu 6.2). His wife may accompany him. He has a fixed abode. He is still bound to perform the obligatory sacrifices, but he has entrusted the entire responsibility of the household management to his heirs. He is consulted by the members of his family and continues to give them advice in worldly matters in accordance with the Dharma. The *Vanaprashtha* renouncer should submit himself to various forms of mortification and give himself over to meditation, study and a religiously minded life. The Vanaprashtha ashrama is dominated by the two last values of human existence, *Dharma* and *Moksha*.

A twice born is fit for the fourth stage, the *Sannyas ashrama*, around the age of 75, after he has paid the 'three debts' - to the Great Sages, to the Manes and to the Gods (Manu 5.257) - through the performance of his ritual obligations.

According to the holy books, the entrance into the new mode of existence as a renouncer should be marked by an imposing ceremony. The renouncer -to-be performs a last sacrifice, after which he throws all his sacrificial utensils into the sacred fire (Manu 6.43) and announces his resolution to be a renouncer (Lingat op.cit.:47). Thereafter, he should shave his head, removing the top knot which many Hindus keep on their crowns (Manu 6.52). He should also remove the sacred thread which distinguishes him from the non-Aryans (Lingat op.cit.:51) and the lower castes. He is thereupon dead to the world and treated as an ancestor. When he actually dies, no funeral rites need to be performed.[4]

> Thereafter he will live without fire, without home, without joy, without protection..., he will wander without care for this world or for heaven... Thus liberated from all ties with the world, indifferent to joy as to pain..., he will only search for the Atman. (Ap.11.9.21.10 and 13)

The burning of the sacrificial utensils and the 'living without fire' are a symbolic expression of the renouncer's *interiorization* of sacrifice. Through the ceremony, the renouncer -to-be is symbolically ritualized out of the world of duties (Dharma) and actions (karma) to the world of indifference, unity, actionlessness (*naishkarmya*) and freedom (Moksha).

> Having reposited the three sacred fires in himself,..., let him...always wander alone,...and in order to attain complete (union with) the (supreme) Soul, (he must study) the various sacred texts contained in the Upanishads,...Let him quit this dwelling, composed of the five elements,..infested by old age and sorrow, the seat of disease, harassed by pain, gloomy with passion, and perishable. (Manu 6.25,42,29,76,77)

The only aspiration of the renouncer is Moksha, to experience the identity between Atman and Brahman - the subjective and objective parts of the Absolute. Through mystical illumination, he will then have suspended the seeming reality of the lifeworld - the maya, the samsara. The sannyasi will then be considered as a-man-outside the-world - overtly outside the structural relations of caste society. He is also believed to be spiritually free from the cosmical lifeworld (maya, samsara). He has become 'the All', free from sorrow, free from karma, free from rebirth.

Devoted Hindus often remain celibate throughout their life and enter directly into the sannyasi mode of existence after finishing their Brahmacharya ashrama. The Gita/Manu however, advocates all four ashramas. A complete life, as propagated in those scriptures, consists in the experience and fulfilment of all four life-stages (Manu 2.224). Each has its due part in life, but in a progressive manner; the pleasurable (kama) is encompassed by the useful (artha) which is in turn encompassed by the

68

moral good (Dharma). All three culminate in Moksha, spiritual liberation, the fundamental value of Hinduism symbolized by the renouncer outside-the-world.

NOTES TO CHAPTER 5

1. The *Smrti* literature is chronologically later than the *Shruti* and can be dated to the Hindu period, from 200 B.C. onwards. They are mostly systematizations, interpretations or manuals for the understanding of Shruti. (Muir 1880 v.2:168) The Smrti literature is comprehensive and refers to the earlier mentioned six Vedangas (auxiliary sciences to the Vedas), the Sutra texts, the six orthodox philosophical schools (*darshanas*, lit. view-points.), the two epic writings (the Mahabharata which includes the Gita, and the Ramayana), the Dharmashashtra texts (lit. treatises on Dharma), among which the Laws of Manu is the most authoritative, and finally the eighteen Puranas (lit. from the old days).

2. Buddhism and Jainism were termed '*nastika*'. *Nastika* is the negation of *astika* (orthodox) and the literal meaning is: 'those who do not believe that it is'. And what did the heterodox religions *not* believe? That the *Shruti* should be a product of revelation which deserved the exalted position ascribed to it by the Hindus.

3. 'Renouncer' (*sannyasi*, literally, one who has given up the Vedic sacrifices): anyone who leaves society and perfects himself in a manner prescribed by the Upanishads. Many orders admit low caste renouncers, although they might not be accepted as sannyasins by the more orthodox circles. It was, however, not only the orthodox scriptures which did not accept Shudras and Untouchables as proper renouncers. Anglo-Indian law followed the orthodox tradition (Dumont 1960:44). Shudras who claimed to be renouncers were often regarded as beggars.

4. If a sannyasi returns to householder life, he will be treated as an untouchable (Brahma Sutra: 3.4.41).

6

NOTES ON THE HISTORICAL GENESIS OF THE LOGIC OF KARMA

The Indologist Kosambi has pictured 'karma' as a religious extension of abstract value. Kosambi thereby indicated the systemic character and function of karma (Kosambi 1956:159). I shall not follow Kosambi in his historic materialist approach to the traditional Hindu world in which karma is explained in a socio-economic context. But I shall maintain Kosambi's idea that karma is a form of abstract value. What kind of abstract value? In my view, it is an abstract value that derives not from the exchange of commodities, but from the exchange of meaning.

Saussure, in his *Course in general linguistics* (1959), has indicated how the concept of value is scientifically relevant also outside political economy:

> Here, as in political economy, we are confronted with the notion of *value*, both sciences are concerned with *a system for equating things of different orders*...To resolve the issue,..., all values are apparently governed by the same paradoxical principle. They are always composed, 1) of a *dissimilar* thing that can be exchanged for the thing of which the value is to be determined, and 2) of *similar* things that can be *compared* with the thing of which the value is to be determined. (Saussure 1959:79, 115)[1]

By abstract value, we shall understand a *common medium*, a common denominator. The best example of a common medium and a common denominator is money, through which all goods can be measured and exchanged.

The task at hand is to go beyond the sacred texts we have scrutinized and try to indicate how 'karma' may have originated historically as the abstract value of Brahmanic Hinduism.

The genesis of the Logic of Karma is a process determined by many variables. One variable is the evolution of material, social, political and religious conditions which took place from the Vedic to the Upanishadic period. The Hindu renouncer originated at the end of this evolutionary process. But most old civilizations underwent a similar transition from the archaic to the historic stage of religious evolution without producing an institution of renouncers as important for their culture as it is for the Indian one. An explanation of a more specific kind is needed to understand the Indian material.

By relying on a diffusionist approach, anthropologists like Fürer-Haimendorf (1953) and Obeyesekere (1980) have proposed to explain the genesis of the *rebirth doctrine* - a main component of the Logic of Karma - as a result of the encounter between the eastward moving Aryans and the tribal peoples of the Gangetic area. Many native tribes of India, today and in the past, share the more general type of rebirth eschatology to be found among various tribal peoples around the globe (Obeyesekere 1980:138). But as Varman states: 'Karma heralds the theory of individualism,... it is opposed to the tribal notion of morality which emphasizes the gens (the communitas) as the unit and which does not concern itself with the apportment of justice according to one's deserts. Thus it can be said that the theory of karma is a great individualistic protest against the tribal canons of morality.' (Varman 1963:35). I agree with Varman. The rebirth doctrine of Brahmanic Hinduism did not evolve out of that early encounter between the Aryans and the tribal people of the Gangetic area.

In his article 'Brahmin, Ritual and Renouncer', Heesterman has tried to picture the growth of karma as a common medium, as a systemic concept, from semantic exchange praxis. Heesterman's hypothesis involves a convergence between perspectives on exchange and evolution. Heesterman is preoccupied with the transition from the pre-classical to the classical sacrificial system, in my terminology, the transition from the Vedic to the Upanishadic period. The preclassical system of sacrifice centred around the symbolic theme of the regeneration of cosmos, the creation of life out of death (Op.cit.:2). The sacrificers were reenacting the mythical drama of the creation of the world from Purusha/Prajapati (Sat.Br./Rig Veda). The system was based on a *reciprocal* exchange relationship between the Brahmin officiant and the patron of the sacrifice. Together they ritualized the drama of life and death by transferring the burden of death and impurity between each other. The receiver of the burden in the sacrificial exchange relationship was the Brahmin officiant. By accepting *dakshina* - gift and food 'payments' for the ritual work performed - the Brahmin officiant took over the sins and the death impurity of the patron. It is no wonder that the Brahmins were very careful about receiving *dakshina* (Heesterman 1964:3). Following Heesterman, there are reasons to believe that Brahmins and Kshatriyas were not originally closed, separate groups (Op. cit.:7). Officiant and patron reversed roles.[2]

The problem in this system was the continuous death and rebirth through exchange and reversal of roles.[3] In search for the continuity of life, the ancient Brahmins and Kshatriyas had to break the vicious circle of mutual dependence between officiant and patron (Op.cit.:12). The solution was to short circuit the bilateral pattern of exchange, to *interiorize* the external exchange relationship into one's own self. The implications of this interiorization process was an individualization of ritual which, according to Heesterman, contributed to the rise and elaboration of the Logic of Karma (Op.cit.:16). The successful outcome of the performance no longer depended on the other participants, but on the correct execution of the automatically working ritual (Op.cit.:14). In this conception, it is no longer possible for a person to transfer bad karma to others; he must digest it himself. The earlier exchange praxis of the pre-classical system based on the obligation to give and return gifts was rejected. Thus it is stated that the best Brahmin is the *shrotriya* who does not accept gifts (S.B. 13.4.3.14).

The new classical system of sacrifice is accompanied by a more rigid system of social stratification, a caste system in which reciprocal relations between, in principle, equal parties have been cut. Consequently, the groups stay fixed in their roles (Op.cit.:16): 'Evil, impurity does not circulate any more between the parties but is fixed at the lower levels of the hierarchy. Disposal of impurity becomes a hereditary specialty.' (ibid) From this stage in the evolutionary process, the tension between Brahmins and Kshatriyas became institutionalized. Hindu theory conceived of these two upper varnas as the manifestation of the antagonistic metaphysical forces of *Brahman* and *kshatra* (imperium).

The role of the Kshatriya

In the post-Upanishadic period (600 - 200 B.C.) of new emerging states and kingdoms, the position of the Kshatriyas was strengthened. The Kshatriyas were the growing intellectual strata with a drive towards conceiving the world as a meaningful cosmos (Weber 1964:124-125). This kind of intellectualism suppressed the belief in magic and attacked the sacrificial ritualism of the Brahmins which involved the slaughter of animals, perhaps even human beings. The result was an interiorization of sacrifice. The Upanishads themselves seem to indicate the specific mission of the Kshatriya in the development of the karma doctrine when it was stated that:

O Gautama, this knowledge has never yet come to Brahmans before you; and therefore in all the worlds has the rule belonged to the Kshatriya only. (Chand.Up. 5.3.7)

Another indication of the relationship between the Logic of Karma, renunciation and the Kshatriyas is the emergence of the two archetypal renouncers, the Buddha and the Mahavira (founder of Jainism). The Buddha was born 567 B.C. He was the heir to the Sakya kingdom in the Himalayan foothills north of the great state of Magadha, present day Bihar. Mahavira, the Tirthankara - literally, the founder of the path - was born the second son of a Kshatriya chieftain in the Magadha state some years before the Buddha. These indications are not to deny that Brahmins played an important role in the formation of mysticism and renunciation in Hinduism. But Brahmanical influence is on the decline in the Upanishadic period, to be restored first in the early Hindu period.[4]

One may conclude that the Brahmins produced ritualism, the Kshatriyas mysticism and renunciation. The former produced the paradigms of the sacrificial action type incumbent upon the ritualists inside the world while the latter produced the paradigms of the meditative karma type which necessitated a life as a man-outside-the-world. The further evolution of Brahmanic Hinduism produced the householder type, a synthesis of the other two categories. The householder type is a normative model for all lay Hindus irrespective of caste and sect affiliation. I hold that the Logic of Karma was historically complete in its essentials when the householder type became fully developed. By that time, karma was established as the abstract - moral/religious - value of the Logic of Karma. People of different orders (varna/jati) could be compared and evaluated through the Logic of Karma as a common medium, a common denominator.

NOTES TO CHAPTER 6

1. Long before Saussure, Hegel also indicated this point (i.e., the production of an ideational common denominator through exchange of meaning) when he compared the structure of spirit with the structure of money.

2. The well known mythical drama of the legendary conflicts between Brahmins and Kshatriyas displayed in the myths of Vishvamitra and Parasurama may reflect such conditions.

3. The Sanskrit term for rebirth in the Vedic period is *punarmrtyu*, meaning redeath. In the Upanishadic period another term is introduced: *punarjanman* = rebirth (see O'Flaherty 1980).

4. Hopkins has a similar perspective on the historical genesis of Hinduism (1971:63).

7

STRUCTURE, PARADIGMS AND IDEOLOGY

We have seen how karma is a common reference point for the three world views explored in chapter four. But we have not yet paid full attention to Dharma. Dharma, as I shall argue, has both an individualistic (*svadharma*) and a holistic (*varnashramadharma*) significance. Dharma as varnashramadharma may, in an anthropological meta-language, be translated as 'social structure'.

The characteristic trait of varnashramdharma as social structure is *hierarchy*. Hierarchy belongs to that order of things which the Hindus accept as given. Even the renouncer who denies ontological status to the lifeworld - the samsara/maya - accepts, as Radhakrishnan has stated it, that the different castes represent members on different stages on the road to self-realization (Radhakrishnan 1980:85). Due to their less favourable *karmic ballast*, the men-inside-the-world must perform their 'natural work' before they eventually, in a later existence or stage of life, may hope to become a renouncer.[1]

THE PARADIGMS OF THE LOGIC OF KARMA

The doctrine of karma consists of five components.

A) A belief in a *universal causality*. All human activity identified as karma commences a causal chain termed *karmabandhana* (lit. 'bound by the chain of actions'). Karmabandhana does not necessarily produce its effects - the fruits of karma (*phala*) - on the completion of an action. Karma is perceived to produce a metaphysical - a karmic-moral - residue (*apurva* lit. not before, *adrshta* lit. unseen) which is accumulated in the person. The sum total of these residues constitutes the *karma ashraya*, the karmic ballast of the person which determines his future destiny.

Brahmanic Hinduism has another mode of presenting the idea of universal causality and karma. This parallel perspective links karma with time. Past karma (*sancita karma*) is the result of all karma accumulated by the person through the ages - i.e., the karmic ballast. Then we have the part of past karma which is supposed to have explanatory relevance for the present destiny of the person, the *prarabdha karma*. And third, we have the karmas performed in the present life (*kriyamana karma*) which will fructify later and produce the future destiny of the person.

The concept of karma may thus be seen to have a wide range of references: Depending on context, 'karma' refers to the action as such. In others, it refers to the residue of actions - the karmic ballast - the destiny of the person.

B) The second component of the doctrine of karma is *ethicization* (O'Flaherty 1980:XI). Good acts produce pleasant results, bad acts produce unfavourable results.(4) The renouncers have an interesting way of describing the ethical quality of actions. Karma is either black, mixed, white or neither black nor white (Yoga Sutra 4.7). Black is bad karma, it is *Adharma* or *papa* - demerit - and leads to rebirth in a lower caste. Mixed karma is neither good nor bad and implies status quo in terms of rebirth chances. White karma is good, it is *Dharma* or *punya* - merit and leads to rebirth in a higher caste. Neither 'white nor black' karma is *non*-karmic producing activity, above the standards of worldly morals, performed by those who have reached Moksha.

C) The third component in the doctrine of karma is the *belief in rebirth* (*punarjanma*) and the wheel of existence (the Hindu lifeworld - samsara/maya). The whole samsaric world is conceived as a gigantic caste system, ranging from the realm of the plants to the realm of the Gods. Each of these domains is inhabited by a certain kind of species, the *jati*. 'Jati' is derived from the root *jan* = to be born, brought into existence, and signifies the form of existence brought about by birth.[3] Etymology here seems to correspond with social reality as the Hindus conceive their caste groups (*jati*) as biological species. Ideology simply states that it is the same principle of demarcation between horses, cows, pigs etc. as it is between the human castes (Cf. Strauss 1966:127). Hence, castes must be endogamous groups.

From the *Garuda Purana* we learn that there are 8.4 million different species in which the soul can be reborn (4.60-62). About 3000 of these belong to the human world. In which of these jatis the soul will be reborn is dependent upon past karma. Good deeds from previous lives qualify for rebirth among the Gods, bad karma qualifies for rebirth among the lower creatures, like worms, insects etc. And as long as any karmic ballast remains, the soul is compelled to enter a new body to experience the fruits of past karma.

D) The fourth component of the doctrine of karma is the *karmic problem*.

The one and only question of Hindu philosophy was, - how could souls be untangled from the web of karma - causality tying them to the wheel of the world. (Max Weber 1967:167)

...but without release from activity the attainment of the goal of man is impossible,.....FOR ACTIVITY IS NATURALLY PAINFUL. (Shankara bhashya Vedanta Sutra 2.3.40 - quoted from Deussen 1972:318)

If karma *is* suffering, then there is a problem - the karmic problem. The problem has two phases: How can present karma production be suspended? And how can the karmic ballast of the past be exhausted? We have already encountered three answers to the first phase of the karmic problem when I presented the world views/interpretative schemes of ritualist, renouncer and householder. As regards the last phase of the karmic problem, the scriptures suggest various interesting techniques as karma transfer and penance. One can often read stories of compassionate saints and Gurus 'digesting' parts of the karmic ballast of their devotees. Karmic transfer is also possible between fathers and sons: 'Father: My deeds (Karma) in you I would place! Son: Your deeds in me I take.' (Kau.Up.2.15) Hard penances are usually also accepted as expiations of past karma. Manu states:

> Penances, therefore must always be performed for the sake of purification, because those whose sins have not been expiated, are born again with disgraceful marks. (Manu 11.54)

For karmic traces of larger crimes, like violating one's Guru's bed (slept with his wife), the Laws of Manu prescribes the following penances:

> He who has violated his Guru's bed, shall, after confessing his crime, extend himself on a heated iron bed, or embrace the red-hot image (of a woman); by dying he becomes pure. (Manu 11.104)

The more extreme forms of the self-mortification, undergone by various types of renouncers (see Glasenapp 1942:62-66), could also partly be understood in this light as attempts to wipe out the more extreme traces of bad karma. Some sects even practised such hard asceticism that it culminated in a ritual suicide (Gombrich 1975:219). Not only penances, but also rites of purification may be seen as instruments to 'burn' up the traces of past karma. Purification can be achieved through fasts, baths, repetition of Vedic Mantras and the use of the five products from the cow.

On the relationship between Karma and Dharma

In order to understand the Logic of Karma as an ideological system,[4] we must take special recourse to Dharma.[5] The double connotation of Dharma, holistic (*varnashramadharma*) and individualistic (*svadharma*, lit. 'own duty'), is well attested to by the believers when they use 'Dharma' to refer to their own individual duties and also to express meanings like eternal law, order and religion. The same double connotation can also be found in the texts of Brahmanic Hinduism.[6]

Dumont defines Dharma as the 'whole' and states that: 'Hindu society is organized around the concept of Dharma in a way roughly similar to modern society around that of the individual' (Dumont 1971:140). Holistic Dharma refers to the structure of duties (norms and rules) pertaining to the various castes and their members, the varnashramadharma - the caste structure - the social set-up of Hindu society. One could say that holistic Dharma, in a functionalist perspective, is an expression of the 'needs' of the 'whole'. Dharma as varnashramadharma contributes to the structuration of the interrelations between the castes, the generations and the sexes by informing the actors about their duties and the correct standards of behaviour. Another function of holistic Dharma is to provide the matrix according to which actions can be morally evaluated. An action which is perceived to deviate from Dharma, that is, from the norms and rules defined by the varnashramadharma and formulated in the Dharma Shastras (Laws of Manu and other texts), is believed to produce demerit. Such morally weak actions are met with sanctions by the society. They are also, as the believers see it, perceived to be sanctioned in the hereafter, either by God[7] or simply by the automatic functioning of the karmic system itself. Hindus as socially competent actors have knowledge of the moral standard of their society and they monitor their actions accordingly. But equally important as the holistic perspective emphasized by Dumont is the individual connotation of Dharma (which is simply overlooked by Dumont, see the appendix).

Svadharma (lit. own duty) is the Sanskrit term which refers to the individual aspect of Dharma. Haradatta, the commentator of *Apastamba Dharma Sutra* defines *svadharma* as follows:

Produced by the act (karma),..., a property of the soul having the name *apurva* (karmic residue), that is Dharma. (Quoted from Lingat 1973:4)[8]

A persons svadharma is not seen to be an arbitrary duty given from power holders above. Nor is it a categorical imperative in the Kantian sense or a kind of narcissistic duty in the modern sense. A person's svadharma refers first of all to his caste duty - the duty to which he is born. Secondly, it refers to his karmic nature (*svabhava*) - to his constitution and inborn qualities as he himself is believed to have produced them through actions performed in his earlier lives. Let us look at it from another angle. Believers state that one can reach the highest goal by following one's caste duties, a position very clearly maintained also in the Gita:

Better (to do) one's own (caste-) duty, though devoid of merit, than (to do) another's, however well performed. By doing the work prescribed by his own nature a man meets with no defilement. (Gita 18.47 - translation Zaehner 1979).

How does Hinduism justify that the individual should remain, once and for all, in the station and calling to which he was born? It is done by positing a chain of connections between the *svadharma*, the *svabhava* (a person's nature determined by karma) and the karmic ballast of a person:
The primary fruit of karma is rebirth in a specific caste (*jati*) determined by the karmic ballast of the person.

It (the karmic ballast - Ø.J.) ripens into life state (*jati*), life experience and life time,.... (Yoga Sutra 2.13)

Birth in a specific caste determines a person's svadharma, the duties, rules, rights and obligations which lead him to enter a certain occupation, lifestyle, network of social relations, social status etc. This position determined by the person's svadharma is, from the spiritual point of view, seen to be the best and most suitable because a person's *svadharma is perceived to correspond to his nature - his svabhava* (lit. one's own becoming') - the karmic ballast of the person (Radhakrishnan 1980:79). Thus, by submission to the duty to which the person is born, (sva)Dharma is that action which permits the devoted Hindu to realize his destiny to the full. It is, to borrow a phrase from Gandhi's interpretation of the Gita, the *natural* work of the individual - the work through which he is able to digest his past karma. By performing one's duty, a person is believed to obtain a better rebirth and finally to be able to solve the karmic problem and reach Moksha.
Hindus do not only fear the sanctions of society when deviating from the prescribed norms and rules for acceptable conduct. They also fear for their rebirth chances. The worldly as well as the other-worldly perspective are both essential for understanding social control and thus the production/reproduction of society.

World construction and world maintenance

I shall now change my perspective and regard karma and Dharma in the light of Peter Berger's (1969) 'world construction' and 'world maintenance' (production/reproduction) perspectives.
First the concept of karma and world construction: I have already presented the 'world constructing' ideas in the Vedic sacrificial system. Karma is indeed world construction and in a double sense. Due to karma, the world is produced in reality as well as in thought. Due to karma, man clings to the created world of maya/samsara.[9] There is an important stanza in the Rig Veda dedicated to Vishvakarma - the world constructor par

excellence (Rig Veda X.82):[10] 'Mighty in mind and power is Vishvakarma, maker, disposer, ...' (Rig Veda X.82.2).

'Vishvakarma' simply means the maker of all things. The world constructing ideas inherent in the myth of Vishvakarma are further strengthened by the fact that technicians and factory workers in present day India - the bearers of industrialization - have their own festival in honour of Vishvakarma.

Regarding 'world maintenance', the following verse is of relevance:

> Dharma is so called because it protects (*dharanat*) everything; Dharma maintains everything that has been created. Dharma is thus that very principle which can maintain the universe.' (Mahabharata, Santip. 109.59 - quoted from Lingat 1973)

By performing one's own duty even the lowest Hindu participates, at least to a humble degree, in the maintenance of the eternal order, of Dharma.

Man as a karmic being

There are two presuppositions which must be maintained to ensure that the Logic of Karma and the intrinsic relation between karma and Dharma can be rationally comprehended. These presupposition are: i) The individual as the agent of action and ii) the individual as soul (personal identity). I shall first consider 'the individual as an agent of action'.

> After hundreds of lives one obtains human birth on earth;....: and who then only provides for and pampers the senses, through foolishness lets slip the nectar from his hand.' (Garuda Purana 6.40)

Hinduism conceives man as a spiritual possibility. In the entire scheme of creation, from plants to the sphere of the Gods, man alone is believed to be the only being capable of producing fresh karma (Walli 1977:164). This is, in my view, the closest we can reach an indigenous definition of man: *Man, the producer of karma, man - the individual agent (ahamkara, kartri)*. But Hinduism does not have a concept of Man as such, universally applicable to all members of Homo Sapiens. Such a notion belongs to the modern world. Hinduism limited the concept of man to people living in the land called Bharatavarsha = ancient India, (Vishnu Purana 3.2.22) or in general to all regions where the varnashramadharma-system operates. So members of the varna system were regarded as men - as capable of producing karma - others were regarded as *mlecchas* = barbarians and *dasas* = slaves.[11]

In CIS no.8 1965 Biardeau presents an analysis of the concept of *ahamkara* - the general term for the ego or the individual in Brahmanic Hinduism. Ahamkara literally means the 'I-doer', the organ which is the cause of individuation, egoism, egotism etc. The ahamkara is the agent (*kartri*) of actions, the first cause in the production of karma. The importance of Biardeau's arguments consists in her linking the doctrine of ahamkara to the men-inside-the-world, while she links the renouncer to the doctrine of Atman (Op.cit.:81), the Universal self, indeed, the negation of the individual. I shall now present Biardeau's arguments which reflect the steps of the Samkhya philosophical system.

The constitution of the individual is conceived of as a process of individuation, a karmic process that first produces self awareness. Self awareness is a product of an initial distinction between Atman - the Universal Self - and the 'I' through the utterance of 'I am' (see Br.Up. 1.4.1). Self awareness occurs in the most refined part of the human psyche, the *buddhi*, which means literally to wake up, recover consciousness. Along with the buddhi comes ahamkara - the 'I doer' - which transforms the higher will of the buddhi to egoism and desires. Then comes the third component of the human psyche the *manas* which establishes contact with the gross object world through the ten senses - the five knowledge senses (*buddhi-indriyani*) and the five action senses (*karmen-indriyani*).

In his spiritual practice, the renouncer seeks to reverse this process of karmic individuation. Accordingly, the stages in meditation are pictured as a kind of involutionary process. The first step towards spiritual freedom commences with the control of the senses (Gita 2.48, Yoga Sutra 2.30,32). Through this practice, the *gross* individuations produced by bodily karma are suspended. The next step involves the practice of suspending the more *subtle* forms of karma, like speech (verbal karma), through the discipline of bodily postures and breathing exercises. The outcome is a detachment (*vairagya, pratyahara*) from external objects which allows the mind and I-doer 'to follow as-it-were' their own nature (Yoga Sutra 2.54). The last step consists of stopping the functions of mental karma, the most *subtle* form of karma. This is done through the practice of meditation. Vyasa, the commentator on Patanjali's Yoga Sutra accordingly describes Moksha - spiritual freedom - as:

Moksha then is only the cessation of the mind from its work.(Yoga Sutra 2.24)

And when the mind stops functioning, it fades away into nothingness. Then the renouncer is established as Atman - the Universal self - as pure spirit released from the limiting individuations of matter (*upadhi*).

If we aspire to understand the ideas and values carried by the renouncers, if we want to converse with them in some manner (Geertz 1973), we cannot ignore their mystical aim of seeking absorption in the Absolute, a spiritual state which involves the extinction of the ego and the suppression of all kinds of karma production. Second, if we aspire to understand the men-inside-the-world, we cannot reject the concept of ahamkara which is the source of individual agency and is conceived as the instigator of the causal chain of actions (*karmabandhana*). Ahamkara, in short, is a Hindu notion which can be compared with our phenomenological understanding of the individual (Bhattacharya 1964:135).[12]

If the concept of the individual is rejected at the level of the caste system, as is done by Dumont (1960), we similarly dissolve the rational basis of Hindu ideology and morality which centres around the idea of individual agency and individual responsibility. In short, by following Dumont one reaches a unidimensional and social deterministic position (see appendix).

I shall now turn to the next presupposition of the Logic of Karma: *the individual as soul* - the issue of personal identity. In the first part of this work I discussed Hume's notion of personal identity. Hume maintained that the individual - the I - was nothing more than a bundle of perceptions flowing with immense speed through the mind. We also saw that reason had no power to intervene in the moral life of the individual. Reason, according to Hume, is, and ought to be, a slave of the passions. Kant could not accept the position of Hume because he believed it undermined the basis for morality and rational conduct. Kant, as we know, restored the notion of the individual as agent and also postulated the transcendental ego as an a priori assumption. There is an analogous opposition as the one between Kant and Hume to be found in ancient India. I am thinking of the extensive debate between the Buddhists, who rejected the ontological status of the soul (*anatmavada*), and the Hindus, who were staunch upholders of this doctrine (*atmavada*). I shall first consider the position of the Hindus.[13]

> Even as a man casts off worn-out clothes, and puts on others which are new, so the embodied (soul) casts off worn out bodies, and enters into others which are new. (Gita 2.22)

Logic seems to demand that there is some form of identity between the individual who sows and the individual who reaps the consequences of his doings. It must be possible to identify the individual who stands responsible with the individual who was the agent. Therefore, one must assume, Hinduism accepted the mobile soul thesis (Herman 1976) to account for the problem of personal identity. The soul, according to this thesis, is that substratum which is believed to be the agent of action, the carrier of the karmic residue and the reaper of the fruits (cf. Halfbass 1980:280). Without the belief in the individual soul it seems difficult to account for morality at all. Jurisprudence itself seems to underscore the point. If the accused has lost his memory, the problem of responsibility is intricate.

The Buddhists rejected the doctrine of the soul (Stcherbatsky 1976). They maintained the doctrine of *kshanikavada* - momentariness. Existence was conceived as a causal chain: A gives rise to B, B gives rise to C etc.[14] There was no substratum securing any form of identity between A and C, it was only a causal chain where the one rose from the other. Many Buddhist schools arose on this issue. Some even came very close to the general Hindu conception.

In a similar manner Buddhism also rejected, or at least was unconcerned with, the problem of structure (*varnashramadharma*). Buddhism was in its initial state a heretical sect of renouncers, growing on the soil of the Hindu social system. They were only to a small degree concerned with the organization of lay social life. The lack of a doctrine of the soul and a doctrine of social structure in Buddhism, is sociologically interesting when seen in relation to the material in Spiro's book *Buddhism and society* (1971). Spiro states that the doctrine of karma is Janus-faced in Burma. It provides *any* social order with a powerful moral authority (op.cit.: 439). He further proceeds to state that Burmese Buddhism in no way adopts such a conservative stance as is offered by the Hindu Dharma theory, which prescribes compliance with caste norms and thereby militates against positional change (op.cit.:441). Spiro therefore concludes that the interpretation of the doctrine of karma as providing powerful support for status quo - and thus being an agent of political conservatism - is only half true (op.cit.:442). This picture might be correct in the Burmese setting, but the picture is not plausible in the context of Hinduism. Without an ideational basis for personal identity (i.e., soul), and without a form of institutionalized social identity (i.e., social structure), Hindu ideology has no *raison d'etre*. It is the intrinsic relation between karma and Dharma and the institutionalized 'freezing' of the social person in his caste position throughout life which provides a basis for social control. In the Hindu scheme of things, the karmic ballast is in principle only convertible at the time of death (Karve 1961:91). The social 'freezing' of the person in the present life is not suspended into a kind of momentariness.

KARMIC IDEOLOGY

The paradigms of the Logic of Karma appear as karmic ideology on the level of the lifeworld. Here, karmic ideology provides answers to questions about the 'why' of institutional and positional arrangements. The first 'why' leads towards the whole - the varnashramadharma - the second towards the karmic history of the individual.

Social structure as a hierarchy - varnashramadharma - is made legitimate by Hinduism by being reified into a divine and eternal institution (Rig Veda X 90). The historical and changing character of the socio-cultural system is thereby denied. Social change as change in structure appears to the believers as impossible.

On the question 'why me', the scriptures of Brahmanic Hinduism have lengthy elaborations on the topic of the relationship between karma and its fruits. The Manu states:

> What wombs (*jati*) this individual soul enters in this world and in consequence of what actions, learn the particulars of that at large and in due order. (Manu 12.53)

Then follows a long list of the different types of karmas and their consequences. A few examples: An untouchable is believed to have murdered a Brahmin in an earlier existence (Manu 12.55). A Brahmin who drinks liquor is believed to become an insect (Manu 12.156). He who has associated with outcasts is believed to be an evil demon. Those who eat forbidden food become worms. For stealing grain, one becomes a rat, for stealing milk, a crow. For relinquishing one's appointed duty without the pressure of necessity, one becomes the servant of *dasyus* (slaves, outcasts, non-Aryans, the enemies of the Gods) after migrating into despicable bodies (see Manu 12.53-81, also Garuda Purana chapter 4,5,6). And for speaking ill of caste and order, one is born a pigeon in a wood (Garuda Purana 5.23).

Following the paradigm of hierarchy, the same karma produces *different* fruits dependent on the status of the actor:

> A Brahmana who has fallen off from his duty (becomes) an Ulkamukha Preta (Preta = Ghost), who feeds on what has been vomited; and a Kshatriya, a Kataputana who eats impure substances and corpses.' 'A Vaisya who has fallen off from his duty becomes a Maitraksgyotika Preta who feeds on pus; and a Sudra, a Kailasaka (preta who feeds on moths). (Manu 12.71-72)

This idea was crucial to Hindu legislation (Manu 8.267-272) and reflects the conception that human beings have unequal karmic ballast and, accordingly, unequal value and unequal chances to absorb the unpleasant results of actions performed.

Another important principle for deciding the proper fruits of karma is based upon the distinction noted earlier between subtle and gross karma. Subtle karma is usually associated with mental action. Verbal karma is less subtle. Bodily karma belongs to the gross type. By solely *thinking* of coveting the property of others one becomes a low caste. And by actually performing it with the help of the body, a man becomes something inanimate (Manu 12.9). Consequently, mental action is supposed to be less fallacious than verbal action and bodily action. The thought is not perceived to be as bad as the deed itself.

(A man) obtains (the result) of a good or evil mental (act) in his mind, (that of) a verbal (act) in his speech, (that of) a bodily (act) in his body. (Manu 12.8)

Hindus are well informed about the relationship between karma and its fruits. But how does one know the karmic ballast of either oneself or one's fellow beings? For those with yogic intuition and knowledge, it is a problem of transexistential memory. There are many stories of renouncers who can recall the actions done in a previous life which are believed to be the cause of one's present destiny. The Yoga Sutra also promises such knowledge to those who undergo the discipline of a renouncer (3.16). For the common people, on the other hand, there is another and easier path:

By external signs let him discover the internal disposition of men, by their voice, their colour, their motions, their aspect, their eyes and their gestures. (Manu 8.25)

Thus they become men and women oozing with leprosy, born blind, infested with grievous maladies, and bearing the marks of sin. (Garuda Purana 4.64)

Thus in consequence of a remnant of (the guilt of former) crimes, are born idiots, dumb, blind, deaf, and deformed men who are all despised by the virtuous. (Manu 11.53)

The fruits of karma produce *external signs*, which are believed to be manifestations of the karmic history of individuals. The etymological meaning of *varna* is interesting in connection with the external signs of karma. Varna means a covering of the soul where colour is the essential aspect. Or varna simply means colour and outward appearance. Each varna of the caste system is associated with a particular colour (Beck 1969:559). The fair Brahmins are associated with white, the ruling power of Kshatriya with red, the Vaishyas with yellow and the Shudras with blue or black.[15] Depending on *moral* quality, karmas have different colours which stamp the soul of its producer. Following the Yoga Sutra, good karma is white (4.7) and people with fair skin like the Brahmin varna are thereby believed to have a good and white karmic ballast. The activity of the renouncer is colourless because it is believed to be non-karmic and because he is outside caste, colour and even moral hierarchy. In a patriarchal ideology like the one to be found in Hinduism, women are also believed to have inferior karmic qualities (Pocock 1972:122). The general picture is quite clear:[16]

Owing to my bad deeds in former lives I got a woman's body, which is a source of great misery. (Garuda Purana 2.41)[17]

Thus, according to Hinduism, individuals are seen to be responsible for their socio-religious destinies. What they have sown, they must accordingly reap.[18] But the doctrine of karma also gives hope to the believers:

(A Sudra who is) pure, the servant of his betters, gentle in his speech, and free from pride, and always seeks a refuge with Brahmanas, attain (in his next life) a higher caste. (Manu 9.335)

The believers can *accumulate* good merit and obtain a better rebirth in a later existence.[19]

The doctrine of karma makes the samsaric world of temporality and suffering into a meaningful cosmos for the Hindu. It provides an explanation for the seeming injustice and the existential suffering of this world. We can conclude with Weber that the doctrine of karma; '..represent the unique Hindu theodicy of the existing social, that is to say, caste system.' (Weber 1967:118)

On the question of the rational limits of Karmic ideology Weber states in his book *The religion of India*:

So long as the karma doctrine was unshaken, revolutionary ideas or progressivism were inconceivable. (Weber 1967:123)

I accept Weber's statement in principle. I shall therefore argue that Hindu reformist sects which deny the validity of varnashramadharma also deny the karmic ideology. The theology of such sects was first of all based on a theism characterized by a belief in an elaborate doctrine of grace (Op.cit.: 179, 187). A full-fledged doctrine of grace implied:

A)   A rejection of the doctrine of karma based on individual responsibility and individual agency.

B)   Non-acceptance of the authority and validity of the orthodox holy books and thereby also:

C)   A rejection of the dominance and God-like character of the Brahmins who are seen as the social carriers of the holy books.

In the book *Krishna: Myths, Rites, and Attitudes* edited by Milton Singer (1971), the problems addressed are those egalitarian ideals in Vaishnava devotion and the canonical status of its scriptural basis - the Bhagavata Purana (500 - 950 A.D., op.cit.:4).[20] The Bhagavatas developed the religious ideal of equality before God:

> He who worships Krishna is not a Sudra, he is a holy man among men; but he of whatsoever caste who does not worship Krishna, he is a Sudra. All the shastras witness this...Wherever there is caste, or pride in intellect, or fear - there *bhakti* cannot exist. (Quoted from Dimock op.cit.:52)

The same attitude can also be witnessed when observing present day Radha Krishna *bhajans* (a form of congregational worship). As Singer says, these bhajans are ritual dramatizations of the ideals of social equality and of supreme devotion to God (Op.cit.:137).

Opposing such religious liberalism were other famous personalities like the *Smarta* Brahmin Bhashkara. He demonstrated how the old-fashioned social conceits of Brahmanism could be imposed on the new soteriologies presented by the Bhagavatas:

> If women and the Sudras were qualified for release, the caste eminence of the Brahman would serve no purpose.... The norm of good conduct in the land of Aryans is conveyed solely by the Brahman's action... The Sudra, etc. cannot be elevated...nor can iron be made into gold by heating it some more... Even the Kshatriya and the Vaisya do not have the same qualification for release as the Brahman. (Quoted from van Buitenen op.cit.:32)

How can the religious liberalism of Vaishnavism and the very conservative stand of Bhashkara both be reconciled as parts of orthodox Brahmanic Hinduism? Hinduism is tolerant in doctrine, but rigid in questions of praxis (Weber 1958:117). In spite of the popular and liberal outlook of Vaishnavism, its praxis is accepted by the standards of Brahmanic Hinduism. I shall exemplify:

As van Buitenen has noted, the Bhagavata Purana strictly follows the norm of correct Sanskrit in Panini's grammar (Op.cit.:23). In form, the Bhagavata sounds Vedic. Regarding the orthopraxis of life cycle rituals, the Bhagavatas follow what is laid down in the Shastras (Op.cit.:38). They accepted the authority of the Vedas and of the Brahmins, but without rejecting the ideal of equality in spiritual matters.

Although the doctrine of grace was well developed in Vaishnavism, Ramanuja gives us a clear answer as to why the doctrine of karma was not rejected. God, the dispenser of grace, is the personification of the doctrine of karma:

The law of karma expresses the will of God. The order of karma is set up by God, who is the ruler of karma (*karmadhya-yaksah*). Since the law is dependent on God's nature, God himself may be regarded as rewarding the righteous and punishing the wicked. (Radhakrishnan 1966 v.2:694)

Ramanuja does not reject individual responsibility. God is not omnipotent. The will of man seems to constitute a limitation of the absoluteness of God (Op.cit.:693). Ramanuja thereby also solves the problem of theodicy - the problem of God's omnipotence and the existence of evil and suffering - by making man responsible for suffering and misery.[21] By the time of Ramanuja, the doubts which might have been raised by orthodoxy on the status of Vaishnavism were no longer relevant. Ramanuja made Vaishnavism fully acceptable to the orthodox and was himself one of the great commentators on the holy scriptures.

The Lingayats, or Virashaivas, of the Kannada speaking region of Mysore, are a well known example of a sect which arose in opposition to the varnashramadharma in the twelfth century A.D (Weber 1958:19, 304-305). The heresy of Basava, the founder of the sect, consisted in rejection of the doctrine of karma (McCormac 1963:61), protest against mediators like priests, Vedic ritual, temples, all in the name of a direct, individual experience. It was a religious movement of and for the underdog, a religion with a full-fledged doctrine of grace and a doctrine of the mystical chosen elect. It was furthermore a religion which replaced social hierarchy by birth with a mystical hierarchy by experience (McCormac 1973:53-54). Basava found the caste system and ritualism of his society senseless (Op.cit.:39). The authority of the Vedas is denied in the theology of the Lingayats (McCormac 1963:69). The superiority of the Brahmins was not accepted. The whole tradition is fiercely questioned and ridiculed by Basava who preached the socio-religious doctrine of equality (McCormac 1973:30,64).[22] But during the course of time, the Lingayats became absorbed into the caste system (Hutton 1946:103, Weber 1958:19-20). The Lingayats now demand the registration of their members according to the four classical varnas.

The struggle between the two great leaders of the untouchables in the 20th century - Mahatma Gandhi and Dr. Ambedkar - provides another example of relevance for the discussion of the rational limits of karmic ideology. Gandhi, as we have earlier noted, accepted the varnashramadharma, but did not accept the ideas of purity/impurity and hierarchy (Zelliot 1972:73). Gandhi rejected the fifth varna and wrote that they should be regarded as Shudras because there was no warrant for belief in a fifth caste (Young India, April 23, 1925, quoted from Zelliot Loc.cit.). Gandhi further writes:

> The law of Varna prescribes that a person should, for his living, follow the lawful occupation of his forefathers,...but with the understanding that all occupations are equally honourable:....A scavenger has the same status as a Brahmin. (Young India, November 17, 1927 - quoted from Zelliot loc.cit.)

A dialogue (quoted from Zelliot loc.cit.) between Gandhi and a Nambudiri Brahmin will, however, underscore that the perspectives of Gandhi were fully within the rational context of the karmic ideology:

> *Gandhi*: Is it fair to exclude a whole section of Hindus, because of their supposed lower birth, from public roads which can be used by non-Hindus, by criminals and bad characters, and even by dogs and cattle?

> *Nambudiri Trustee*: But how can it be helped? They are reaping the reward of their karma.

> *Gandhi*: No doubt they are suffering for their karma by being born as untouchables. But why must you add to the punishment? Are they worse than even criminals and beasts?

> *Nambudiri Trustee*: They must be so, for otherwise God would not condemn them to be untouchables.

> *Gandhi*: But God may punish them. Who are we human beings to take the place of God and add to their punishment?

> *Nambudiri Trustee*: We are instruments. God uses us as His instruments in order to impose on them the punishment that their karma has earned for them.

Dr. Ambedkar, whom Nehru described as a revolutionary (New York Times, December 6, 1956 - quoted from Lynch 1972:109), reacted against Gandhi's position, which he thought was not sufficiently radical. Gandhi wanted to reform Hinduism, Ambedkar rejected it. In his book *What Congress and Gandhi Have Done to the Untouchables* (1946) Ambedkar writes:

> To the Untouchables, Hinduism is a veritable chamber of horrors. The sanctity and infallibility of the Vedas, Smritis and Shastras, the iron law of caste, the heartless law of karma and the senseless law of status by birth are to the Untouchables veritable instruments of torture which Hinduism has forged against the Untouchables. These very instruments which have mutilated, blasted and blighted the life of the Untouchables are to be found intact and untarnished in the bosom of Gandhism. (Ambedkar 1946:308)

Consequently, Ambedkar, in one of his most dramatic rejections of Hinduism, burnt the Laws of Manu in public in 1927. This cost Ambedkar the approval of all but the most radical of his caste Hindu supporters (Zelliot 1972:82). In 1935 Ambedkar announced his vow to leave Hinduism entirely and to convert to some other religion. In 1956 he converted with 3000 Jatavs of Agra to Buddhism and founded the Indian Buddhist society (Lynch 1969:146). The conversion of Ambedkar and the Jatavs was motivated by the belief that only in leaving Hinduism could the people free themselves from the burden of pollution and untouchability. By 1966-67, 3,5 millions of India's former untouchables had converted to neo-Buddhism (Fiske 1972:113). Neo-Buddhism became the symbol of the oppressed.

Kanshi Ram, one of the followers of Dr. Ambedkar and the supremo of the political party BSP (Bahujan Samaj Party), the low caste party in power in Uttar Pradesh 1994-95, stated as follows in an interview with India Today, June 30. 1995:

> He [Mahatma Gandhi] was a *Manuvadi* [follower of the laws of Manu]. He forced the Poona Pact on Dr. Ambedkar who was fighting for the cause of the oppressed....[BJP (Bharata Janata Party) is a] Manuvadi [party] number two. Congress I is number one. Janata Dal number three. They are all Manuvadi...Uttar Pradesh is the cradle of Brahminism. It is the land of Ganga and Jamuna, it is the land of Manu. It is the land of *Rishis* and *Munis*. So it is the most important area of the enemy. So we thought we should acquire strength and catch the enemy by the neck.

The role of karmic ideology is obviously as relevant in the political discourse today as before.

Notes to Chapter 7

1. This kind of thinking is subsumed under the doctrine of *kramamuktih*, progressive liberation, and is accepted by Shankara as the lower but necessary approach for the caste Hindus (Deussen 1972:436).

2. For the ritualists, good and bad are not so much concerned with inner disposition, intentions etc. as they are with "orthopraxis". They judge karma by its external manifestation and by the degree of deviation from "orthopraxis".

3. In a philosophical language, *jati* connotes the term genus in opposition to species - that is, a class of a greater scope than the species subsumed within it. Or it connotes the species in opposition to the individuals (see Dravid 1972).

4. 'Ideology', as earlier defined (chapter two), refers to a system of ideas which justifies, conceals or reifies social structure and thereby make status quo appear as a legitimate order.

5. *Dharma* is derived from the verbal root *dhr* = the action of maintaining, supporting (Lingat 1973:3) and its primary meaning would be: duty, eternal law, order, religion, the whole etc.

6. See Kunst in his article 'Use and misuse of Dharma' (1978), who correctly underscores the individual and the collective interpretation of Dharma. See also Lingat 1973: *The Classical Law of India*.

7. In the theism of the householder, God is conceived to be the controller of the law of karma (*karmadhyayaksah*).

8. Kunst seems to underscore this interpretation of the concept of Dharma: 'This *Dharma* is dependent upon cultivation, and cultivation is dependent on action (karma). Therefore *karma* is the chief means of *Dharma*.' (Kunst 1978:12) Kunst proceeds: 'The Upanishadic internalization of ontological processes and the emphasis on the individual *Dharma* as a reflection of the cosmic *Dharma* of the Vedas seem to have contributed to the breakthrough by which the concept of *svadharma* has come to the forefront.' (Op.cit.:8)

9. The Gita also stresses the world constructing power of karma in several of its verses: '...as the creative force known as works (karma - ØJ) which gives rise to the (separate) natures of contingent beings.' (Gita 8.3)

10. Vishvakarman can probably be compared with the Demiurgeous as he was presented in the works of Plato.

11. Such notions are reflected in the theoretical categories of the Hindus which distinguish between *karmabhumi*, lit. 'the land and sphere of karmaproduction' and *bhogabhumi*, lit. 'the lands and spheres where the souls reap the fruits of past karma' (Walli 1977:152-154). To be born in a human body in the regions where the human varna system operates - in *karmabhumi* - was a unique possibility for a devoted Hindu aspiring to reach heaven or final emancipation.

12. The reader should notice that in various contexts the term *ahamkara* can be substituted with *kartri* which I have translated as the individual agent.

13. The reader is referred to Beidler's book *The vision of self in early Vedanta* (1975) for a thorough debate on the various notions of soul in Brahmanic Hinduism.

14. 'This being, that arises; because this comes into being, that also comes into being; when this is absent, that too is absent; because this disappears, that too disappears...' (Khuddaka-Nikaya Udanta, quoted from Na-Rangsi 1976:185)

15. 'The most interesting contrast..., is that between white, red, and yellow taken together, and the fourth colour category, blue/black. This opposition can be thought of as paralleling the separation of the twice born castes (Brahmin, Kshatriya, Vaishya) from the once born Shudras. Following this logic, blue occupies the bottom of the colour hierarchy... We know

from the classical texts that blue/black has an association with dark or lower class skin colour.' (Beck 1969:559-560)

16. '...; a woman is never fit for independence:...For women no (sacramental) rite (is performed) with sacred texts, thus the law is settled; women (who are) destitute of strength and destitute of (the knowledge of) Vedic texts, (are as impure as) falsehood (itself), that is a fixed rule.' (Manu 9.3,18)

17. Old medical texts also explain disease as a result of past karma (Filliozat 1964:95).

18. 'Karma which has been made, whether good or evil, must inevitably be suffered. Karma not suffered does not fade away even in tens of millions of ages.' (Garuda Purana 5.57)

19. This progressive, accumulative approach towards the highest goal is termed *kramamuktih* in Sanskrit.

20. The *Bhagavata Purana* reflects a progressive development of the religion of the Bhagavatas which gave rise to the Gita. One of the historical novelties in the Gita was its theism and religious liberal outlook: 'For whosoever makes Me his heaven, base born though he may be, yes, women too and artisans, even serfs, theirs it is to thread the highest way.' (Gita 9.32)

21. On the problem of evil in Hinduism, see O'Flaherty 1980, Hermann 1976.

22. In short, McCormac finds many analogous traits between European protestant movements and the Bhakti religions of the Lingayats (Op.cit.:53).

8

THE HIERARCHICAL STRUCTURING OF THE HINDU LIFEWORLD

The present chapter examines *how* the paradigms of the Logic of Karma structure the Hindu lifeworld. I shall first deal with the hierarchical structuring of time and space.

TIME AND SPACE

The lifeworld is the world of time and space. Brahmanic Hinduism underscore this point:

> There are, assuredly, two forms of Brahma: Time and the Timeless. That which is prior to the sun is the Timeless (*a-kala*), without parts (*a-kala*). But that which begins with the sun is Time, which has parts. (Maitri Up.6.15)

> Within Nescience (*avidya*) which is the cause of the phenomenal world, there emerges, first of all, the phenomenal world (samsara) consisting in the appearance of differentiation. Differentiation is spatial and temporal... (Helaraja's commentary on Bhartrihari, quoted from Iyer 1969:123)

Time and space are, as Leach notes, man-made products (1961:133), produced and reproduced by the paradigmatic actions of the system - by specific forms of socio-cultural rhythms.[1] Thus, as phenomenological concepts, time and space are perceived and structured differently from culture to culture and even between different social groups of the same culture.

The most characteristic trait of the Hindu perception of time and space is *hierarchy*. The hierarchical structuring of time and space appears in the context of Hinduism first and foremost through the sacred/profane continuum.

The sacred and the profane

The sacred manifests itself in the lifeworld as a *hierophany* (Eliade 1976). Hierophanies establish the spatial, temporal and human reference points -

the 'centres' of time and space - around which the lifeworld of Hinduism is structured. Hinduism provides us with three forms of hierophanies; *spatial* hierophanies, like temples and places of pilgrimage, *temporal* hierophanies, like festivals and auspicious moments, and *human* hierophanies in the form of holy men. The most important human hierophanies are the hierophants themselves, - the priests and the renouncers. They constitute the human 'centres' of caste and sect respectively.

Hierophanies are either direct manifestations of the sacred like the *avataras* (incarnations) of Vishnu, or human reproductions of the heavenly prototypes. Examples of the last are temple constructions and ritual actions which are seen to be modelled after celestial structures or actions performed by divine personages and culture heroes in mythical time. *Dharma* could be conceived in this light. A dharmic action (good action in accordance with Dharma) is that action which maintains the world order, which repeats the actions instituted by the sacred itself in the beginning of time. A karmic action (bad action not in accordance with Dharma), on the other hand, is a deviation from the sacred patterns.

Sacred time and sacred space are bounded units which 'cut up' the spatio-temporal world and transform it into a hierarchical structured whole. Sacred time and space are also the centres in which the possibility of intimate contact between the different regions of the cosmos exist. They are 'openings', points of transmission to something beyond, something quite different. The sacred is the eternal present, the immobile centre in which there is no succession, no action, no change, birth, decay and death. Following the belief of the Hindus, the sacred is an object of direct experience when the person is in a state of religious freedom, in a state transcending karma. The religious Hindu is said to be thirsting for the sacred world, a world saturated with Being. He seeks to abolish profane space and time, to be in the eternal present, in the centre. He seeks to transcend the world of maya and samsara to become one with Atman/Brahman.

Kala (Time) and Karma

Panikkar has emphasized the relationship between *kala* (time) and karma in the Hindu tradition (Panikkar 1972, 1974, 1976).[2] This relationship between kala and karma are significant in three ways.

A)   Karma *constitutes* time: 'If the priest did not offer up the sacrifice of fire every morning, the sun would not rise.' (S.B. II,3,1,5) The sun is one important symbol of time in Hinduism.

B)   Time is a *pre-supposition* for karma: 'From Time flow forth created things. From Time, too, they advance to growth. In Time, too, they do disappear. Time is a form and formless too.' (Maitri Up. 6.14)

C)   Karma *is* time. The expression 'sacrifice is the same thing as the year' occurs frequently in the Brahmana texts. Another frequent statement is 'Prajapati is the year'.[3] Prajapati is an important deity in the *Brahmana* texts who, like the cosmic giant Purusha of the Rig Veda, immolated himself in the primordial sacrifice. In this act, the year and its intrinsic divisions were born. The Vedic fire altar was identified with time:

> That fire-altar also is the Year, - the nights are its enclosing stones, and there are three hundred and sixty of these, because there are three hundred and sixty nights in the year; and the days are its yagushmati bricks, for there are three hundred and sixty of these, and three hundred and sixty days in the year....this fire-altar is Prajapati, and Prajapati is the year. (S.B. X,5,4,10 and VIII, 2,1,17-18)

Even the smallest unit of time, the *muhurta*, equalling a period of 48 minutes - the thirtieth part of a day - was given its symbolic expression in the Vedic altar (Basu 1969:263).

The point to note is the neat parallelism between the sacrifice and the calendar. The Hindu calendar, which is based on solar and lunar movements, is presented in the language of ritual time. In the Brahmana texts we find prescriptions on the *Gavamayana* sacrifice which lasted 361 days. Following the north/south movement of the sun, the rites performed during the first 180 days were directed north, while those of the last 180 days the rites were directed south. In between the two periods of six months (*uttarayana* and *dakshinayana*), there is the *vishuva* day when the sun is in equinox (21/3 and 23/9). Every six days completed one rite called *Sadaha*, meaning a collection of six days. Thus each Sadaha stood for a week and five of these made 30 days - a solar month. The lunar month was divided into two fortnights, the black fortnight (*krishnapaksha*) starting with the full moon and the light fortnight (*shuklapaksha*) starting with the new moon.

These divisions of time were paralleled by important events in the religious life of the Hindus. An important observance for most religious minded Hindus, was, for instance the fast called *Ekadashi* on the eleventh day of each fortnight. Another important observance was the monthly *shraddha* ritual to ancestors between the 10th and 13th day of the dark fortnight (Manu 3.276).

The day was divided by the three important rituals collectively called *Samdhya*, lit. holding together, union, junction etc. These were performed at sunrise, noon and sunset. They were often accompanied by the recitation of the *Gayatri mantra* (prayer).[4] The six seasons which divide the year, spring, summer, the rainy season, autumn, winter and the cold season, are also linked to different forms of religious activities. Spring is the season of the Brahmins (S.B. 13.4.1.3) and summer the season of the 'hot' Kshatriyas (S.B. 13.4.1.2).

The division of the year into the northern and southern passage of the sun, each of six months, deserves further attention. This division seems to imply various important ideas, beliefs and ritual practices connected with *auspicious* time (*subh*) in Hinduism.

> Now I shall tell thee,..., of the time (*kala*) travelling in which the Yogis return, (and again of that, taking which) they do not return...Fire, flame, day-time, the bright fortnight, the six months of the Northern passage of the sun - taking this path, the knowers of Brahman go to Brahman.... Smoke, night-time, the dark fortnight, the six months of the Southern passage of the sun - taking this path the Yogi, attaining the lunar light, returns. (Gita 8.23-25)

Why is the period of the sun's northern passage preferable? An interesting light has been thrown on the question by Tilak in his theory of the arctic home of the ancestors of the Aryan race.[5] The words *pitryana*, the path of the fathers, and *devayana*, the path of the Gods, appear many times in the Rig Veda (see X.88.15). But the introduction of the north as the abode of the Gods and the south as the abode of ancestors and death, as well as the belief in the inauspicious period of the southern passage of the sun, and the auspicious period of the northern passage, was unknown to the Rig Vedic people. This distinction appeared first in the Upanishads (Br.Up. 6.12.15, Chand.Up. 5.10.1-3). It probably evolved after the fair Aryans, coming in from the north, had encountered the dark people - the *Dasas* (fiend, demon, savage, slave) - coming from the south. As we have heard earlier, skin colour was a symbol of the karmic ballast - the moral quality of people. The step was not far before the south became connected with the darker forces of existence and the southern passage of the sun became an inauspicious period of the year.

It is of significance in this picture that the annual shraddha ritual of ancestor remembrance took place in the dark fortnight of the month *Ashvina* (September/October). It thereby marked the commencement of the six-month period when the sun was in the southern hemisphere. The shraddha ceremony was a period when the dead were believed to return to the village[6] to supervise that ritual offerings (*pinda*) were made to them as well as gifts of food to the Brahmins. The Brahmins who were indispensable as ritualists were believed to be the friends of the manes (Lewis 1958:213). The southern passage of the sun would secure the proper return of the manes to the abode of Yama, the God of death, along with the ritual food offered.

The four festivals and the four castes

Though the festival cycle varies from region to region, four sacred periods have Pan-Indian relevance and seem to be more important than the others (Marriott 1976:131, Sharma 1965: 83-84). Each of the four festivals is connected with one of the four varnas in a regressive manner.

A)   The first festival is the *Rakshabandhan* on the full moon day at the end of the month of *Shavana* (July-August). This festival marks, according to Hindu conceptions, the point of transition between the old and the new agricultural year. This is emphasized by its popular name, *Salono*, derived from Persian *Sal-i-nau* - new year (Mukerji 1918:91).[7] Rakshabandhan also marks the transition from the rainy season to the autumn. Sisters will first take a ceremonial bath, make a *rakhi* (wrist band of thread) and put it onto the hands of their brothers. In return, the brothers should give money and clothes. The festival is widespread among the higher castes in India. The second component of the 'charm tying festival' is linked to the *jajmani* system. The Brahmin *purohit* (family priest) will visit all his *jajmans* (clients) and put a rakhi onto their hands. In return, the jajmans will provide *sidha* (gifts of flour or grain to Brahmins) and money to their family priest. As the jajmani system is on the retreat, the family aspect is at present the most important part of the festival (Jaer 1995).[8] Rakshabandhan is primarily a festival connected with the Brahmin varna. The tying of the thread on well-to-do people in return for grain or cash symbolizes the interdependence as well as the superiority of the Brahmins. The jajmani system is instituted afresh for the next agricultural year. Between brothers and sisters, the charm tying festival symbolizes solidarity which shall last after the girl has moved to her husband's village. This festival also concludes a fortnight when married sisters return to their natal village to stay with their parents and siblings (Marriott 1955:198).

B)   *Vijayadashami* (lit. 'the tenth day of victory'), popularly known as *Dashahra* (lit. 'the removal of the ten heads'), takes place in the month of *Ashvina* - September-October. Dashahra is a festival reenacting the victory of Rama - the champion of righteousness - over Ravana, the king of Lanka, the leader of demons and evil-doers. It is a festival with a specific relevance for the Kshatriya. The festival symbolizes the traditional Kshatriya duty of protecting the Dharma. Worship of weapons used to be a common component of the festival (Lewis 1958:215). But the most important part of the celebration is the performance of the *Ramlila* where the actions of Rama, Sita, Hanuman and the other personages of the *Ramayana* epos is reenacted. An outstanding performance of the Ramlila in India today is screened in Varanasi under the aegis of the Maharajah of Ramanagar (Varanasi). It attracts a huge mass of visitors. The Maharajah leads the procession, often seated on an elephant. Finally, on the tenth day of the festival, the complete victory of Rama over Ravana - of good over evil - is reenacted. On this day, a big procession carrying an enormous figure of Ravana proceeds to the place where they will burn the demon king Ravana to ashes.

C)   The third festival is *Deepavali*, the festival of light. It takes place in the month of *Karttika* - October-November. This festival marks the return of the Goddess Lakshmi (the Goddess of wealth). She is honoured by being offered oil lamps. In Varanasi on this occasion, the whole Ganges River is covered with small burning oil lamps - a beautiful sight indeed. Lakshmi is, first of all, the Goddess of the Vaishya caste. The festival of light is of specific relevance to the Vaishya varna. Traders give sweets to their neighbours and start new account books on Deepavali (cf. Lewis 1958:223).

D)   The fourth festival is *Holi*, the festival of sprinkling colour, playing pranks and merrymaking. It takes place in the month of *Phalguna* (February-March). According to Hindu mythology, on this very day Holika, the sister of the demon king Hiranayakashyapa, was burnt. The story will have it that the king's infant son, Prahlad, was a great devotee of Vishnu. This was resented by the demon king, who wanted to punish his son with death. A device was found. His sister had received the boon of immunity from fire so she was asked to sit on top of the flame with the infant on her leap. But God so willed that she herself was burnt and the infant came out safely (Pandey 1969:117). This great event is celebrated every year with the enactment of the religious drama presented in the myth.

The Holi festival is a *new year* celebration. It marks the position of the sun entering the northern hemisphere. The myth tells us that the old year, symbolized by Holika, is burnt into smoke. But Prahlad, the good infant who was a great devotee of Lord Vishnu, was saved from the fire. And with this symbol of goodness, purity and innocence, the new year starts, released from the accumulated burdens of time and sin of the old year (Eliade 1971). The Holi is a saturnalian festival whose structures seem to be precisely the inverse of the social and ritual principles of routine life (Marriott 1966:210). The festival involves a symbolic return to chaos before the cosmos of the new year is re-created (Eliade 1971:51-62). It is an institutionalized festival for the *abolition* of the karma accumulated through the year (Eliade 1971:117, Babb 1975:170) - an abolition of both individual and group karma.

McKim Marriott reports that the villagers of Kishan Garhi believe Lord Krishna taught them to celebrate the festival of Holi (1966:207). There is, however, no scriptural information regarding the Holi festival in the

Bhagavata Purana where the sports of Krishna (*Krishna lila*) are described. But the description of the play of Krishna with Radha and the other cowherd maidens at Vrindavan, Mathura, must have provided an orthodox archetype and thereby an orthodox acceptance of a very ancient festival of the common people.[9] 'Under the tutelage of Krishna, each person plays and for the moment may experience the role of his opposite; the servile wife acts as the domineering husband, and vice versa; the ravisher acts the ravished; the menial acts the master;... Each actor playfully takes the role of others in relation to his own usual self.' (Marriott 1966:212)

Lewis reports from Rampur that the women there have the significant privilege of using sticks to beat up the men, including those of the higher castes. Low caste women, often intoxicated by *bhang* (hemp) or liquor, hold up men passing through the streets and demand money from them. If money is not forthcoming, they will be severely beaten. Wives take the opportunity to return the beatings they have received from their husbands throughout the year (Lewis 1958:232).

Holi is also the feast of love. It is an occasion with sexual excesses which probably are survivals from orgiastic elements of the Holi festivals of the past. Even the most orthodox Brahmin might turn up on this day to utter the most vulgar language in public. The period around Holi is believed to be very auspicious for weddings.

The Holi is the sacred period of the year primarily related to the Shudra varna (Marriott 1966:201, Lewis 1958:229, Sharma 1965:84).

The regressive character of social time

Festivals are condensations of sacred time. They are periods when the community might transcend profane duration - forget time and temporarily 'lapse' into a moment of eternity. But the sacred has different attributes and different implications according to which varna - which part of the cosmical man (Purusha, the symbol of the caste system as an organism) - the individual is attached.

Each of the four festivals occurs during a period when the social accumulation of karma (*samasti karma*) corresponds to the degree of impurity supposedly inherent in the varna with which the festival is identified. While the Rakshabhandan is a 'subtle, light, cold and pure' festival, the Holi is full of impurities, gross, hot and chaotic. This does not mean that each festival is only celebrated by its respective varna. The other varnas also take part. It could be said that the Dashahra, for instance, is the period when all participants assume the role of a Kshatriya. At the Holi they assume the role of the Shudra. The four festivals remind the believers of the organic nature of the caste system and of the 'spiritual unity in physical diversity'. It also reminds the believers of the hierarchically organized purity/impurity phenomenology of the Hindu jajmani system defining the various occupations and their social carriers as well as the substances with which these are interrelated.

The regressive character of cosmical time

The regressive character of social time through the festival cycle has its parallel in the regressive character of cosmical time through the *four ages* (*yugas*) of the world.

A)   The golden age has two names in Brahmanic Hinduism: *Satyayuga*, the age of truth and *Krtayuga*, the age when everything is well done, proper etc. According to the laws of Manu, the golden age is that period when the conduct of man was in perfect harmony with his prescribed duties - his *svadharma*. The golden age was the period of the culture heroes of Hinduism, those Rishis who laid down the pattern of conduct for the succeeding generations.

B)   The silver age is called the *Tretayuga*, meaning the age of triads when the bull of Dharma only had three legs and not four as in the preceding age.

C)   The bronze age is called the *Dvaparayuga*, meaning the age of two, i.e., when the Dharma bull had only two legs.

D)   The last age, the dark iron age in which the Hindus believe to find themselves at present, is called the *Kaliyuga*. Kali is the symbolic expression of the number one and accordingly denotes the age when the Dharma bull has only one leg. Kali also means the losing die in the game of dice while the treta and dvapara mean the die with three and two dots respectively.[10]

The Krtayuga is supposed to last 4000 divine years, the Treta 3000, Dvapara 2000 and the Kaliyuga 1000 divine years, which together make a complete cycle spanning 12 000 years - a *mahayuga* (a divine year = 360 human years). A thousand such mahayugas constitutes a *kalpa*; fourteen kalpas make a *manvantara* (the period or age of Manu). A kalpa is equivalent to a day in the life of the creator God Brahma; another kalpa to a night. A hundred years of Brahma constitute his life. And still the life of Brahma does not succeed to exhaust time, for the Gods are not eternal (Eliade 1971:114). They are also *subject to* the law of karma and the cosmic creations and destructions succeeding each other in a cyclical fashion.

The decrease in the duration of each new yuga corresponds to a similar decay on the human plane:

(Men are) free from disease, accomplish all their aims, and live four hundred years in the Krita age, but in the Treta and (in each of) the succeeding (ages) their life is lessened by one quarter...., Dharma is deprived successively of one foot, and through (the prevalence) of theft, falsehood, and fraud the merit (gained by men) is diminished by one foot (in each) (Manu 1.83,82)

The present Kaliyuga, which is supposed to have begun 3102 B.C., and which shall last 360 000 human years, is the last age of this great cosmic cycle (*mahayuga*). It is supposed to end with a *Pralaya*, a Ragnarok of destruction. The cosmic fire will purify the whole creation: All created things and forms will be reabsorbed into the stomach of Vishnu and digested for further purification before the *karmic seeds* after one night of cosmic sleep by necessity causes a new great cycle to emanate from the creator God.

'The terror of time'

Why does the festival cycle commence with the light and pure festival of Rakshabandhan of the Brahmin varna to proceed to the Dashahra of the Kshatriyas and the Deepavali of the Vaishyas and finally to end in the more chaotic and 'impure' new year celebration of the Holi, associated with the Shudra varna? Why, furthermore, does the cosmical cycle commence in the pure and perfect golden age of the Rishis of Hinduism - the forefathers of the Brahmin varna - to decline into the impure, chaotic and shudra like iron age of the present? Why, in short, does the structure of social and cosmical time appear as a temporal *reflection* of the varna hierarchy? I suggest that we should interpret the hierarchical structuring of social and cosmical time in the context of the Logic of Karma - in more general terms in the context of what Eliade has called the 'burden of history, the terror of time' (Eliade 1971, 1957).

Time is profane duration, the medium in which actions (karma) take place. As time passes actions seem to deviate progressively from the archetypes - the Dharma - which were instituted in the beginning of time. The passage of time and the conduct of actions result in the accumulation of sin and impurity, in short, karmic ballast. The laws of Manu in the above quoted verse (Manu 1.82) seem to underscore my interpretation. Dharma is deprived successively of one foot because of moral depreciation. Thus, perfection is not, as in the linear millenarian Christian conception of history, to be conceived in the future.

There is one seeming exception to this native theory of socio-cosmical regression. This is the well known doctrine of the *avataras* - the incarnations of Vishnu. It makes its first appearance in the Gita:

For whenever the law of righteousness withers away and lawlessness arises (*aDharma*), then do I generate Myself (on earth)....For the protection of the good, for the destruction of evil-doers, for the setting up of the law of righteousness I come into being age after age. (Gita 4.7-8)

'The justification of the avatara is precisely because cosmic history, the accumulations of social and cosmical karma, shows a kind of negative inertia. The world decays in a spiritual and moral manner something which requires the intervention of the divine - of the nonkarmic - again and again in order to reverse the trend.' (Panikkar 1972:42) But although the avatara gives comfort and knowledge to his devotees, he cannot stop the inevitable decline of the cycles, whether cosmic or annual, towards the Pralaya and the Holi. But regeneration will again commence. There will, in the Hindu scheme of things, always be a new creation and a new year and so on ad infinitum (Pocock 1967:313).

'Degeneration' and Sanskritization

Lingat has presented an explanation of relevance to the belief in the degeneration of cosmos and society. His explanation is of importance because it provides an understanding of how karmic ideology can be related to the process of Sanskritization (Lingat 1962, 1973:189). Lingat takes his point of departure from the indigenous theory of *kalivarjya*; 'according to which certain practices, even though admitted or even prescribed by the *smriti*, are forbidden in the Kali age, a theory which has been used ... since the 12th century, as a justification for the abolition of certain customs ... ' (Lingat 1962:9). The scriptural basis of the kalivarjya theory are two famous stanzas from the Laws of Manu:

> One set of duties (is prescribed) for men in the Krita age, different ones in the Treta and in the Dvapara, and (again) another (set) in the Kali, in proportion as (those) ages decrease in length....In the Krita age the chief virtue is declared to be (the performance) of austerities, in the Treta (divine) knowledge, in the Dvapara (the performance of) sacrifices, in the Kali liberality alone. (Manu 1.85-86)

One example is the prohibition on the slaughtering of the cow and the eating of beef which probably occurred during the early Hindu period (Lodrick 1980). In the Vedic period the sacrifice of the cow was a normal thing. We learn from the *Brihadaranyaka Upanishad* that the great renouncer Yajnavalkya enjoyed eating beef.

Other examples are linked to the fact of cultural diversity and geographical spread. Many examples of customs and usages of the little traditions which fail to tally with the rules of Dharma prescribed by the Great Tradition. The verses 172-173 of Book 9 of Manu regard the marriage of a boy with his maternal uncle's daughter or his paternal aunt's daughter as a grave sin. Still, it was a common match among South Indians. Thus, what was Dharma for southerners was Adharma for the peoples of the north (Lingat 1973:169-170). The problem for the orthodox believers was to explain how the eternal and universal Dharma which had its ultimate source in the Veda, could be reconciled with historical change and geographical diversity?

The theory of *kalivarjya* on the decline of the moral capacity of mankind through the four yugas proved to be a good solution. The theory of kalivarjya allowed for the existence of 'unity in diversity' because it was based on the idea of hierarchy. In the words of Lingat: 'If the rule of *Dharma* cannot abrogate the customary rule, the latter certainly cannot abrogate the rule of *Dharma* as such, that is to say as instrument of the law of karma.... Even when not followed, the rule of *Dharma* always appears to the Hindu as a model towards which one should tend, for it is a principle of classification. A caste rises in the social hierarchy only as it approaches the usages practised by the higher castes, i.e. those who most respect the traditions set out in the *smrti*.' (Lingat 1973:202-203)

The processes of Sanskritization involve interactions between the Great Tradition and its social carriers on the one hand and the many little traditions and their social carriers on the other. These 'interactions' are one of the moving forces of Indian civilization and history. They undoubtedly involve a continuous deviation from the archetype models constituted by the Rishis, the forefathers of the Brahmins inhabiting the original land of Hinduism, the *Aryavarta* or *Brahmavarta* as the laws of Manu call it.[11]

Following Lingat, I will suggest that the process of Sanskritization is indeed what is reflected in the theory of kalivarjya. The moral quality of the Hindu is believed to be declining because the original culture has spread throughout the Indian region as a whole and also into the heart of the religion of the common people.[12]

The past as the golden age

The past does not only refer to the golden age. It also refers to the golden land and the golden people, the land and the period of the purest and best of Brahmins.

The sociology of knowledge thesis that the regressive perception of socio-cosmical time reflects social hierarchy is strengthened when we analyze the value orientation towards the past in the Hindu conception of time. The past *is* the golden age, the age of perfect wisdom and perfect morality. The past provides the model for the present. Actions performed should be guided by the paradigms institutionalized in the past. Morality should be judged according to the deviation from the norms institutionalized by the culture heroes (Rishis) in the beginning of time. Who are the prime *social carriers* of the past in Hinduism? First we have the ritualists - the *Smarta*

Brahmins - who, as followers of the *smritis*, were the staunch upholders of the ritualistic tradition of the Vedas. The Sanskrit terms *Smarta* and *smriti* are both derived from the verbal root *smr* meaning remember, recollect etc. The Smartas, then, are those who uphold the prescriptions laid down in the category of scriptures called smriti, what is remembered. The Smarta ritualists are, as it were, believed to be the 'oldest' in Hindu society. They should be able to trace their genealogy back to the seven Rishis - the culture heroes of Brahmanic Hinduism - who instituted the exemplary models for proper Hindu life. The ritualists are also believed to be spiritually mature. Lower castes often call their superiors, even of their own age, Baba, meaning father's father (Cohn 1969:62). The old man is believed to be wise because he is a man of the past.[13]

The individual and time

While social change as change in *structure* is a phenomenon without any rational basis in Hinduism, the idea of individual change and progression is indeed an essential element of the karmic ideology. From the perspective of karmic ideology, the destiny of a person, his place in the social hierarchy and his misfortune and suffering, not only find a meaning but also acquire a positive value. The suffering of one's present life is acknowledged to be *deserved* because it is the result - the fruit - of past karma. In short, the socio-cosmical 'biography' of the individual - his own karmic history - explains his present situation. On the other hand, suffering acquires a positive value because the karmic debt that burdens the individual can be liquidated. The individual is thus given a hope for future improvement.

Karmic ideology links the individual to the three modi of time, but to a different degree depending on social adherence.[14] The ritualist, for example, has a special connection with the *past*. The social function of the ritualist is to inform the present by the past. But as individuals concerned with their own religious liberation, ritualists are also concerned with the future. They hope to produce fresh, good and white karma in order to improve their future destiny. The aim of the householder is to act in harmony with the eternal order (Dharma) by subscribing to the models instituted at the beginning of time. The householders seek to *repeat* the past in the present in the hope of 'lapsing' into eternity. But on a more practical level, the householder is also devoted to karma accumulation in order to produce good karma to improve his rebirth chances. The renouncer has a special connection with the *present*. To reach the perfect state of *jivanmuktih* - liberated while alive - the renouncer performs yoga with bodily postures, breathing exercises and meditation. The purpose of breathing excersizes is the prolongation and rhythmization of the breathing process. Breath (*prana*) is regarded as the essence of man. The more harmonious his breathing, the more tranquil is his mind. Furthermore, respiration corresponds to an internal time through the mastering of which the renouncer may hope to transcend time altogether. The *Kalachakratantra* text seems to reflect this attitude:

(The Yogi) relates inhalation and exhalation with day and night and then with fortnights, months and years gradually working up to the major cosmic cycles. (Quoted from Panikkar 1976:72)

Then suddenly, when his body is neutral and completely firm, his breath in harmony with the rhythm of the cosmic wind and his mind tranquil without any modifications, the renouncer 'leaps' into transcendence and timelessness.

The renouncer is associated with the Sanskrit term *kshana*, meaning the instant, the moment, the smallest unit of time (twinkling of an eye). The mystical schools following the Upanishads take the instant, kshana, as their fulcrum for the 'leap into timelessness.' (Panikkar 1976:72) By halting the moment and by suppressing the activity of thought, time no longer flows. The renouncer then lives in an eternal present - the *nunc stans*. Vyasa, the commentator on Patanjali's Yoga Sutra states: 'For the wise there is cessation of the successions of the universe. Not for the others.' Yoga Sutra bhasya 4.33) By making the *kshana* their fulcrum for spiritual liberation, the renouncers naturally rejected the *kramamuktih* - the progressive, accumulating form of liberation practised by householders and ritualists. Thus, the renouncer as a cultural value symbolizes the eternal present free from the past and unconcerned with the future. The renouncer in his most sublime spirit disparages and even rejects the reactualizations of auroral time, which are so typical of the householder path.

The high cultural value put on the present is, as I shall now argue, also reflected in the usage of Sanskrit. Although classical Sanskrit developed a highly subtle system of verbal forms, the present and the aorist tenses predominate. This 'present orientation' is often referred to as the 'substantive' character of Sanskrit. The aorist is the very close past addressing repetitive acts which, although out of sight of the listeners, are still well known to them (Gonda 1962:273). This kind of 'present orientation' is also witnessed in the Hindi use of the word *kal*, which means both yesterday and tomorrow, the day before yesterday and the day after tomorrow. The important characteristic is the distance from the centre 'today', which is in itself non-temporal (Baumer 1976:79). This form of 'present orientation' is probably related to the tendency found in classical Sanskrit to show a preference for static as opposed to dynamic relationships (loc.sit.). Verbal forms are often transformed into action nouns and other substantive or adjectival expressions. Furthermore, there is a tendency to stress passive rather than active verbs. In the passive construction, the logical subject - the agent - is put in the instrumental case. He is grammatically transformed from the karmic responsibility of being an agent to the liberating condition of being an instrument.[15] One can certainly ponder whether the development of karmic ideology influenced the Sanskrit language towards its tendency to eliminate action - the verb as such.[16] However, the reader must not think that classical Sanskrit resembles some of the American Indian languages analyzed by Whorf (1976). The verb, as well as all its tenses, are highly developed in Sanskrit. What I am suggesting is that there was a tendency in discourse to choose some forms instead of others, linguistic forms that seem to reflect the cultural value of eliminating karma as such.

The renouncer as a cultural value offers some interesting points on the relationship between social structure and time. The renouncer is a man-outside-the-world. He is overtly released from the hierarchical relations of caste society. He is also released from the structure of time. The ideal renouncer is the symbol of complete transcendence, liberated from the chain of karma evolving from the past through the present into the future. The renouncer is a person who is believed to be *here and now* [17] outside the structural hierarchies of time and space.

The hierarchical structuring of space

The spatial dimension of the cosmos is also structured around the sacred. The sacred hierophani can best be described as the 'centre' (Eliade 1974:374). As an analogy to the sacred structuring of time, the centre of space may be conceived internally, as with the renouncers, or externally, as with ritualists or householders. I shall start the presentation with the renouncer and his 'mystical space'.

It is primarily within Tantric Yoga that the symbolic *interiorization of space* was fully developed. We can read about the sacred space of the renouncer:

> Here (within this body) is the Ganges and the Jumna... here are Prayaga and Benares - here the sun and the moon... I have not seen a place of pilgrimage and an abode of bliss like my body....Imagine the central part (or spinal column) of the body to be Mont Meru,...
> (Tantric texts quoted from Eliade 1969:227, 235)

The sacred geography of the Hindus is symbolically conceived as the *centres* of the body. Mount Meru, the holy mountain of Hinduism, represents the spinal column - the *Sushumna*. The Sushumna is perceived as an *axis mundi* and 'the Great Way' (*Mahapatha*), the passage between 'earth' and 'heaven'. At the base of the spinal column is the *Muladhara chakra* (lit. the centre being the root of the stream), symbolized by the element of earth, the downward sign of the *yoni* (female genital organ) and the *linga* (the male genital organ). Coiled eight times around the linga and blocking its mouth is the *Kundalini* - the serpent or sexual power. Through various forms of disciplines, like *Hatha Yoga* (body yoga), breathing exercises etc., the adept aspires to purify the Sushumna in order that the Kundalini may rise to reach the bodily 'heaven', the *chakra* (centre) called *Brahmarandhra* at the top of the head. It is here that the final union is reached. In theistic terms, this is the union between *Shiva* (the male principle) and *Shakti* (the female principle) - the union between the God and the Goddess. The union between Shiva and Shakti is a 'spatial' analogy to the union between Brahman and Atman of the Upanishads.

'To hasten the ascent of the Kundalini, some Tantric schools combined corporal positions with sexual practices. The underlying idea was the necessity of achieving simultaneous 'immobility' of breath, thought and semen.' (Eliade 1969:248). The renouncers, whether they belong to the Tantric or Upanishadic schools, seek to reach karma annihilation - 'immobility' - by stopping the karma of mind, breath and the sexual act (no discharge). In this light, the sexual rituals of the left hand Tantrics (whose main aim was to prolong and finally stop the emission of the semen altogether) may have a cultural rationale. If the semen is emitted, the renouncer falls under the law of time and death, like any common libertine (Op.cit.: 268). In that case, the renouncer should retrieve the semen discharged (Briggs 1938:298).

The men-inside-the-world - the ritualists and the householders - have an *external* conception of sacred space. We have already seen one example of this external conception of sacred space in the case of the Vedic horse sacrifice. Newly conquered territory was consecrated by erecting the Vedic altar with its sacrificial post as the sign of victory. The locus of the ritual was consecrated to be the centre of the newly conquered land. Similar construction rites can be observed when temples and houses are erected, as they are also perceived to be 'centres of the world' for the people concerned. Stevenson in her book *The rites of the twice born*, reports that before a single stone is laid, whether house or temple, the astrologer points to that spot in the foundation which is exactly above the head of the snake that supports the world (Stevenson 1920:354, quoted from Eliade 1971:19). Before constructing a temple, a diagram (*vastumandala*) of the cosmic man Purusha should be drawn on the ground. The temple is erected according to this diagram to ensure that the various parts of the temple correspond to the various parts of the cosmic man (Harashananda 1979:13). Accordingly, the temple has a hierarchical structuring which symbolizes the four varnas: One first enters the least sacred part of the temple where one can buy articles of worship. Then the devotee proceeds to the next part, a narrow passage which sacralizes the devotee for the entrance into a big hall used for congregational religious acts like singing, dancing, recitation of mythological texts, religious discourses and so on. The most sacred part of the temple is the *garbhagriha*. The garbhagriha is the *sanctum sanctorum* containing the images of the temple deities. The whole temple is usually surrounded by a high wall which completely marks off the sacred cosmos from the profane and impure world outside. The 'fifth varna' - the untouchables, who are perceived to be born *'outside* of the cosmic man' are, according to Brahmanic Hinduism, not allowed to enter a Sanskritic temple. The untouchables are regarded as so impure by orthodox Hinduism that the 'field of purity' which a temple represented is believed to be defiled by their presence or touch.

In a similar manner, when a Brahmin builds a new house, he will always construct it from the sacred wooden post (*vastupurusha*) (Harper 1964:179) which will make up one of the right corners in the kitchen. As Srinivas reports from the Coorgs, the purest and most sacred part of the house is the kitchen. This is, of course, where the food is prepared. It is also the room that contains the household fire. Also, the kitchen may be an ancestral shrine (Srinivas 1965:76-77). When the women of the house are in their periods or when child birth occurs, they should not enter the purer parts of the house (Harper 1964:158). A few decades ago, in most areas of South India, rules dictated which part of a high caste man's house people could enter (Srinivas 1980:11, cf. Mayer 1966:56).

Hinduism perceives the temple, the house and the human body as a micro-cosmos organized around a consecrated centre of the world. The ritualist is established in the temple. He is the priest functioning as the mediator between lay Hindus and the Gods. The householder is established in the house. He is the producer of the necessities of life. He is dependent upon the ritualist in connection with life cycle rituals and for approaching the Gods of Brahmanic Hinduism. The ritualist and the householder who are 'external to the sacred' should perform pilgrimage (*yatra* - lit. march, advancing) to sacred places (*tirthas* - lit. passage, way). The law teacher Gautama (200 B.C.) declares all mountains, rivers, holy lakes, abodes of seers etc. as *sin destroying localities* (Bharati 1963:137). Most Indian scriptures make ample mention of pilgrimage. As always when the injunction for an observance is given, the account of the merit which accrues from them is extensively elaborated. In particular, the accounts of the merit producing and health bringing qualities of pilgrimage centres seem to be interesting examples of traditional forms of marketing (Bharati 1963:145). Most Hindus accept seven primary centres of pilgrimage in India (Kashi, Prayag, Mathura, Hardwar, Ayodhya, Dvaraka and Kanchipuram, op.cit.:160). Even the Southerners regard northern India to be the most auspicious part of the country. The most prestigious of the seven centres is Kashi, the canonical name for Banaras.[18] Banaras is the eternal city which is believed to survive even the universal dissolution (Eck 1983). To die in Banaras is believed to secure the best rebirth possibilities and to secure straight passage into heaven. In India, important centres of pilgrimage are believed to be connected with other centres of pilgrimage elsewhere. The Ekambareshvara temple at Conjeevaram, Madras, has a little low corridor closed by a small gate said to be the subterranean connection to Kashi (Banaras), 1500 miles away (Bharati 1963:165). In this manner the culture area of Brahmanic Hinduism is integrated through its great centres of religion.

The renouncer, on the other hand, has no need for making any spatial advance towards a sacred place: 'Here (within this body) is the Ganges and the Jumna... here are Prayaga and Banaras...' (loc.cit.) The renouncer as a value has, in principle, *interiorized* the spatio-temporal world. The breath is his internal time (Panikkar 1976:71). The spinal column is his axis mundi. And he has reposited the three sacred fires in himself (Manu 6.25). This means that the ideal renouncer is believed to be *his own 'centre'*. He does not need to move in order to approach it. It further means that he needs no form of mediums for reaching final liberation. The renouncer's modus in time is the *kshana* - the moment. Analogous hereto: his modus in space is the 'centre'. The Manu states:

> Let him always wander alone...He shall neither possess a fire nor a dwelling, he may go to a village for his food, (he shall be) indifferent to everything, firm of purpose, meditating and concentrating on Brahman. (Manu 6.42-43)

The ideal renouncer, as can expected, should not have connections with any specific territory. He is, in principle, above the compartmentalization of space since he is overtly outside the hierarchical relations of caste society.

The directions in space

The distinction between right and left is used for classifying castes and sects in India. It is also employed for classifying the body for the purpose of ritual. For instance, there are clearly formulated rules on the proper use of the right and the left hand. The direction of movement in these rituals is also clearly specified. Veena Das has analyzed the *Grihya Sutra* texts and provides us with various examples on the symbolic value of the right/left opposition (1977:91-113).

When the twice born hangs his sacred thread from left to right, he is performing rites to the Gods. In the rites performed for ancestors and for protection from serpents, the performer has to wear his sacrificial cord suspended from the right shoulder towards the left side of the abdomen. The direction of these rituals is also from right to left. When demons are ritually driven away, the performer proceeds by throwing holy grass towards the left using the left hand for the purpose.

The *right* seems to be associated with propitiation of divine beings who are friendly and benevolent. The *left* is identified with the unfriendly and frightening supernatural beings who are believed to inspire terror and cause harm if they are not regularly propitiated (Op.cit.:99). Veena Das further states that the opposition left/right and ancestors/Gods can be associated with pairs like odd/even, night/day, vegetables/meat and others.

In the study of Konku society, Beck (1972) has argued that the right/ left division is an important principle behind the organization of caste in South India. She finds that the deities of the left hand castes are usually female, associated with death, sorcery, serpents and darkness. Harper's analysis of the Havik Brahmins in the Malnad part of South India also attests to the importance attached to left and right in questions of purity/impurity: The lowest indigenous caste is sometimes referred to as 'left-handed untouchables' to distinguish it from the higher 'right-handed untouchable' caste (Harper 1964:179).

Right is associated with the auspicious cardinal points, north and east, while left is associated with south and west (Das 1977.:106). The north, as mentioned earlier, probably received its status from being the direction of the arctic home of the Aryans (Tilak). It became associated with the abode of the Gods. The east is the place of the rising sun. It is the point in space symbolizing re-creation and life. For example, the sacred fire is placed to the east of the house for the rituals of marriage, pregnancy, childhood and initiation. Persons undergoing such life cycle rituals must be seated on holy grass pointing northward. During the performance of these rituals, the movements have to be made from south to north. During the birth ritual, the mother passes the child to the father from south to north (Das 1977:105).

The south is the abode of *Yama*, the dwelling place of the ancestors. The west is also associated with ancestors, as can be observed during the ancestor festivals when the ancestors are believed to enter the world of the living from the west. Ordinary mortals are not allowed to use the same direction for entry. Hence the rule that a house should not have its main entrance facing the west. The south and west are the important directions in rituals concerned with ancestors as well as rituals concerned with prosperity and fertility (Eliade 1974:352). Ancestors symbolize the continuity of life. The shraddha festival which, as noted earlier, marked the entrance of the sun into the southern hemisphere, is also a harvest festival. In connection with the ritual of death (*antyesthi*), it is the south/ north direction which assumes importance. Following the *Garuda Purana*, the dead body should be taken to the cremation ground and placed with its feet facing the south, its head facing the north. During the course of the cremation, the skull of the dead should be split open to provide an opening for the soul in the direction of the abode of the Gods in the north (10.16,56). The contradiction between the belief in the south as the abode of ancestors and the head of the dead body facing the north, reflects the hope that the deceased has enough merit to travel by the path of the Gods (*Devayana*). Then we have the rituals symbolizing *social* death: When a caste member is excommunicated, his relatives perform certain rituals as if he were dead (Manu 11.183-188). The direction of the ritual is the south. When a person has decided to leave his routine life to become a renouncer, he performs a last sacrifice in which his sacrificial utensils are burnt (Lingat 1973:47). He is then treated as dead by his relatives. The direction of the ritual is the north.

In the lineage temple belonging to the Pramalai Kallar in Kokkulam, the vegetarian Gods are situated to the north and the meat eating Gods to the south. The vegetarian Gods belong to the Sanskritic pantheon; they are the pure ones. The meat eating Gods belong to the pantheon of the little tradition. They are impure. Hence, the temple needs two kitchens and two priests, a 'Great Traditional' priest and a 'little traditional' priest (Dumont 1959:82). This mode of structuring the divine needs to be considered in relation to the social order. *Diet* is symptomatic of the hierarchical structuring of castes. The two kinds of Gods in the temple - the vegetarians and the meat eaters - are each related to the superior and inferior castes respectively. The pure vegetarian Gods are located in the north of the temple. The impure meat eating Gods to the south. The temple thus reflects social hierarchy in a simplified form (Dumont 1959:83).

Hierarchy and territory

Most anthropologists agree that there is a spatial distribution of castes in the villages which to a large extent corresponds to their occupational specialization and mutual ritual rank (Gough 1971:18, Mayer 1960:56, Srinivas 1965:29, Srinivas 1976:186-187, Jaer 1995). The localized, territorial unit occupying a caste quarter of the village will most often be a sib or a clan constituted by a set of males and their families who believe themselves to be descended from a common male ancestor. Such for example is the *biraderi* in parts of Uttar Pradesh (Cohn 1968:24). These territorial units are exogamous and intermarry 'horizontally' (Srinivas 1965:215).

The question now is whether it is possible to recognize any of the aforementioned spatial categories at the level of the village organization. If we turn our attention to the untouchables we shall definitely find some correlation between spatial categories and residential patterns. Even today they will be situated in the harijan hamlets outside the village proper. The Laws of Manu states:

> But the dwellings of Kandalas and Svapakas (untouchables ØJ) shall be outside the village...Their dress shall be the garments of the dead (they shall eat) their food from broken dishes, black iron shall be their ornaments, and they must always wander from place to place. (Manu 10.51-52)

Following karmic ideology, the untouchables should live outside the village because they are not regarded as being created from the cosmic man Purusha (Manu 10.48). They are regarded as so impure that they would defile the village if they entered inside it. In relation to the untouchables, the village is a 'field of purity' which needs to be isolated from the danger of impurity.

Based on the deductions to be made from the ideal model, one could expect to find Brahmins to be settled in the northern part of the village and the Shudras in the southern part. And to complete the picture, the Kshatriyas could be expected to occupy the eastern part and the Vaishyas the western part of the villages. Lewis' ethnographic description from Rampur can give us an idea of the state of affairs in that area. The dominant caste of the Jats is clustered together in the centre of the village. Some Brahmins are living with the Jats, but there is also a group in the northern part of the village. The middle castes, Nais and Banias, are also in the centre of the village. The lower castes of Rampur are all situated at the outskirts of the village (Lewis 1958:19). In Kumbapettai, a Brahmin Tanjore village described by Gough, the picture seems to be organized more closely to the ideal model. The Pallan untouchable group serves as watchmen around the village. The Brahmins live in the northern part of the village not far from the other clean non-Brahmin castes. The more polluting castes are generally found farther to the south (Gough 1971:19). In Karchana village in Eastern Uttar Pradesh where I performed my fieldwork in 1985-86 (Jaer 1995), the Brahmins and Thakurs (Kshatriyas) occupy the area towards the north of the village. The Vaishya trading castes are settled around the bazaar area, southwest of the upper caste area. The majority of the Vaishya agriculturalists occupy the western part of the village. The Shudras live more or less in all directions around the main high caste area. The avarnas, like the large Chamar community, occupy several hamlets outside the main area of the village proper in the south-eastern direction.[19]

Interesting verses in the scriptures have relevance to village life and its relationship to the cardinal points:

Let him carry out a dead Sudra by the southern gate of the town but (the corpses of) twice born men.., by the western, northern, or eastern (gates). (Manu 5.97)

The righteous go into the city of the King of Justice (Dharma) by three gateways, but the sinful go into it only by the road of the southern gate. (Garuda Purana 4.3)

In Kumbapettai, for instance, the Brahmin cremation ground, is situated to the extreme north of the village. The cremation grounds for the lower castes are situated in the southerly direction. The same pattern can be observed in Banaras where the Manikarnika ghat is found in the northern part of the city. This is a famous burning *ghat* traditionally used for twice born castes. To the south, at the Harishandra ghat, we find the other cremation ground which has traditionally been restricted to the Shudras.

The examples above seem to indicate a significant correlation between the spatial distribution of the castes and the values put on the north and south. Material on the east and west indicates no such correlation. A proper study on the correlation between the ideal model based on the principles of ritual separateness and the values put on the directions, and the empirical picture of spatial distribution, would also have to take into account that an Indian village is not a static entity. Groups leave and others arrive. In practice, only a new village can embody the ideal model (cf. Srinivas 1976:187). Another variable which is of relevance and which runs counter to the implications to be deduced from the ideal model is the practical requirements of the jajmani system based on functional interdependence. Servicing and menial castes often have to live close to their masters. The problem of which jati belongs to which varna will also complicate the investigation.

Hierarchy and territory - the patterns of mobility

In a short article on caste and territory in Malabar, Miller found a territorial unit - the *nad* - comprising a number of villages. Miller stated that: 'For all lower castes the chiefdom (nad) was the limit of social relations within the caste, while their relations with other castes were largely confined to the village.' Only the superior castes had an internal organization which extended throughout the nad and beyond. 'Complete freedom of movement was denied to all but Nambudiri Brahmins, who helped to maintain a unified system of values throughout the Malabar coast.' (Miller 1954:416, 419). Miller further suggested that the territorial divisions which he found in Malabar were an essential concomitant of the traditional caste system (Loc.cit.). Miller's hypothesis seems to be strengthened by the process of Sanskritization. Ritualists and renouncers were the models and carriers of this process. At least from the beginning of the Christian era, these types of people must have spread from their prestigious homeland in the northern part of India (cf. Manu 2.18-24) to the other parts of the continent. Taking a village perspective, the relationship between the Great and the little traditions appears as a question of levels. In the pantheon, for instance, there will be supernatural beings with significance only for the household. These will be encompassed by the deities of the local sib. Then again we have the deities of the regional jati having intervillage significance. The regional jati will on account of its traditional occupation and rank, be defined within the Pan-Indian varna hierarchy and thereby adhere to its respective deities in the Sanskritic pantheon. In addition to this kind of *horizontal* enlargement of territorial significance illustrated by starting from household to sib, then to jati and finally to varna, there is also *vertical* enlargement of territorial significance. That is, many deities cannot be said to belong to any particular group or section of society. They are the Gods of the whole rather than any part. There will be deities stressing village solidarity, regional solidarity and Pan-Indian solidarity. Babb concludes his analysis of the pantheon in Chhattisgarh, Raipur, Madhya Pradesh as follows: 'Thus embedded within the temple organization of Chhattisgarh is a hierarchy of objects of worship associated with the social and territorial segmentation of Chhattisgarhi society...' (Babb 1975:187 - cf. Harper 1959, 1964).

In general, the village and the region will have temples and shrines representing the various levels and aspects of Hinduism. But the Sanskritic temples and deities will definitely be served by Brahmin ritualists, because their deities are those with greatest territorial and social spread. They are also regarded as the most pure and the most powerful deities. They are the superior deities having the highest rank in the divine hierarchy. Accordingly, they must be served by the purest and 'best' of men. The less pure and less powerful deities, with more restricted territorial and social significance, will be served by religious functionaries recruited from non-Brahmin castes. In Chhattisgarh, the Baiga is the priest of the less pure temples associated with the more 'pragmatic' (Mandelbaum 1966) village deities (Babb 1975:119).[20] Territorial spread increases the higher up in the hierarchy we focus our attention. Whether we are concerned with the human or the divine hierarchy, the purest are those closest to having an All-India relevance. The renouncer as a value has in principle transcended spatial divisions altogether.

THE KARMA LOGIC OF THE CONCRETE

The opposition between the pure and the impure is identified by Bougle and Dumont as the organizing principle of the caste system (Dumont 1970:43). I agree with Dumont in his emphasis on the importance of the purity/impurity idiom in the Hindu context. But I do not accept the structural status given to these notions by Dumont. I regard the pure and the impure as collective representations on the level of the lifeworld and not as categories with a structural status. A study of the pure and the impure tell us something fundamental about the way the Hindus *perceive* hierarchy and not how they explain it. Dumont confuses structuralism with phenomenology (see appendix).

The pure and the impure

There are three kinds of pollution: caste pollution, act pollution and relational pollution (Orenstein 1968:116, Das 1977:128). *Caste pollution* is, as the term indicates, a permanent state lasting from birth to death. It involves a degree of defilement which is 'inborn' to caste members. This degree is socially defined by the caste's relative position in the caste hierarchy. *Act pollution* is a temporary state of pollution (Harper 1964:152) incurred on the part of individuals by touching impure substances, by deviating from prescribed norms etc. In such cases, the person is in need of purification in order to regain his normal condition. On the other hand, individuals may have been put in a higher state of ritual purity by undergoing entry rites for the performance of religious activities. Individuals may also, on account of their prestige, their behaviour and religious learning, be regarded as more pure than the average member of their caste. Finally, *relational pollution* means the state of impurity which incurs on kin members on the occasion of birth and death. It is a temporal state of pollution related to the nature of life itself.

The impurity incurred at birth and death increases as we go down the varna hierarchy. The law books prescribe 30 days of impurity for Shudras or half that length for well behaved caste members. They prescribe 10 days for the Brahmins (Orenstein 1968:120). Yet, in the conduct of his daily affairs, such as eating, social interaction, morality and so forth, it is the Brahmin who is the most vulnerable. To give an example from the law books: If a low caste man is bitten by a dog, he merely needs to salute a number of Brahmins, who purify him by looking at him. If a 'superior Brahmin' is bitten, he must as penance and purification first wash and then recite the highly sacred *Gayatri mantra*. If one is bitten while engaged in a religious rite, one must fast three nights, take clarified butter and drink sanctified water (Orenstein 1968:121). The rationality here may be as follows: In the same way as weak people need more time to recover from sickness, the Shudra, who is conceived as impure by caste, needs a longer period to return to a normal state after the crisis of life. The Brahmin on the other hand, is so pure and 'strong' that the crises of life do not affect him to the same degree. The Brahmin is more vulnerable to the act pollution. He is purer than his surroundings. He may easily be defiled if he does not exert proper caution. He is expected to live more in accordance with the prescribed norms of Brahmanic Hinduism. Any deviation on his part is more 'costly' than that of the Shudras and other low castes. One can certainly ponder to what extent 'to be bitten by a dog' is a kind of *self-inflicted* act pollution. Whatever the case may be, events are not perceived to happen at random in the Hindu scheme of things. One is bitten by a dog because of previous karma. We can thus easily imagine that to be bitten by a dog, is a disgrace to a high ranking person - a disgrace which might even put his status in doubt.

The notions of purity and impurity are of special relevance to the Hindu jajmani system. As the term indicates, the jajmani system is modelled after the Vedic sacrificial organization whereby persons recruited from different jatis perform different functions (Mahapatra 1978). The main relationship is between the *jajman* (from *yajamana* = the person paying the cost of sacrifice - the patron) and his clients. The relationships are usually stable and inherited. The jajmani system binds together different castes living in a village or group of neighbouring villages. Marriott reports from Kishan Garhi that even a poor householder retains six or seven servants of different castes to serve him in ceremonial ways and thus demonstrates his own caste rank. Householders and their servants formally address each other with courtly titles. The Brahmin ritualist is called 'Great King' (*Maharaj*) or learned man (*Panditji*), the potter is called 'Ruler of the people' (*Prajapat*), the barber 'Lord Barber' (*Nau Thakur*), the carpenter 'Master Craftsman' (*Mistri*), the sweeper 'Headman' (*Mehtar*) or 'Sergeant' (*Jamadar*) etc. (Marriott 1955:190).

The jajmani system is not exactly coextensive with the caste system in general. The artisan and commercial castes do not seem to be integrated into the jajmani system to the same extent as other castes (Wiser 1936:143, Pocock 1962:87). The reason may be, as Pocock suggests, that the artisan and commercial castes do not take part in the ritual handling of purity and impurity. They provide material goods and not religious services (Pocock op.cit.). The essential aspect of the jajmani system is not economy (cf. Pocock 1962) but its *ritual organization*. The Brahmin ritualists, as hierophants and spiritual mediators, must be kept pure enough to transact with the Gods on behalf of the whole community. Hence they are in need of clients who can handle the impure tasks and substances of the life process.

The division of labour surrounding the holy Indian cow is an excellent illustration of the jajmani system: The Brahmin ritualists use the products of the cow, like coagulated or sour milk, butter and the liquid and solid excreta, in religious rituals. These substances are believed to have great purifying qualities. The Chamars, on the other hand, are the leather workers. Their duty is to fetch dead cattle (Cohn 1955:64) and carve the skin. The Brahmin ritualists have the highest rank in Hindu caste society while the Chamars are generally described as untouchables (op.cit.:60). Why is this so? The white cow was the means of production of the once pastoral nomadic Aryans. In the Vedic period, the white cow, and the horse were main symbols of domination. As the caste society developed, the horse lost its significance and the white cow became the *symbol* of a hierarchically integrated society.[21] I believe the white cow has the same symbolic function for the jajmani system as the primeval giant Purusha has for the varna system. The Chamars make up an untouchable caste because they handle the extremely impure dead cow. The Brahmin ritualist is at the other extreme of the hierarchy because his occupational function involves the handling of the pure products of the white cow. Together the Chamar householder and the Brahmin ritualist make up the living extremes of the social hierarchy. In between those extremes is, as I shall argue below, no exact agreement on relative rank.

On the relationship between karma and the purity/impurity complex

Dumont and others have argued that the '...elementary and universal foundation of impurity is in the *organic* aspects of human life and from this the impurity of certain specialists is directly derived; in the veneration of the cow we have already encountered one criterion, which is evidently bound up with the distinction between pure and impure,...' (Dumont 1970:55). I cannot accept Dumont's *reductionism*. Anthropological research tells us that it is impossible to find a universally valid list of substances which are pure and impure. If biology could explain the logic of the pure and the impure, then such a universal list should be possible to find. I do not believe we shall be able to grasp the rationality behind the pure and the impure by relying on organic factors alone. Marriott reports that flour ground by a woman leather worker in her own house and sold or given away by her cannot be eaten by Brahmins. But flour ground by her when she is working as an employee in a Brahmin's house is quite acceptable to the same consumers. 'There does not appear to be any *physical* principle that determines which substances hold impurity and which merely transmit them.' (Harper 1964:173, my italics). My understanding of caste pollution and act pollution does not totally reject organic factors, but rather it takes its point of departure from karmic ideology, morality etc.[22] As Gough has observed from Kumbapettai in the Tanjore district, high ranking castes are often called 'good' while low ranking castes are called 'bad' (Gough 1971:51).

The Gita provides us with the key native terms to understand the relationship between karma and purity/impurity:

The fourfold caste was created by Me, by the differentiation of Guna and Karma...' (Gita 4.13) The essential terms in this verse are *guna* and *karma*. The meaning of the term guna is ambiguous. In the context of the Gita it can be understood to mean quality and substance. There are three gunas: *sattva, rajas,* and *tamas.* They are the constituents of *prakrti,* a term we earlier translated as 'matter' or 'nature'.

> Sattva, Rajas and Tamas - ... born of Prakrti, bind fast in the body the indestructible embodied one (Soul)....Of these Sattva... binds by attachment to happiness and ... knowledge....Know Rajas to be of the nature of passion ... it binds ... the embodied one (soul), by attachment to action....And know Tamas to be born of ignorance ... it binds fast ... by miscomprehension, indolence and sleep. (Gita 14.5-8)

The defining criteria of *sattva* are purity, subtleness, goodness, wisdom and harmony. Of *rajas* they are greed, unrest, desire (Gita 4.12). Regarding purity/impurity, the *rajasika* is believed to be in the middle of the scale. *Tamas* denotes impurity, grossness, heaviness, inertia, dullness etc. Sattva is believed to be white in colour, rajas red and tamas black (Davis 1976:9). All kinds of beings, from plants to Gods, consist of a certain mixture of the three gunas. One can speak of sattvik, rajasik or tamasik persons, intellects, modes of thinking (Gita 18.29), actions and actors (Gita 18.19) foodstuffs and diets (Gita 178-10).

Davis, in his article: 'A Philosophy of Hindu Rank from Rural West Bengal' (1976), has ethnographic material which supports the thesis on the relationship between guna and the purity/impurity complex in Hindu indigenous thinking: '... the philosophy of Hindu rank presented here is neither esoteric doctrine nor sterile logic but ... a shared construction of reality that is considered authoritative...In brief, the entire Bengali cosmos is ordered by a premise of ranked inequalities; all life forms within the cosmos are defined by the same radical material substance (gunas) and the behavioral code or *Dharma* appropriate to those *gun*(as). The same is also true, significantly, of Bengali perceptions of human society. All persons are viewed as belonging to a number of birth-groups (*jati*) arranged in a series of ordered ranks. And these birth-groups are defined according to that nature, which are viewed as a duplex criterion of rank....Davis concludes that the pure and the impure refer to a summary evaluation and statement of the *gunas* and *Dharmas* that characterize an activity or substance or birth-group as a whole (Davis 1976:7, 11, 16).[23]

The concept of the *substance-code* used by Davis is, in the terminology followed in this book, equivalent to the following: 'substance' = *svabhava* = *gunas* = karmic ballast. 'Code'= *svadharma* = *Dharma*. Let us have a closer look at the chain of meaning connections involved here. A person is believed to consist of a certain mixture of the three gunas. This mixture is seen to constitute a person's nature - his *svabhava*.[24] This is a term I earlier identified with a person's karmic ballast. Thus, a person's karmic ballast - his svabhava - created through earlier karmas is, in the idiom of the gunas, the person's guna mixture. A person's guna mixture - his svabhava - provides him with certain *dispositions* for action types in his present life. These dispositions are defined by the person's *svadharma* - the duties which are appropriate to him. The more perfect his realization of his svabhava by living according to the duties defined by his svadharma, the better will be his rebirth chances. If the person is sattvik, that is, if sattva is in preponderance in his nature, he ought to devote much of his time to meditation, contemplation, priestly functions and teaching. If he is rajasik, he ought to be a man of action who protects the Dharma. And if he is tamasik, he ought to perform tamasik occupations and handle tamasik substances. If the person chooses to *realize* his destiny to the full, he will reap what he has sown in earlier incarnations. And through experience he is cleansed. That is a paradigm in Hinduism.

An illustration: The Brahmin ritualist and the leather worker are the human extremes of the pure/impure hierarchy. The holy cow is a symbol of hierarchical integration: The Brahmin ritualist is connected with the five products of the cow in his priestly functions and the leather worker is connected with the dead cow. The leather worker is impure, as the believers perceive it, because he has a tamasik karmic ballast which *deserves and requires* an impure occupation bringing him in touch with impure substances. The Brahmin ritualist, on the other hand, is believed to have a sattvik nature. He needs and deserves a pure occupation which involves only the handling of clean substances.

> The duties of the Brahmins, Kshatriyas and the Vaishyas, as well as the Shudras, have been divided according to their inborn qualities, Arjuna' (Gita 18.41).

The individual should perform his caste duty, his svadharma (Gita 3.35), because this is believed to be that type of action which *corresponds* to his karmic ballast (svabhava) - the persons specific guna mixture. By performing one's duty, karmic ideology promises religious liberation or at least rebirth in a better caste.

Sanskritization and caste climbing

In the following account, my focus will be on the *cultural forms*, the '*dress*' which any claim to higher rank must assume in order to be acceptable and understandable to society.

Srinivas has defined Sanskritization as follows:

> A low caste was able in a generation or two to rise to a higher position in the hierarchy... by Sanskritizing its ritual and pantheon. In short it took over, as far as possible, the customs, rites and beliefs of the Brahmins. (Srinivas 1965:39).

It seems obvious that the caste groups who attempt to sanskritize themselves contribute to the *maintenance* of *Dharmashastran* values and karmic ideology (cf. Barber 1968:33).

Some ethnographic accounts of processes of Sanskritization will be of value here:[25] Cohn reports from Madhopur in Uttar Pradesh how the *Jaisvara Chamars* (leather workers) began to outlaw the eating of beef and the carting of manure in order to try to raise their social status. In the first instance, they were compelled by the dominant caste (the Thakurs) to leave the village, but later they were permitted to return and were excused from the manure work which they had perceived as degrading. The outcome of the process was at least a passive recognition of the Chamars' claim to higher status and in addition, Cohn adds, a gain in their vital dimension of self respect (Cohn 1955:72-73).

Another partly successful movement was undertaken by the *Noniyas*, a Shudra caste found in Madhya Pradesh, Uttar Pradesh and Bihar (cf. Rowe 1968). Traditionally, the Noniyas were salt producers and 'earth diggers'. On account of the new opportunities provided by the colonial administration in building government roads, bridges etc., an increasing number of Noniyas acquired considerable wealth during the last half of the nineteenth century (Rowe 1968:70). Dissatisfaction with the noticeable discrepancy between their low ritual rank and their newly acquired economic wealth led to a self-conscious caste mobility organization - the *Chauhan* movement. The Chauhan movement involved initiation with the sacred thread and the writing of a body of literature providing mythological legitimation of their claims to twice born status. They claimed Rajput status through the last Hindu King of Delhi, Prithiviraj Chauhan, who, in the twelfth century, was defeated by the invading Muslims. This movement spread quickly especially after World War I. As early as 1924, the local leaders of a Noniya community in Sanghaipur, Jaunpur district, donned the sacred thread - the symbol of twice born status and, accordingly, the 'symbolic justification' par excellence in caste mobility movements (Rowe op.cit.:71).

Cohn reports from Madhopur how the local Noniya communities there also donned the sacred thread and called themselves by their long claimed title of Chauhan Rajputs. Their action was met with violence by the lords of the village, who beat the Noniyas, broke their threads and threatened further violence if the act was repeated. Ten years after this first unsuccessful claim to higher status (1947) the Noniyas again put on the sacred threads, this time without overt reaction from the lords of the village (Cohn 1955:73). By the mid 1950s the 'new' Noniyas were being served by Brahmin priests. Their Goddess was now vegetarian, no longer demanding blood sacrifices. They kept their brides in *parda* (seclusion). These changes were indeed signs of having undergone a process of Sanskritization. From holding a rank bordering on the untouchable category, the Noniyas had risen in the village caste hierarchy to a rank of tenth or eleventh (Rowe 1968:68).

The *claim* to higher social prestige usually provides the caste group with an awakened consciousness and higher sense of group solidarity. But social mobility movements are not of much value if the claims are not at least partly accepted by the other castes. Srinivas presents us with an interesting example: 'The Smiths of South India ... call themselves Vishvakarma Brahmins, wear the sacred thread and have sanskritized their ritual ... This does not,..., explain why they are considered to belong to the Left-hand division of the castes, and no castes belonging to the Right-hand division, ..., will eat food or drink water touched by them... Normally Sanskritization enables a caste to obtain a higher position in the hierarchy. But in the case of the Smiths it seems to have resulted only in their drawing upon themselves the wrath of all the other castes.' (1970:43) 'An attempt by the Smiths to assert their equality with the others usually led to a fight between them and the others. Fifty years ago, the Cheluvadi (Untouchable) of Kere beat a wealthy Smith from Mysore who walked into the village wearing red slippers. The Smith was rich and had lent money to the extent of Rs. 50.000 to the villagers.' (Srinivas 1960:31) This example calls to mind the inherent conflict between status and power in the Hindu context.

Transactions and karmic transfer

The claim to higher social recognition takes place in the form of ritual transactions focusing on food and services (Marriott 1968). Such ritual transaction seems to be based on the assumptions that a) food and services are believed to transfer the karmic quality of actors, and b) that different kinds of food and services have unequal quality with respect to their capacity as mediums of karmic transfer.

We have earlier encountered the belief in karmic transfer in connection with the ancestor rituals. The doctrine of karmic transfer is significant also between the living members of caste society:

...one eats the faults of one's host. (Quoted from Mauss 1974:125)

Marcel Mauss notes that: '...in this system of ideas one gives away what is in reality a part of one's own nature and substance, while to receive something is to receive a part of someone's spiritual essence.' (op.cit.:10) Food and services are seen as the *vehicles of the spiritual and moral quality* of actors.[26] Regarding the unequal quality of the mediums of karmic transfer, Beteille notes how silver is considered to be, relatively speaking, 'pollution proof'. Orthodox Shri Vaishnavs, he states, offer water to their Smarta guests in silver tumblers and food on silver plates (Beteille 1978:285). Harper, observing the Havik Brahmins in Malnad, Mysore, notes how silk is regarded as superior to cotton as a ritual isolator from impurity. He also notes how modern shirts in themselves are regarded as impure (Harper 1964:154-155).

The Hindus have an extensive classification of food. Raw food is best in relation to the purity/impurity idiom. Raw flour, sugar, clarified butter or whole fruit forming the materials for a complete meal may be sent as a gift to Brahmins or other high caste patrons for preparation in their own houses. Such gifts earn the donor spiritual merit (Marriott 1968:143). Less honorific is *pakka* food, which is cooked in clarified butter. This is the superior category of cooked food which can be offered in feasts to Gods and to guests of high status. Third comes inferior cooked food (*kachcha*). The dry-baked cakes of barley are typical examples. They are used as ordinary family fare or as daily payment to artisans and servants (op.cit.:114). To accept this kind of inferior food as a gift is to *accept* one's inferiority.[27]

Marriott notes that it is difficult to focus on services as a transactional idiom indicative of caste rank (op. cit.:147). One reason, he states, is simply the complexity of services which makes analysis difficult. A barber does not merely shave and cut hair. For some he offers manicure, pedicure, massage, surgery, messenger service, cooking, dish washing and various other kinds of ritual assistance at ceremonies of the life cycle (op.cit.:147). Marriott also poses the question whether a kingly caste which commands many services must be regarded as having higher rank than a Brahmin caste which commands fewer. The artisan and commercial castes, furthermore, are not fully integrated into the jajmani system. Their occupations seem to have a more neutral status in relation to the purity/ impurity idiom. The Vaishya does not limit his profit by refusing to deal with certain castes, nor does he lower the price of his product when dealing with a Brahmin. Nor will the artisan refuse to supply anyone who can pay him (Pocock 1962:87). Still they take part in the caste ranking game by communicating their subjective meaning on rank through the transactional idiom of food.[28]

Now, following the assumption that ritual transactions in food are indicative of caste rank and that caste rank betokens the social definition of the karmic ballast of persons and groups, we should expect that high ranking castes would not accept gifts of food from lower ranking castes. To accept a gift, in this line of reasoning, would signify that one is prepared to 'eat the faults of one's host'. That would be an irrational mode of behaviour if the ritual distance between the parties involved is too great. To stress the problem, we could say that everybody wants to *receive good karma and avoid bad karma.* Mauss is to the point when he states as follows regarding the Brahmins: 'A whole caste which lives by gifts pretends to refuse them, then compromises and accept only those which are offered spontaneously. Then it draws up a long list of persons from whom, and circumstances in which, one may accept gifts, and of the things which one may accept; and finally admits everything in the case of a famine - on condition, to be sure, of some slight purification. The bond that the gift creates between the donor and the recipient is too strong for them.' (Mauss 1974:58) The high ranking Brahmin should be careful even to receive gifts offered by kings (Manu 4.218). 'O king, to receive from kings is honey at first but ends in poison.' (Quoted from Mauss (op.cit) Indeed, the highest ranking Brahmin is the *shrotriya* who should *not* accept gifts. This is ideal picture seems to support the following hypothesis: The high ranking Brahmin wishes to withdraw from reciprocal exchange praxis because he is at the zenith of the hierarchy. He does not want the burden of an inferior karma intruding into his soul to degrade his spiritual level and social prestige.

The strategy of interaction

But being a man-inside-the-world, the Brahmin, as all other members of caste society, must organize his life according to the rules of separation and interdependence regulating intercaste behaviour. So it is a practical as well as ritual necessity for the Brahmin ritualist to interact with his jajmani masters and servants. Following the values and ideas of karmic transfer, the ideal Brahmin ritualist strategy is to *minimize* transactions and only accept substances of perfect form, such as gifts of land, money, and whole grain.[29] Marriott is quite correct in classifying the transactional strategy of the Kshatriyas as *maximal* (Marriott 1976:26).[30] As a social category referring to the dominant castes,[31] the Kshatriyas are, as Marriott observes, Hindu groups who enjoy '*hot*' diets and temperaments (ibid). They are usually meat eaters, have a 'hot' pantheon etc.[32] This overt picture of the Kshatriyas fits well with conceptions of karmic ideology. The karmic nature of the Kshatriya varna is believed to have a preponderance of rajas (Davis 1976:12).[33] A rajasik nature is hot, extrovert, active and highly transactional. According to the Laws of Manu, it is an important duty of a Kshatriya to give, while for the Brahmin it is the duty to receive gifts (Manu 1.89, 10.77-78). Furthermore, a rajasik nature needs rajasik food to stimulate those dispositions which are necessary for the fulfilment of one's rajasik duties like governing, protection of the people and warfare.

> Prowess, boldness, fortitude, dexterity, and also not flying from battle,
> generosity (*danam*) and sovereignty are the duties of the Kshatriyas
> born of (their own) nature. (Gita 18.43)

The duty to give is a necessity on the part of the dominant caste. Its members are invested with sovereign right over the land and they must redistribute food in return for services. The more they give, the more they manifest their caste attributes. And the more the servant castes give of services in return for gifts and food, the more they manifest their dependence and their inferior caste attributes. From the perspective of the maximal strategy of the Kshatriyas, food givers are indicative of superior rank while service givers are indicative of inferior rank (Marriott 1968:170).

The *life-style* of the Kshatriya is apparently quite impure. Kshatriyas usually eat meat, drink liquor, and, as warriors indulge in violence (cf. Kolenda 1978:80). They may be seen as considerably less pure than many castes ranked below them. To solve this inconsistency, Dumont, who identified the purity/impurity dichotomy as a basic structural principle, turned to another dichotomy, that between status and power. The Kshatriya received his second rank in the hierarchy because of his secular power.[34] But 'secular' power also requires a cultural 'dress' - a karmic rationalization to turn power into legitimate authority. This cultural dress is related to the fact that the pure/impure are highly *relational* notions. What is impure for one caste might not be considered impure for another. Meat, for example, is not impure in itself. It is impure for the Brahmins, but neutral or even necessary for the Kshatriyas.

If we change our perspective from the collective to the individual, we shall also learn that purity/impurity are highly relative notions:

> Better is one's own Dharma, (though) imperfect, than the Dharma of
> another well performed. Better is death in one's own Dharma: the
> Dharma of another is fraught with fear.' (Gita 3.35, Manu 10.97)
> Devoted each to his own duty, man attains the highest perfection.
> (Gita 18.45)

What is considered pure/impure must be seen in relationship to the individual's Dharma. The Gita is clear in its classification of actions and agents with respect to the purity/impurity idiom. The Gita calls those actions sattvik i.e. pure, where the agent is freed from egoistic inclinations (18.26). Actions performed with egoistic motives, greed, passion - pursuing the fruits of actions instead of simply performing one's duty - are called rajasik (Gita 18.27). And the tamasik action is impure because the agent is deluded, proud and vulgar, a cheat who procrastinates (*dirgha-sutri*) to use the adjectives offered by the Gita (18.28).

The Sattva-abiding go upwards, the Rajasika dwell in the middle, and the Tamasika, abiding in the function of the lowest *Guna*, go downwards.' (Gita 14.18)

We are reminded once again that organic explanations of purity/impurity are not healthy. Substances are not pure/impure in themselves. They are pure/impure as symbols of the moral quality of actors. Thus, it is a mistake caused by the organic perspective to label the Kshatriya as impure. It is his Dharma to kill and eat meat.

The logic of caste ranking

Regarding the logic of caste ranking, Marriott states that '...high rank always deriving from the giving, low rank from the receiving of foods. Serving relationships, ..., appear to create rank by a complementary logic: givers of services are lower than receivers, ...' (Marriott 1968:170 also 142, 146, 147) To what extent are the propositions of Marriott's interactional theory of caste ranking correct?

Let us return to the earlier noted ambivalence of the Brahmins. Beteille, for example, reports from Sripuram, Tanjore district how Smartas and Sri Vaishnavs reduce their transactions with non-Brahmins to a minimum. Rather, their life-style revolves around the cultivation of scriptural knowledge and the performance of individual and family rites, both of which are associated with high social esteem (Beteille 1978:292). But if the Brahmin completely withdraws from exchange relations, he would not be able to perform his social duties. Indeed he would be defined in the category of renouncers who are relieved from the duties of caste society. According to the Laws of Manu, it is the *duty* of a Brahmin ritualist to sacrifice for others and to teach the sacred knowledge. In return, he receives his sacrificial fee and gifts from pure men (Manu 10.76). The Brahmin, the apex of the hierarchy, is thus supposed to give services and to receive gifts - acts which, following Marriott, should put him in an inferior position.

The Sanskrit term *dakshina* (sacrificial fee to a Brahmin) has an interesting etymology. It is derived from *daksha*, which means 'dwelling in the south', and it is also related to the term *dakshinayana* (the southern passage of the sun), which I dealt with in the previous section. The term *dakshina*, indeed, signifies ambivalence: During the ritual, the Brahmin priest places himself to the south, that is, he accepts a symbolic and temporal inferiority to the patron of the ritual.[35] On the other hand, the Brahmin ritualists are givers of the greatest of all gifts, the sacred knowledge of the Vedas. It is through his priestly services that the Brahmin restores his ritual supremacy as the living 'vehicle' of the sacred knowledge. As receiver of gifts, the Brahmin ritualist is put in a vulnerable context in which he also accepts his situational inferiority to the givers. As a giver of services, he manifests his superiority. But the Brahmin ritualist should not be prepared to enter into transactions with castes below the twice born level:

> For he who explains the sacred law (to a Shudra) or dictates to him a penance, will sink together with that (man) into the hell (called) Asamvrita. (Manu 4.81)

The bond that the ritualist would have created between himself and the lower castes is too *vulnerable* for him.

The gift of a maiden is regarded as the greatest of all gifts by the Hindus. Thus the widespread practices of *anuloma* (lit. 'following the hair') marriages, in which the wife givers are inferior in status to the wife receivers. This phenomenon also needs to be tested against Marriott's proposition. High caste men marry women of inferior status. As stated in the Manu, a Brahmin may marry four wives, one from each varna, the Kshatriya may marry three, the Vaishya two and the Shudra only his equal (Manu 9.149, 157). Great merit is believed to come to the woman and her kin when she is given to superior castes. This certainly does not make the wife givers superior to the wife receivers, although the latter will communicate his ambivalence towards the transaction. If the transaction is reversed to *pratiloma* (lit. 'against the hair') marriage, that is, if a woman is married below her status, great demerit is believed to accrue on the wife givers and the offspring of the relationship.[36] The rules of Hindu marriage, according to which wife givers are considered inferior reflect the doctrine of karmic transfer. No 'substance' is seen to be more vulnerable to karmic transfer in Hinduism than women. Through their women, the exogamous group may be defiled and 'destroyed' (Gita 1.41-42).

We have seen that the logic underlying intercaste transactions and caste rank is more complicated than McKim Marriott's propositions above. The Brahmin stands supreme in spite of being a receiver of gifts and a giver of services.[37] He is greater than the Kshatriya who is the giver of gifts and a the receiver of services. The interactional theory of caste ranking, as Marriott is well aware of, is not sufficient to explain the empirical picture. There is a need for an attributional theory derived from the ritual status index of the Great Tradition.

The objective meaning framework

This attributional theory was proposed by Marriott in addition to the interactional model presented above (Marriott 1976:114). But Marriott conceives the relationship between the interactional and the attributional model differently from me. For Marriott, the two models seem to represent alternative approaches. The former, following Marriott, seems more fertile when analyzing rural systems of stratification. The latter seems more appropriate when analyzing urban systems (Marriott 1968: b:114). Marriott also adds that the interactional ranking might be expected to give way to an actual spread of attributional ranking through the process of Sanskritization (ibid). As I see it, the two models presuppose each other. The attributional theory reflects the context of objective meaning of caste climbing while the interactional theory provides the patterns of the various subjective meanings of rank.

The attributional theory of rank is based on the varnashramadharma scheme of the Great Tradition. Most anthropologists believe that this Pan-Indian structure provides the common idiom of hierarchy and its various attributes (Kolenda 1978:95, Srinivas 1962:7, 63, 1976:169, Dumont 1970:73). The varna scheme constitutes a 'lingua franca' by means of which all Hindus can communicate about social structure.[38] Furthermore, the varna scheme establishes a matrix of diacritical attributes which facilitates the social definition of people. Individuals also establish their self-understanding within this context as the varnas index a person's stage of religious realization (Srinivas 1962:151). Knowledge of the attributional theory of the Great Tradition is a necessary mental outfit for all Hindus, whether urban or rural, high caste or low caste, man or woman, in order to be able to operate as a competent Hindu.

Life style models as channels of communication

How is the varnashramadharma scheme of the Great Tradition communicated to the lay Hindus? It is communicated through the life-style models which the ideal ritualists, renouncers and householders represent.[39] The ritualists represent the life-style model of Dharma, the renouncers the life-style model of Moksha and the householders represent the Moksha/Dharma model. The concept of the life-style model is not foreign to the Laws of Manu and the Gita:

> From a Brahmana, born in that country, let all men on earth learn their several usages. (Manu 2.20)

The Laws of Manu upholds the Brahmin ritualist as the main life-style model. The Gita, on the other hand, does not seem to emphasize any peculiar type: 'Whatsoever the superior person does, that is followed by others. What he demonstrates by action, that people follow.' (Gita 3.21) In short, we can say that a caste raises in the social hierarchy only when it copies the usages practised by those who most respect the traditions set out in the holy scriptures (Lingat 1973:203).

The highest ranking among the Brahmin ritualists are those who have traditional education in Sanskrit scholarship (Beteille 1978:280). They are believed to be the most erudite in matters of sacred knowledge. Their traditional occupational functions are in the areas of instruction, teaching, ritual services and legislation.[40] As 'orthopraxis' (Harper 1964) Brahmins, the purity/impurity complex is naturally very important to the ritualists. The Brahmin ritualists inform the lay Hindus about purity/impurity and the ideology of hierarchy. Their stress on vegetarianism, teetotalism, the performance of Sanskritic life cycle rites and religious piety in general have become an important standard for correct 'dharmic' behaviour. As astrologers, the Brahmin ritualists make the lay Hindus aware of their own karmic history (Berreman 1963:222). Being the life-style models of Dharma, the ritualists inform about the spiritual value of performing one's ascribed duties.

Then we have the renouncer:

> The *sannyasi*, the man who has renounced the world to pursue a life of prayer and contemplation, commands very great respect among Coorgs. He leads a celibate life, and in his case bachelordom does not constitute a drawback. The rules which apply to ordinary men do not apply to him. Preference for the *sannyasi* is found everywhere in India among the Hindus. (Srinivas 1965:241)

The highest ranking among the renouncers are the *siddhas* and the *jivanmukthas* - those who are liberated while alive. They teach the lay Hindus the value of sexual abstention, the suppression of bodily appetites, the value of fast, prayer and meditation (see Srinivas 1976:303). They also modify the information the lay Hindus have received from the Brahmin ritualists regarding hierarchy. Through the sect, the renouncers propagate spiritual equality. The caste system belongs to the world of *maya*. In reality, from the perspective of *Atman/Brahman*, equality, unity and non-differentiation are the fundamental facts. But the renouncers have also taught the lay Hindus the reasons for inequality. They have informed the lay Hindus about the workings of the law of karma and the various ways to solve the karmic problem. The renouncers have also taught the lay Hindus about the eternity of the soul. Some of them live on the cremation grounds where they meditate on death and the transitoriness of the body. Through this form of meditation, it is believed that they 'see' the eternal, undying principle in man - the soul.

The great places of pilgrimage - Prayag Raj located on vast sandbanks between the Ganges and Yamuna rivers on the outskirts of Allahabad city in Eastern Uttar Pradesh, Banaras and others as well, as the great bathing festivals, the *Kumbh Melas*, are what we may call civilizational centres in time and space, where the dialogue between the renouncers and the householders is intensified. The reader is referred to the appendix for a presentation of how centres of pilgrimage serve as information channels between the Great Tradition and the living Hinduism of the local community.

Finally, we have the life-style model of the householder. *Sthitaprajna* is the Sanskrit term used to denote the perfect householder. *Sthitaprajna* means 'established in wisdom' (while performing the duties). By synthesizing the Moksha ideal of the renouncer and the Dharma ideal of the ritualist, the sthitaprajna should remain unmoved, undisturbed, and self controlled while performing his duties. In order to attain this state of affairs the first prerequisite for a sthitaprajna is to renounce both the spring and purpose of action:

Whose undertakings are all devoid of plan and desire for results,....
(Gita 4.19 also 2.51, 6.2 and others.)

The Gita introduces a new term for renunciation; *tyaga*. Tyaga refers not to the renunciation of action as such, which was the meaning of the earlier term *samnyasa*, but to the renunciation of the fruits and purpose of action (Gita 18.13). *Tyaga*, in the vocabulary of this book, is a value based on activity, subordination, devotion and *holistic* karma. Samnyasa is a term connected with mysticism which advocates inactivity and extinction. The second prerequisite of a sthitaprajna is his indifference to the experience of the dualities of existence (*dvanda*): 'Having made pain and pleasure, gain and loss, conquest and defeat, the same...' (Gita 2.38) The third prerequisite of a sthitaprajna is non-attachment and self-control: 'But the self-controlled man, moving among objects with senses under restraint, and free from attraction and aversion, attains to tranquillity.' (Gita 2.64) The fourth mark of the wise man as conceived in the Gita is the absence of *egoism* and the feeling of mine: 'Forsaking egoism, power, pride, lust, wrath and prosperity, freed from the notion of mine and tranquil - he is fit for becoming Brahman.' (Gita 18.53) And, at last, the sthitaprajna performs his caste duty:

Devoted each to his own duty, man attains the highest perfection...(Gita 18.45)

This attitude and mode of understanding apply to all householders, whether Brahmin or Untouchable; by trying to discipline themselves in this manner, the householders may hope for a better rebirth. And by further sanskritizing their customs by becoming vegetarians and teetotallers, they may also succeed in the caste climbing game of the lifeworld.

The Gita and its conception of the *sthitaprajna* has been in the forefront of discussion among nationalists and intellectuals of modern India. One of the most influential interpretations was delivered by Mahatma Gandhi.[41] How can Gandhi's conception of *ahimsa* - non-violence - be reconciled with the heroic Kshatriya warrior outlook of the Gita, which concludes by advising Arjuna to fight against his teachers and relatives? Gandhi is clear in his answer. He gives a symbolic interpretation of the Gita:

> What is described is the conflict within the human body between opposing moral tendencies imagined as distinct figures. (Gandhi 1926:16)[42]

With this interpretation, the ideal model of the householder -the sthitaprajna - can function as the main guide for Gandhi.[43] We should also note Gandhi's attitude towards duty (*svadharma*). Gandhi's interpretations here are important for understanding his views on the caste system. Speaking on the sweeper, Gandhi comments:

> The man who cleans lavatories as carefully as he does the utensils in his home observes his Dharma in the truest manner. (Gandhi 1926:105)

Gandhi *preserves* the classical idea of the varnashramadharma system as a functional organism. But Gandhi does not accept that the caste system should be regarded as a hierarchy. Each person, whether cleaning lavatories or functioning as a ritualist, has equal value (Gandhi op.cit.:124). Consequently, Gandhi did not accept the idea of pollution and untouchability. Gandhi stresses the importance of individual duty (svadharma) which he defines as that which society assigns to the individual (Gandhi op.cit.:301). *Gandhi defines varna as the definition of the individual's natural work* (Gandhi 1926:298). The ascribed duty of a person is a definition of the kind of activities which the person will be able to *digest* (Gandhi 1926:302) without producing additional karma. It is also a token of the individual's natural talents by means of which it is easier to learn to function 'automatically as a machine':

> When we have learnt to function in this manner, like a machine, we shall have gained the true end of human effort. (Gandhi op.cit.:124)

To modern man, Gandhi's metaphor '*like a machine*' is probably inappropriate. But for many Hindus in present day India, Gandhi is the archetype of a sthitaprajna. The question, however, remains whether the life-style model of the householder makes man a machine or a saint.

Whatever the case, the behaviour appropriate to a householder maintains the world of Brahmanic Hinduism.

Notes to Chapter 8

1. Astronomical, solar and lunar time as well as the rhythms of nature and agrarian time contribute to a more unified, cross-cultural experience of time, at least in the measurement and calendric structuring of time. The universal experience of birth, growth, decay and death gives humanity some common experimental substratum. But if we are concerned with the differentiation between cultures, the naturalistic perspectives offered by Bloch in his article: 'The past and the present in the present' (Bloch 1977:284-285, 287) are of little value to us. Bloch's advice of focusing on practical activity for securing common universal concepts gives little insight into the experience of time in Capitalism as well as Hinduism. The world of industrial production and capital has produced its own socio-economic rhythm. In Hinduism, the main producers of culture - the ritualists and renouncers - were completely *released from* all kinds of practical activity.

2. '*Karman* as that which remains as the subtle structures of temporal reality, ... as that which all existing beings have in common and in which they share.' (Panikkar 1972:31) '*Karman* is a sort of condensation of time, a cosmic link of universal solidarity on that level of reality which we call precisely temporality.' (Panikkar 1974:162)

3. On the relationship between Prajapati and time, see Panikkar 1976.

4. 'That desirable (splendour) of Savitri - May we mediate upon (that) splendour of the God! And may he inspire our thoughts!'

5. Appeared in *Prabuddha Bharata* vol.9:160. Quoted from Gita Advaita edition 1976:193.

6. The re-entrance of the ancestors is a common phenomenon in agrarian societies (see Eliade 1974).

7. In the agricultural calendar instituted by Akbar *Asharh* (June - July) is the first month (Whitcombe 1971:21).

8. From Rampur in Delhi state, Lewis has described this festival as follows: 'A Brahman ties a *ponchi*, or wrist band of coloured thread, around the wrist of the head of the family. In return he is given a handful of grain, or sometimes as much as a *sir* of grain. Girls also tie *ponchis*,..., around the wrist of their brothers..., receiving from a few annas to 5 rupees in exchange.' (Lewis 1958:208)

9. It is of significance that Gopala Krishna, one of the three faces of Krishna, is believed to be a Shudra (Hopkins 1971:124).

10. The symbolic identity of the yugas and the game of dice is significant in that the whole of creation is conceived as the great play - the *lila* and the *maya* of the Gods.

11. Cf. the verse from Manu: 'From a Brahmana, born in that country, let all men on earth learn their several usages.' (2.20)

12. A similar kind of logic can be observed in the status evaluation of the Kanya Kubja Brahmins. Khare has noted that one criterion for rank is how far one lives away from the original centre of the Kanya Kubja culture (Khare 1970).

13. The relationship between social structure and the conception of time has earlier been suggested by Bloch: 'Here too the amount of social structure, of the past in the present, of

ritual communication is correlated, with the amount of *institutionalized* hierarchy and *that is what it is about.*' (Bloch 1977:289)

14. Gurevich, in his article 'Time as a problem of cultural history', has noted that the conception of time does not only differ between the various societies and cultures. 'It does not pass uniformly in the consciousness of the various classes and groups, which all perceive and experience it in their own way, functioning as they do at different rhythm.' (Gurevich 1976:238)

15. Liberation through the conception of oneself as an instrument in the hands of God or society - the holistic karma type - was developed in the Gita.

16. The Sanskrit grammarians regarded the verb as the grammatical expression of actions (Iyer 1969:338). Actions which are complete are expressed in one of the past tenses. Actions which have begun, but are not yet completed, are expressed through the present tense. Undertakings yet to come belong to the future tense.

17. Cf. the early Buddhists, the renouncers par excellence whose philosophy was termed the *kshanikavada* - the followers of the doctrine of momentariness - by the Hindu philosophers.

18. The *Kashikhanda* of the *Skandapurana* states about Banaras: 'Though situated on the earth, it is not earthly. Though established below, it is higher than the heaven; though bound to earth, it is the giver of freedom; the mortals living in it becomes immortals.' (Quoted from Pandey 1969:142)

19. Karchana is thus an example of the hamleted village type (Cohn 1971). Hamlets populated by lower castes are dispersed around the main settlement area. The hamleted pattern is, according to Cohn, quite common in villages with mixed rice/wheat cultivation (ibid.:142), as is the case with Karchana.

20. The *Baiga* is what Mandelbaum has termed a religious functionary serving the pragmatic complex of religion (1966). He is a curer and exorciser. In many regions he has a clearer shamanistic character (see Berreman 1964) involving spirit possession, journeys to the abode of the spirits etc., all in order to find remedies for the suffering of his customers. The Brahmin ritualist, on the other hand, serves the transcendental complex of Hinduism. He performs or directs virtually all that part of village religious activity which is of the learned, literate and Great Tradition (Berreman 1964:55). These will comprise inter alia life cycle rituals and other periodic religious observances such as festivals. The transcendental aspects of Hinduism are represented through the Sanskritic temples, deities and scriptural tradition, and are believed to be important for maintaining the long term well being and solidarity of the society as a whole.

21. I find Harris' explanation of the sacredness of the white cow (1978) untenable. I am unable to find that which makes the white cow more practically useful for the Hindus than the buffalo. I therefore suggest that the sacredness of the white cow need to be explained in a sociological and historical perspective.

22. See Douglas who states that pollution has indeed much to do with morals (Douglas 1980:129).

23. Davis is a follower of the non-dualistic ethno-sociology of Marriott and Inden (Kolenda 1978:71). For a short critique of this school, see the appendix.

24. The etymology of *svabhava* is symptomatic. It is a composite of *sva* = one's own and *bhava* = becoming. 'Nature', then, is 'one's own becoming'.

25. We should note that the process of Sanskritization is increasing in this century, at least on the part of low caste Hindus (cf. Marriott 1968.113 - Srinivas 1965.229).

26. Apart from these foodstuffs which, according to Marriott, are the best transactional mediums indicative of rank (Marriott 1968:151, 158), one should also mention the 'purifiers' like water and the five products of the cow. To bathe in the Ganges is believed to clean the

sinner of his guilt. Harper notes that the more severe types of pollution are removed by eating the five products of the cow, changing the sacred thread, taking a bath and changing clothes. The Laws of Manu provide an extensive list of purifying substances (Manu 5.110-146).

27. Silver and silk have higher economic value than, for example, cotton. Hence they stand out as symbols of higher rank. Raw food is less cultivated than cooked food. In India the cooking process is seen as the beginning of ingestion. Therefore, cooking is susceptible to pollution in the same way as eating (Douglas 1980:1265). Raw food is also more easily convertible than cooked food and therefore carries its stamp of social structure to a lesser degree than cooked food. The higher position of *pakka* food than *kachcha* food probably derives from the symbolic value of *ghee* - clarified butter - being the product of the cow. Ghee is also costly in modern India. Regarding the purifying effect of water, I suggest that one be careful about adopting a 'concrete' explanation. For a Westerner, the holy rivers may not appear very clean. Another reason is probably the mythological conception of water as the material substratum of the creation. By bathing in the holy rivers, the devout Hindu is immersing into the 'origin of things'.

28. Marriott states that the transactions of the *pakka* category of food provide some of the most comprehensive and public dramatizations of caste rank (op. cit.:151). But later he adds: 'If one had to choose a single transactional medium as an indicator of rank, *kachcha* food would be the medium to choose in Kishan Garhi. However, such a simple index would be quite incomplete, for transactions in garbage add two further distinctions to these nine, and transactions in *pakka* add still one more distinction, bringing the total number of distinctions by food transfer to twelve.' (op.cit.:158)

29. The Brahmin ritualist, regarded as the purest and highest ranking in the hierarchy, is in great need of withdrawing from caste transactions. Why is purity so *vulnerable* to impurity? Why does impurity seem to be more potent than purity? (cf. Dumont & Pocock 1959:24). This is the impression left us when we observe the ritual transactions of Hindu society. This phenomenon is consistent with the Logic of karma. The soteriology of the Logic of Karma involves a kind of 'emptying' - a striving towards some form of actionlessness and immobility. The static and passive are regarded as more sacred than the dynamic and active. Ritual purity in this perspective is accordingly some kind of empty state; an *absence* of defilement. This hypothesis is strengthened when we note what Leach called the 'negatively privileged' (1971): The higher the status of a caste, the more numerous are the types of food it cannot eat, occupations it cannot pursue, and the avoidance enjoined upon it (see also Cantlie 1977:263). It is the value of renunciation which here filters back into caste.

30. 'But a Brahmana unable to subsist by his peculiar occupations just mentioned, may live according to the law applicable to Kshatriyas; for the latter is next to him in rank.' (Manu 10.81) By following the law applicable to Kshatriyas, Brahmins loose their ideal caste attributes. Such Brahmins may then constitute the dominant caste of the village (Srinivas 1959, Dumont 1970:162) and their rank is now to a greater extent derived from secular power rather than from status (cf. Dumont 1970). Accordingly, their transactional behaviour is better analyzed in the context of the Kshatriya model. Marriott's approach will, as noted below, be quite correct in their case.

31. The Kshatriya varna is, as I noted in the example of the Noniyas, 'open' in the caste climbing game. It is as much an achieved as an ascribed status. In general, one is a Kshatriya because one possesses the *kshatra* - dominion, military or reigning order. That is, one has relatively eminent right over the land. The other characteristics of the dominant caste are power to grant land and to employ members of other castes in agricultural capacities, to build up a large clientele (Dumont 1970:162). It also has judicial authority: The notables of the dominant caste are often entrusted with the arbitration of differences in other castes or between different castes (see Srinivas 1959). The relationship between the Brahmin ritualist and the dominant caste is modelled on the relationship between the Brahmin and the King.

32. *Shakti* is important in their pantheon. Shakti is the Goddess with various manifestations who symbolizes the 'hot' and active principle in Hindu cosmology. In various myths, the king is pictured as married to Shakti - the Earth (Dumont 1971).

33. It is even plausible that the Sanskrit term for king, *Raja*, is derived from the same verbal root as *rajas*, i.e., *ranj* or *raj*, meaning to be affected, moved, to redden, be charmed etc. (Monier Williams).

34. Secular power is a residual component in Dumont's model (Dumont 1970:38-39). It intrudes into the ideal picture, which is a religious hierarchy where the Brahmin ritualist constitutes the apex.

35. 'Therefore at the Rajasuya ceremony (the ceremonial anointing of a king) the Brahman sits below the Kshatriya.' (Br.Up. 1.4.11)

36. The Laws of Manu conceives the growth of the caste system as an outcome of mixed marriages which produced the many jatis out of the four original varnas (Manu 10.25-45).

37. The results reached by Marriott and four other anthropologists, when comparing caste rank in villages of West Bengal, Bihar, Maharastra and Uttar Pradesh, are as follows: 'Out of 176 castes in these villages occurring in regional lists of 36 each, only nine types of castes were common to the four regions: Brahman, Rajput, Merchant, Barber, Potter, Weaver, Washerman, Oilman and Leather worker. These nine castes form a similar hierarchy of just five ranks in the different regions. With Leather worker at the bottom; Weaver and Washerman and Oilman always above Leather worker; Barber and Potter always above them; Rajput and Merchants always above Barber and Potter; and Brahman and Rajput always ranked at the top.' (Quoted from Singer 1964:102-103) Unfortunately, we are not informed here about the internal ranking of the Brahman and the Rajput. The picture from my own work in Karchana village, Eastern Uttar Pradesh was very clear. The 5 kinds of Brahmin groups of the village were all ranked above the Thakur Kshatriya (Jaer 1995).

38. According to Ghurye, there are about 200 caste groups in each linguistic region. These groups are further sub-divided into 3000 smaller units, each of which is endogamous and constitutes the area of effective social life of the individual (Ghurye 1950:28).

39. My concept of 'life-style model' has many similarities with Damle's (1968) 'reference groups': 'The reference group acts as a frame of reference for self-evaluation and attitude formation, whether the group is one in which ego has membership (...) or one in which he himself is not a member (...) ... A group may also be selected as a *negative* reference group, where the attempt is to avoid all identification with it... There must be patterned ways in which people become acquainted with the norms and activities in the groups which they select as evaluative and comparative frames of reference.' (Damle 1968:96-97)

40. Khare, in his monograph *The Changing Brahmans* (1970), stresses that the real indicators of Brahmanhood for the Kanya Kubja Brahmins, like any other Brahmin group, lie in acquiring and choosing those modes of behaviour that are consistent with the values prescribed by the holy scriptures. As cultural norms, these modes of behaviour are uniformly emphasized, but as ideals in general, they are only imperfectly reached (Khare 1970:24, 102, 106).

41. About the Gita Gandhi states: 'Then arose a great and lofty minded man, the composer of the Gita, who gave to the Hindu world a synthesis of Hindu religion... for forty years I have been seeking literally to live up to the teachings of that book.' (Tendulkar 1961:180)

42. Consequently, Gandhi reinterprets the very first verse of the Gita: 'It is the human body that is described as Kuruksetra, as Dharmaksetra.' (Gandhi 1926:16)

43. Not without reason, Gandhi considers the last 19 verses of chapter two in the Gita as the essence of Dharma (Gandhi 1926:9). These verses give the main description of the *sthitaprajna* in the Gita.

PART III:

A COMPARATIVE EXERCISE

9

HINDUISM AND CAPITALISM COMPARED

ACTION - KARMA

We have seen from the first part that Kant regards individual agency, individual responsibility and autonomy as transcendental, a priori presuppositions for a valid concept of man and morality. There are many examples to be found in the philosophical discourse of Brahmanic Hinduism which emphasize that the same presuppositions also have an important significance in the Hindu tradition of knowledge.[1]

In the Hindu tradition we find determinist schools of thought and schools which uphold the freedom of the will. We find ideas centred around the problem of predestination and we find schools believing in the mechanics of nature. In the Buddhist Sutras we can read of wide ranging religious/philosophical discussions between the determinist schools (*Ajivika* - see Basham 1951) and the Buddhists who were staunch advocates of the theory of karma (Na-Rangsi 1976). The determinists claimed that the individual was altogether unable to alter his cosmical destiny while the followers of the doctrine of karma maintained personal responsibility and thus a possibility for the individual to alter his religious quality and future destiny.

Kant defined 'autonomy' as subjection of the will to its own law - the categorical imperative - i.e. self determination, self legislation in front of the moral law. The philosophers of Brahmanic Hinduism also entered into an elaborate analysis of the problem of autonomy (see Maitra 1963:80-183).[2] Their problem was: what is the relationship between the moral imperatives embodied in the code of scriptural duties and the moral agent? Within the matrix of these imperatives, what makes the actor assume the status of a moral agent? To answer this question, the philosophers of Brahmanic Hinduism examined the nature of *volition* (*pravrtti*). According to their view, volition arises in the agent with a knowledge of the sense of duty and the will to do it.[3] As a karmic being, man is conceived as an autonomous agent, not in front of Kant's moral law which, in Kant's philosophy, constitutes Man as such,[4] but in front of the scriptural imperatives which, when obeyed, define the actor as a Hindu.[5] We can look at this issue from another point of view:

Freedom and necessity

Freedom, as we saw it in the case of Hegel, is a kind of *sociological apperception*, an understanding of the necessary relationship between I and We, and We and I (see chapter one). This kind of insight gives the agent an understanding of the workings of the socio-cultural system and of the interdependence between participants. Seen against the background of growing individualism and the emerging success of liberalist ideology at the time of Hegel, the idea of the 'sociological apperception' is significant.

Freedom in the context of Hinduism, is a kind of *religious apperception*.[6] It is religious because the 'We', the collective dimension of the system, is conceived in the idiom of a religious language. It is conceived of as the *varnashramadharma*.[7] The religious apperception involves insight into the relationship between a person's ascribed duties and his karmic ballast, that is between his *svadharma* and *svabhava*. The more the Hindu 'acts out his destiny', the more his activity will approach the fundamental value of non-karmic actions - religious emancipation. The immanent relationship between freedom and necessity present in the philosophy of Hegel as well as in karmic ideology, gives rise to values like self discipline, self control and self knowledge.[8] Naturally, such values are important for a proper understanding of social control because they guide the actor towards world maintenance.[9]

DIFFERENT VALUES

Individualism and holism

Individualism is a value in Capitalism. The individual should, according to the spokesmen of classical liberalism, deliberately pursue his *own* interests.[10] The individual is praised as the centre of things - a being which perceives himself as a substance independent of the social relations of society. And the concept of society is reduced to an aggregate of such individuals.

In Brahmanic Hinduism 'society' = *varnashradharma* is praised as that 'holy whole' within which the individual should strive to accommodate himself. 'Society' is not regarded as an aggregate or sum of individuals, but as a whole, an independent instance of reality. The individual (*ahamkara*, *kartri*) is seen as the root cause of karma production and suffering. The individual is regarded as that entity which *counteracts* the 'needs' of the whole - the collectivity - through selfishness and egoism. The conception of the individual and individualism as it appeared in classical Capitalism is highly disregarded by Brahmanic Hinduism.

There is one point of convergence between Capitalism and Brahmanic Hinduism with respect to the 'individual'. The notion of the *biography* of the individual is of importance in both contexts.[12] Psychoanalytic theory regards the formative processes of personality to start from child birth.

Compared with Hinduism, where the remembrance of previous lives (the *cosmic* biography of the individual) is seen as a great value,[13] the point is interesting. Both Hinduism and Capitalism have a kind of 'psychoanalytic' approach though with a totally different notion of where the story starts and ends.

The past or the future

The passage of time is, as Eliade notes, a metaphysical burden on religious man (cf.Eliade 1971). Accordingly, the renouncer seeks to live in an 'eternal present' by trying to replicate the rhythm of the timeless. For the ritualist and householder, on the other hand, the past emerged as the golden age while the present is devalued to the iron age of Kali. The spiritual and moral qualities of the world and men are seen to have degenerated through the four yugas (cosmical periods). To repeat the archetypal patterns (Dharma) instituted by the culture heroes at the beginning of time is seen as the highest value. Activity in accordance with Dharma - in accordance with the eternal archetypes - is regarded as non-karmic actions which lead to religious liberation. The Hindus uphold the glory of *old age*, whether it refers to old people in general or, more symbolically, to high caste people who are believed to have a genealogical connection with the mythical past. Old people are wise people. They are believed to have knowledge and experience of the constitution of the world. They are seen as the more sacred and spiritual. In Hinduism, it is the past which shines forth in the present, while in Capitalism it is the future in the present (cf. Bloch 1977).

In a secular, desacralized cosmos in which modern man finds himself, time and space have few bounded units and inner differentiations of social, intellectual or religious significance.[14] The notion of the sacred/profane which is of such importance to Brahmanic Hinduism, is of little significance to modern man.

In opposition to Brahmanic Hinduism, in which time is perceived as a *quality* that is either good or bad for doing things (Madan 1985), time in the context of Capitalism is perceived as a *quantity* of which man has more or less. '*Time is money*' is a rather telling expression in this regard. Modern man values efficiency and rational organization of time. Since the growth of the Protestant ethic, waste of time has become almost sinful (McHale 1979:89). The slogan of the day is to save time because time is money. In Hinduism, on the contrary, no one is afraid of wasting or losing time, precisely because *lost time is Being regained* (Baumer 1976:83).

The Western concept of time discloses, as Eliade has noted, a kind of quantitative eschatology (1971), a belief in the coming of the 'sacred' whether it be the saviour or the new society. This idea of social and cultural *progress*, crucial to the value system of classical Capitalism (McHale 1979:88 - Collingwood 1970:321), has its roots in Christian theology (Augustine) and its linear concept of history. The idea matured in the nineteenth century Europe with thinkers like Marx and the Victorian evolutionists.[15]

The idea of progress and future orientation is functional in connection with the socio-economic 'need' for accumulation and growth. This *systemic* need manifests itself on the level of the actors as the 'unending' drive towards profit and accumulation of wealth.[16] It also manifests itself as a drive towards technological change and intensification of the labour process. Systemic equilibrium is impossible. The outcome is as follows:

> The tendency to create the *world market* is directly given in the concept of capital itself. Hence the great civilizing influence of capital, ...(Marx 1973:407)

This 'historic mission of capital' creates, as Marx saw it, the possibilities for a higher stage of society in the future.[17]

In Hindu society economic life and material production had not the sense of setting their own goals and being its own masters such as we have seen it in Capitalist society. The ultimate aim of economic production was man - production for use and not for exchange (Sahlins 1972). In Capitalism, on the other hand, the ultimate aim of economic production is the accumulation of wealth.[18] Modern man puts high value on using time efficiently because it is in the future that his purpose shall be realized. The reference to the past came to be of declining importance in a world view based on the idea of progress (cf. Jeanniere 1977). Capitalism stresses the future, prizes youth and devalues old age.

The end of times

Hinduism believes in *Pralaya* - the cosmic destruction - in which the whole of creation is reabsorbed into the stomach of Lord Vishnu for a thorough purification. But after one cosmic night in the unmanifest state, a new cycle commences afresh on account of the unripe karmic seeds in need of fructification. In the Western tradition, the Christian conception of the day of judgement has turned into a more concrete horror, an economic breakdown of the Capitalist system, a nuclear Ragnarok, an ecological disaster. Prophecies like Nostradamus', forecasting 1995 A.D. as 'The end of time' have become a part of the general mind. The difference between the traditional and the modern conception is that modern man does not conceive 'The end of time' as an outcome of cosmic necessity (the law of karma) or God's wrath. He sees it as a product of his own creative activities.

Marx has an interesting perspective on 'the end of time' in his theory on the 'decline in the general rate of profit'(Marx 1959:213 - 1894), where it is stated that the interest obtained from investments of capital tend to decrease due to the development of productive forces.[19] This suicidal (Marx 1973:750) tendency of the capitalist mode of production is held by Marx to be the most important law of political economy (Marx 1959:211).[20] When the rate of profit is declining:

> ... the capitalist mode of production...comes to a standstill at a point fixed by the production and realization of profit, and not the satisfaction of requirements. (Marx 1959:259 and 258 - 1894)

Profit is the rational motive for economic actions. Without a reasonable interest on invested capital, capital will either move to other branches and countries or be left idle (Marx 1959:250). If there are difficulties in the expansion of the market and growth of the G.N.P., economic depression and unemployment may become the order of the day. Marx saw two solutions to the problem: Either a violent overthrow - a revolution - or a depreciation of capital and reduction of the value of labour power to awake the actions of capital, guided by the rate of profit, to a new cycle of life. Ultimately, according to Marx, the recurrent problems will lead to the downfall of Capitalism - to the end of time (Marx 1973:750).

DIFFERENT IDEOLOGIES[21]

Fetishism

Comparing Hinduism and Capitalism, *fetishism* is an interesting phenomenon:

> In that world (the religious world - ØJ) the productions of the human brain appear as independent beings endowed with life, and entering into relation both with one another and the human race. So it is in the world of commodities with the products of men's hands. (Marx 1887:77 - 1867)

The Hindu is alienated under his *ideational* objectivations - 'the products of the human brain' - while modern man is alienated under his *material* objectivations - the 'products of the hand'. The fetishism of Hinduism as well as the fetishism of Capitalism are both products of human activity, though with different sources of origin. The social construction of reality is indeed different in the two worlds we are investigating.

The traditional Hindu lives in a world where material production is transparent, unconcealed, existing for the sake of man and, as long as the powers of nature do not intervene, controlled by man. The religious world, on the other hand, is endowed with powers, extended to all domains of life, and mystified.[22] The Brahmins stand supreme in the Hindu world. They possess the sacred knowledge which is, as it were, their 'private property'. And they command and manipulate, as the law books put it, the magical and spiritual forces. The Brahmins are invested with religious privileges which dispossess and alienate the rest of the people from the products of their 'brains'. It seems fit that Hindu theism puts special emphasis on the attitude of subordination to God which, according to the orthodox view, means subordination to the rules of the caste system and hence service to the superior castes.

Modern man is not living in a world of supernatural fetters. The religious world is demystified and unconcealed. Here, it is the world of commodities - the *market* - which appears as an independent source of energy and creativity. It seems as if money has the power to multiply by itself, to increase through interest without any effort on the part of the subjects.[23] The Capitalist stands supreme in the modern world. The institution of private property gives him the right to appropriate the objectivations of the producers. This institutional arrangement of not being in control over the products of one's own labour gives rise to the experience of alienation in which modern man feels that he has lost contact with his action essence - his being.[24] Man-made products appear as external forces - as fetishes - turning their back on the producers themselves.

Fetishism is not a mode of consciousness incumbent on the disprivileged strata of a population only. It is a systemic arrangement making its impact on everybody. However, the upper strata finds itself more comfortable in this state of alienation. Its members believe they are the ones to manipulate the fetishes; the capitalist as the economic entrepreneur intervening in the market and the Brahmin ritualist as the magician trying to coerce the spiritual forces of samsara/maya. Fetishism is based on a permutation of social relations and the products of labour - mental or physical labour - into things in themselves (Marx 1887:77 -1867), independent beings endowed with life. The conventions of everyday life - the *habits* to use an important term in the epistemology of Hume - make it a commonplace that social relations assume the shape of things (Marx 1970:34 - 1859).

Reification

Reification is a 'social construction of reality' which transforms the man-made to appear as given by Nature or given by God - that is, as eternal, unchangeable laws.[25]

Capitalism reifies *man* into a '*homo economicus*'. Man, irrespective of time and place, appears as an instance of 'homo economicus' (cf. Alavi 1973). By thus reifying 'man' into an abstract individual, his socio-cultural and historical character is concealed. One implication of this mode of philosophical anthropology is that the institution of the market economy appears as the '*best of all possible social worlds*' seen in relationship to man's nature as a homo economicus.

Karmic ideology, on the other hand, does not reify man. Man's nature is conceived as *svabhava* (lit. one's own becoming'), as a kind of historical, self-produced human 'nature'. Karmic ideology reifies the *whole* - the caste system as such - and thereby conceals the man-made and historical character of society. The caste structure appears as an eternal arrangement instituted by God. Status quo gets the fixed and immutable character of being a manifestation of the Divine itself.

Reification in both contexts implies that fundamental change seems impossible. The laws of God or the laws of Nature cannot be changed through human effort. The outcome of the ideological process of reification is that the exercise of power and the asymmetrical relations of domination appear to the participants as *inevitable and thus legitimate*.

Concealment

The ideology of Capitalism informs its social carriers that they are living in a socio-cultural system based on equality and freedom. From the individualized perspective of the market, everybody seem to enjoy equality and freedom. The individual is regarded as responsible for his socio-*economic* destiny: One is rich because of hard work, one is poor because of laziness.[26] But Capitalism, if we are to believe Marx, conceals social structure and social determinism which reproduce inequality behind the backs of the individuals (Marx 1973:244 - 1857-58). The ideology of Capitalism holds that there is no such thing as a class *structure*. The socio-economic forms of the lifeworld are seen as the aggregated outcome of individual efforts.

The picture is quite the opposite in the Hindu world. Here the participants are informed about inequality and hierarchy as the essence of social being. Social structure is not concealed. It is the acceptance of the superiority of the Brahmins and their sacred knowledge which, as we have heard, actually defines a Hindu from the native point of view. But following karmic ideology, the Hindu is perceived to be responsible for his socio-*religious* destiny. This perspective is quite similar to the ideology of Capitalism, which perceives the individual as the creator of his socio-economic destiny. In the context of both karmic and capitalist ideologies, man is seen to be *responsible* for his own destiny. He is invested with the possibility of improving his future lot.

Ideology and action

Karmic ideology informs its believers that they are born unequal because of past karma. Everybody has received his social status and experience of pleasure and pain as deserved. Thus, within the context of Hinduism, a person cannot appeal to a proportional form of justice based on the principle of equality and claim that one as a sweeper should be treated equally with a Brahmin. Social critique of existing institutions is beyond the rational limits of karmic ideology. In Capitalism, the picture is reversed. Here inequality is concealed by the dominant ideology. The outcome of the capitalist world view stressing equality and freedom is that social critique is a legitimate and rational activity. One can appeal for 'justice' with reference to the ideology itself. Indeed, socialist ideas rose on the foundations of a the ideology of Liberalism. Within the context of capitalist ideology, the struggle for radical social change is as rational as the struggle for status quo.

Capitalism, as perceived by Marx, is a system based on contradictions. The contradiction between the ideology of Capitalism informing its social carriers of equality and freedom and inequality as a *social fact*, gives rise to social critique, to a willed and planned effort for social change, to detachment from former modes of actions. In Hinduism on the other hand, the dualism between appearance and reality gives rise to a religious striving, to a willed and planned effort for *individual* change - to improve one's rebirth chances and finally to attain religious freedom. In the case of the renouncer, the dualism gives rise to a renunciation of 'social life' altogether.

Ideology and social relations

What precisely distinguishes capital from the master servant relation, is that the worker confronts him as a consumer...and possessor of money,...' (Marx 1973:420)[27]

Capitalism regards the working man as an independent and free actor. The working man enters the market to sell his commodity, his labour power, to whom he may choose. Furthermore, he can buy in the market what he needs for himself and his family according to his means. He enjoys in this sphere a *formal* equality with other buyers and sellers. Legally, the working man is accorded the same rights as the others.

But the social relations of Capitalism is quite contrary to the relations of personal dependence (cf. Marx 1973:158) found in Hinduism. Hinduism subscribes in principle to a form of authorization over persons which is direct. The superior castes do not encounter their servants on an equal basis as sellers and buyers. They encounter their servants as beings of an unequal kind, *born* to perform inferior occupations and to remove ritual dirt from their superiors. Hence, since the various castes do not share any common attributes like workers and capitalists who must both be buyers and sellers in the market, there is no basis for an ideal of equality. On the contrary, Hinduism conceives hierarchy as the essence of social being and informs its believers accordingly. But it would be a mistake to regard Hindu servant castes as similar to slaves. Slaves are the property of their masters. Slaves are in principle considered more or less as animals without human responsibility and agency. Hindu servants are not the private property of their superiors. They adhere to their caste groups and enjoy, in comparison with the slave, some degree of freedom. However low they may be on the social scale, they are regarded as Hindus, as karmic beings who contribute to the reproduction of the eternal Dharma. They are also perceived to be invested with the possibility for religious emancipation.

Idealism or materialism

The ideas of the ruling class are in every epoch the ruling ideas, i.e. the class which is the ruling *material* force of society, is at the same time its ruling *intellectual* force. (Marx 1970:64 - 1846)

This one-to-one relationship between material force and intellectual force is problematic in Hinduism where the Brahmin varna control the spiritual and intellectual production. Brahmin domination is based on the control of the holy scriptures and on the belief that they also thereby control the spiritual/religious forces. Brahmin domination is *not* based on the control over the material forces, which is in principle governed by the Kshatriyas. Thus, a kind of Historical Materialism upholding the material base as the only explanatory principle is not feasible in the case of Hinduism.

THE ECONOMIC OR THE RELIGIOUS PROJECT

The borders of experience: Life and death

One peculiar characteristic of the Hindu tradition is the idea that men can become Gods (cf. The 'Man-God' - Eliade 1969). The renouncer is the social manifestation of this idea. For the liberated renouncer, the Hindus believe there are no limitations in time and space. Through religious praxis one can remember earlier lives, one can see the thoughts of others, one can fly etc. At least so say the Hindu texts and such are the beliefs of the Hindus. The Hindus do not perceive the borders of experience as we do. What *we* would conceive as metaphysics beyond perception is regarded as entities of experience for the Hindus.

The Hindu conception of the lifeworld (maya/samsara) is not restricted to this life only (and to the succession of generations). For the Hindu, the lifeworld signifies both society and cosmos, this life and the life hereafter. This 'metaphysical' *extension* of the lifeworld concept is linked up with another mode of perceiving human existence in Hinduism. The following quotation provides a general illustration of the point:

> The personality before birth is purely spiritual; it becomes completely profane or unspiritual in the earlier periods of its life, when it is classed socially with the females, gradually becomes more and more ritualized and sacred as the individual grows older and approaches death, and at death once more becomes completely spiritual and sacred.' (W. Lloyd Warner, quoted from Eliade 1977:13)

It is significant in this picture that the Sanskrit terms for religious freedom, *Nirvana* and *Moksha*, also signify death. It is common in modern India to hear phrases like 'He reached his Nirvana on...', meaning that the person died on that day and, furthermore, that the person, at least for the sake of courtesy, is said to reach his final emancipation after death. For modern man on the other hand, the following ironic statement is probably not totally out of place:

> We are born mad; then we acquire morality and become stupid and unhappy; then we die. (Anonymous British psychoanalyst, quoted from ibid.)

Modern Western existentialist philosophers supply us with the best source for understanding modern man's perception of death. Nietzsche's statement 'God is dead' is symptomatic. The metaphysical world is *devoid* of content. Death and the hereafter are perceived as non-being. After death there is nothing, no judgement, no return. Heidegger's description of human existence as 'Being unto Death' (Sein zum Tode) is probably one of the more well informed statements of the existential situation of modern man.

The Yogi and the Actoman[28]

In a world view where religion and metaphysics are losing their importance as sources of comfort, hope and meaning, the 'project' stands out as the more rational solution to the problem of meaning. Modern man ought to be an actoman forever thrown into activity like Sisyphus in the Greek myth. The man of action is highly praised by Capitalism. He is the person who contributes to social life. He is the person who is believed to develop the 'land'. Contemplative, inactive people are often seen as strange or even as a burden to society.

One possible point of departure for an understanding of the actomanic lifestyle is to examine the secularized world view of modern man: 'God is dead'. Given this perception of man's cosmological situation, modern man interprets the fundamentals of existence as a problem of nothingness (Heidegger 1974:11). The only existential answer which seems to be of an absolute kind for modern man is Death. This metaphysical and cosmical state of affairs may give rise to an experience of dread. Dread, as we have learnt from the existentialist philosophers (cf. Kierkegaard 1844), is indeed defined by being the *experience of Nothingness*. Thus, the comparative situation is as follows: While the Yogi is confronted with Being and the demands which Being puts on him, the Actoman is confronted with Nothingness and the experience of dread which 'nothingness' produces. 'Being' is something which the Yogi believes he will experience when his karmic life has come to naught. The Actoman, on the other hand, meets 'Nothingness' through the existential apperception of Death and the experience of dread. He is, as it were, thrown back into the positive evaluation of this worldly life - into actions and projects. If not, the Actoman is left in dread and absurdity. In order to escape 'Nothingness', the Actoman is bound to externalise himself into the world of objects and continuously to engage in actions. The Actoman must be a creator - a project-maker - to confirm his existence as a human being. The Actoman must *fill* himself through projects directed towards the world of objects. The Actoman seeks to *expand* his own self by enlarging his properties in the world of objects. He is usually a self-interested person who regards society as a means to his own ends. Even the religious minded capitalist, as portrayed by Wesley, is devoted to material wealth:

> ..., we must exhort all Christians to gain all they can, and to save all they can, that is, in effect, to grow rich. (Wesley, quoted from Weber 1976:175)

The Yogi, on the other hand, should be *introvert*. He seeks to internalize his life-practise by turning away from the world of objects and actions to cultivate his inner Self. The Yogi seeks to *empty* himself of possessions, desires, actions, memories etc. Actions perceived to serve individual or sectional interests are regarded as karmic actions which lead to rebirth and suffering. By being empty of karma, the Yogi is believed to reach Being - the Absolute - and experience Moksha. The Yogi seeks to transcend temporality and obtain the eternal present. As a symbol of time, the Yogi represents the present - the moment. The Yogi symbolizes, furthermore, the centre of space and should not be on the way to or from somewhere. His spinal column is portrayed as his axis mundi.

The actomanic experience of space and time is best described through the notion of speed. The Actoman seeks to traverse longer and longer distances in the shortest possible time. The things which need to be done are continuously increasing for the Actoman. Lost time is lost life. This, indeed, is in contrast to the yogic saying that 'lost time is Being regained'. The Actoman with his projects and his *intentional* mode of being can hardly dwell in the moment. He throws himself into the flood of time, consumes it and is oriented towards his goals in the future. The ideal of the Actoman is not to repeat eternal archetypes, but to seek detachment from former modes of action. The Actoman pursues change for its own sake and soon gets bored with the old. He secures his individuality by creating something new and identifying himself with something new. He conceives novelty as the possible source of an ultimate experience. An old person's experience is of little value to modern man. Old people are no longer held to be the carriers of the wisdom of the past. They are not any longer the models for action. The Actoman should create his own life, cultivate his individuality and choose his own way.

A real Yogi is usually an old person. He should, following Brahmanic Hinduism, have successfully passed the first three stages of life. First in the fourth stage - in the *sannyasi ashrama* - is the person seen as ready and matured to become a real Yogi. Life itself is thus seen to have a progressive development in which old age is the period closest to the finalization of the human goal: Freedom from the world of actions and objects - a religious experience in the form of a *unio mystica*.

Sartre has formulated the general condition of the Actoman as follows:

To be is to act, and to cease to act is to cease to be. (Sartre 1975:613)

Compared with the earlier quotation from Shankara:

...but without release from activity the attainment of the goal of man is impossible,... FOR ACTIVITY IS NATURALLY PAINFUL.' (Shankara bhashya Vedanta Sutra 2.3.40 - quoted from Deussen 1972:318)

we may again clearly see how the values of Brahmanic Hinduism and Capitalism are the reverse of each other, but with action/karma as the identical third - the bridge of translation between the two.

NOTES TO CHAPTER 9

1. In the case of Kant it is a matter of *a priori* presuppositions while in Brahmanic Hinduism it is a matter of *other-worldly* presuppositions. It is the same structural principle operating within two different systems of thought, the first rational, the second religious.

2. I am thinking of the *Prabhakaras* belonging to the ritualist branch. The point, however, is that the Prabhakaras have a much more 'internalized' view than the externalism of Kumarila (Maitra 1963:99).

3. Kumarila, the ritualist philosopher, used the term *shabdabhavana* (lit. causality from words) to identify the relationship between scriptural injunctions and the agent. Maitra (1963:136) interprets Kumarila's position as mechanistic.

4. The main difference between the position of Kant as a representative of the West and the voices of Brahmanic Hinduism, is the *universalistic* conception of Man held by Kant and the '*nationalistic*' concept of man prevalent in Brahmanic Hinduism (cf. the earlier noted statement of the doctrine of karma as limited to the region of *Bharatavarsha*).

5. One native definition of a Hindu is he who accepts the authority of the Holy scriptures and the Brahmins.

6. For a relevant anthropological discussion on the 'concept and state of freedom', see Fürer-Haimendorf 1963: 'Freedom and conformity in tribal, Hindu and Buddhist societies of India and Nepal', in Bidney, D. (ed.): *The concept of freedom in anthropology*, The Hague, pp. 107-129.

7. The 'collective' is according to our Durkheimian assumptions on the relationship between society and religion, divinized and reified.

8. The Sanskrit term *yoga* denotes self discipline, self control, self knowledge. For example, *karma-yoga* means discipline in actions.

9. Hegel's philosophy is often perceived as a form of legitimation of the Prussian state. Similarly, the concepts of karma and Dharma make up the karmic ideology which justifies the caste system.

10. 'Only in the eighteenth century, in "civil society", do the various forms of social connectedness confront the individual as a mere means towards his private purposes,...' (Marx 1973:84 - 1857-58)

11. Cf. the notion of the abstract individual, Lukes 1973.

12. It also informs us of an important difference to Christianity. I am thinking of the doctrine of original sin, which teaches us that there will be a collective punishment.

13. The *Jataka* stories of Buddhism are examples of the importance attached to earlier lives. By describing the 'cosmic biography' of the Buddha, lay people may see a road to religious emancipation.

14. There are certainly qualifications of time and space even in the modern world. The liturgical calendar of the Christian church still contributes to the structuration of the year. We differentiate between work time and spare time. In our structuration of space, we still have the notion of the fashionable West End and 'proletarian' East End.

15. Marx did not, as Hegel before him, regard 'the present' as 'the end of history' (cf. Hegel and the Prussian state). For Marx, the 'present' was a contradiction. The capitalist system could accordingly reach identity with itself only by developing into a new mode of production where the present contradictions would be suspended.

16. 'Die *Funktionen*, die der Kapitalist ausubt, sind nur die mit *Bewusstsein* und *Willen* ausgeubten Funktionen des Kapitals - .... Der Kapitalist funktioniert nur als *personifiziertes*

Kapital, das Kapital als Person,...' (Marx 1969:17)

17. Marx has a twofold perspective on Capitalism: It creates possibilities, but is based on exploitation and systemic contradictions which will in the end lead to its downfall. Among the negative effects noted by Marx is the lot of the labourer: 'It follows therefore that in proportion as capital accumulates, the lot of the labourer, be his payment high or low, must grow worse. The law, finally, that always equilibrates the relative surplus population, or industrial reserve army, to the extent and energy of accumulation, this law rivets the labourer to capital more firmly than the wedges of Vulcan did Prometheus to the rock.' (Marx 1887:604 -1867)

18. 'Accumulation for accumulation's sake, production for production's sake: by this formula classical economy expressed the historical mission of the Bourgeois, ...' (Marx 1887:558)

19. If, as argued by Marx, profit has its source in the production of surplus value through the exploitation of labour, it follows that the relatively smaller portion of total capital being invested in labour power in proportion to machines, robots etc., must as a general tendency lead to the decline in the rate of profit.

20. It is a question whether this theory can be empirically tested at all. First of all because the rate of profit and rate of surplus value are counteracting tendencies (Marx 1959:219). Another reason is the continuous expansion of the capitalist system to less developed spheres of production and to foreign countries where the rate of profit is higher (Marx 1959:258). Of importance for counteracting the decline of the rate of profit is also, according to Marx, the increase in the production of unproductive waste, capital which does not serve to instigate the development of the productive forces.

21. The reader is referred to chapter two for a definition of ideology.

22. The idea of a universal causality within the field of morals is an example of a man made construction of ideas and representations which assume power and independent life over its producers.

23. 'Because it is value, it has acquired the occult quality of being able to add value to itself. It brings forth living offspring or, at the least, lays golden eggs.' (Marx 1887:152 -1867)

24. It is important that we do not fall into the Hegelian track and define *alienation* as identical to objectivation (Marx 1975:387-392). Alienation has its roots in specific social conditions. Alienation is caused by an underlying process through which some actors are dispossessed to the benefit of others.

25. The passive epistemology of empiricism remains, if we are to believe Marx, in the grip of fetishism and conceals the products of history into immutable laws of nature (Marx 1973:87 - 1857-58). The implications of such modes of thinking are ethnocentrism: 'Hange ich ihnen daher den Namen *Kapital* an in der Zuversicht,..., so habe ich *bewiesen*, dass die Existenz des Kapitals ein ewiges Naturgesetz der menschlichen Produktion ist und dass der Kirgise, der mit einem den Russen gestohlenen Messer Binsen abschneidet und aus diesen Binsen seinen Kahn flicht, ganz ebenso gut ein Kapitalist ist, wie der Herr von Rotschild.'

26. The ideology of individualism, freedom and equality which is peculiar to Capitalism is, according to Marx, an idealized expression of the market: '...*equality and freedom*. As pure ideas they are merely the idealized expression of this basis (i.e. the market, ØJ),...' (Marx 1973:245 - 1857-58)

27. Hence the contradiction in Capitalism which, on the one hand, tries to press wages below the value of labour in order to increase immediate profit, but which, on the other hand, sees the need for the working class to demand consumer products.

28. 'Actoman' - the person who always must act. I am indebted to Prof. Arne Martin Klausen for this nice, new word.

APPENDICES

PILGRIMAGE AS A SOURCE OF KNOWLEDGE

The people of Karchana village in Eastern Uttar Pradesh, where I did fieldwork 1985 - 86 (Jaer 1995),[1] travel to many places of pilgrimage and for several reasons.

The majority of the villagers attend one or several of the local Melas which take place throughout the year in surrounding villages of Karchana. Such Melas appear like a blending of markets, fun fairs and religious events and have a purely *local* significance. People who are troubled by evil spirits too powerful to be handled locally will travel 30 kms to Shankargarh, a place of *sub-regional* significance (Allahabad district only). Women who desire sons travel to *Sarada Devi's*[2] place in Maihar, Madhya Pradesh about a days journey (200 kms) away. For the same reasons, and also if parents have small children said to be troubled by the evil eye (*nazar*) or witchcraft (*jadu tona*), people will travel to Vindhyachal about 60 kms away from Karchana towards Banaras. Maihar is a place of pilgrimage with a *regional* significance. Vindhyachal has a *supra-regional* significance

Most people in Karchana will visit Prayag Raj for at least one day during the annual *Magh Mela* festivals and for several days during such important events as the *Kumbh Mela*. People go there for spiritually - transcendental, rather than material - pragmatic reasons.[3] The month of *Magh* (January) attracts somewhere between four and eight million pilgrims annually (Information provided by Mela administration, 1986) to Prayag Raj. Every sixth year, a half *kumbh* festival is celebrated and the congregation of pilgrims is at least doubled. Every twelfth year, when the sun is in Aries and the planet Jupiter is in Aquarius (*Kumbh*) and when the month of Magh arrives, the Kumbh Mela is celebrated at Prayag Raj. The last one, the Kumbh Mela of 1989, attracted more than 40 million visitors. On the most auspicious day of this month, the *Mauni amavasya* (new moon day), on the sixth of February, around ten million people were estimated to have taken a dip in the holy rivers at Prayag Raj (Times of India 7.2.89).

The most holy place at Prayag Raj is the *Sangam* (the confluence of the two rivers) and the most holy time was 3.18 a.m., the correct bathing time settled by the *Pandits* (learned men). At this auspicious moment, more than 2.5 million people were reported to have taken their dip in the restricted area of Sangam (Op.cit.). In addition, as devout Hindus told me, 33 million Gods and Goddesses were also present to enjoy the heavenly nectar of the holy rivers at this extraordinary juncture of sacred time and sacred space.

A centre for the Great Tradition

The enormous congregations of people from all over India, the presence of all the religious specialists and sects of all denominations within the Hindu fold, the performances of the epic dramas, Vedic styled sacrifices and sermons transmitting the core values, ideas, symbols and methods of Brahmanic Hinduism, finally, the sadhus - the renouncers - who demonstrate the 'truth' of Hinduism, attest to the fact that Prayag Raj is a primary centre in the civilizational network of India. The force of cultural and civilizational integration which reside in centres like Prayag Raj and events like the Kumbh Mela are emphasized by many (Cohn and Marriott 1958, Bharati 1970, Bhardwaj 1973, Preston 1980).

When we recall that 72% of the population in Karchana are illiterates (reference year 1985-86. The figure is close to the average picture of village India), that the majority of them do not yet have access to TV or even radio, but that many of them visit centres like Prayag Raj and the Kumbh Mela, then it seems reasonable to conclude that pilgrimage is one of the more important sources of Great Traditional knowledge. The information received, the experiences undergone, the things seen and done during a pilgrimage to a holy place like Prayag Raj at the Kumbh Mela, will have impact upon the making and re-making of the world view and attitudes of pilgrims. The members of the grown up and older generations will particularly reinforce and revitalize their cultural competence and belief while the younger generations will acquire new knowledge. What the pilgrims, young and old, have experienced during pilgrimage will have significance for their life back home and be disseminated to others.

Participants

Men and women, towns people and villagers, seem to be equally represented. The pilgrims arrive from every part of India. But the majority of the people are from Uttar Pradesh, Bihar and Madhya Pradesh. My data from Karchana village, 20 kms away from Prayag Raj, reveal that most of the higher castes (Brahmin, Kshatriya, Vaishya) and quite a few from the Shudras, visit the Mela during the festival period. But few Avarnas visited the Kumbh Mela. The preponderance of higher caste pilgrims is probably, as Bhardwaj concludes, due to the correlation between the status of the place of pilgrimage and the caste composition of the pilgrims (1973:175). Prayag Raj is a Pan-Indian, Sanskritic and Great Traditional place of pilgrimage. Hence, a preponderance of higher castes is to be expected.

Besides the householders visiting Prayag Raj as lay pilgrims, we also find many Brahmin ritualists and renouncers - sadhus. The *panda* is a low ranking Brahmin priest serving at places of pilgrimage. The panda is supposed to help the pilgrims to perform the traditional rites associated with the place. In return for his services, the panda receives gift/fee (dakshina) from his clients. I was told that around 1400 families of pandas are living in Allahabad. Around 300 of them are registered pandas working as priests in the Mela area. The *sadhu* (lit. 'doer of good acts') is a person who adopts an ascetic way of life, as prescribed by his *Guru* and the subsect to which he belongs. A sadhu is furthermore, in principle, pledged to the performance of social good as part of his obligations. A sadhu is thus a person who leaves his family and home to become, as Dumont has phrased it (1960) a renouncer - a man-outside-the-world. He wears sectarian marks, drawn on his forehead with sandal wood paste or sacred ashes. Most sadhus have very long hair and beard, but some are completely shaven. Sadhus should not wear sewn clothes and the *Naga* sadhus of all denominations should not wear any clothes at all. Sadhus should, furthermore, perform socio-religious duties, like observing fasts, food taboos and other ascetic or self-purificatory acts pertaining to their sect. He should worship daily, listen to religious discourses, study the scriptures, visit centres of pilgrimage and perform social service. A sadhu is usually dependent on the earnings of others, either through begging or donations from disciples or other lay people. Sadhus may become leaders of sects - i.e. sect Gurus. The believers perceive the sect Gurus more or less as Godlike people.[4] Gurus of repute are often charismatic and powerful people, in command of considerable wealth and not infrequently wielding significant political influence. People in important positions might be among their followers.

A cultural logic

The cultural competence needed, reinforced and developed when pilgrims visit a pilgrimage centre like Prayag Raj is rooted in the cultural Logic of Karma. The Logic of Karma is drawn upon by the pilgrims as a kind of 'cultural lingua franca' by means of which Hindus throughout India may understand each others. The Logic of Karma is also drawn upon as a cultural repertoire - a set of interpretative schemes, values and ideas - in order for them to understand and orient themselves in a place like Prayag Raj. It is within the context of the Logic of Karma that the interpretative schemes of 'merit accumulation', 'cause and effect' and 'karma annihilation' should be understood.

Merit accumulation

Rich and poor, high caste and low caste, men and women, young and old, go through serious hardships to undertake a pilgrimage to Prayag Raj.

Long journeys of three to four days in overcrowded trains and buses are not uncommon. Only the more wealthy pilgrims can afford a proper shelter, and the nights are cold in January. Pilgrims fear robbers and accidents. For the poor people, a pilgrimage to Prayag Raj is also expensive. Pilgrims go through such hardships *because* they feel a great desire to reach Prayag Raj during the Kumbh Mela. Why?

The reasons given by the pilgrims for undertaking the pilgrimage to Prayag Raj and the Kumbh Mela is not pragmatic but transcendental. Pilgrims inform that they are *accumulating merit - good karma* - to improve their rebirth chances. They ultimately believe that bathing in the holy rivers at the appropriate time and place will finally clean away their sins and secure direct passage to heaven.[5] The pandas (river priests) guide the pilgrims in merit-accumulation by imposing on them the actions described in the *Prayag Mahatmya* - the Puranic text on Prayag Raj. Among other things, this text promises release from 10 000 rebirths for every hair above the chin, which finds its rest in the Ganges. Naturally, a pilgrim ought therefore to cut his/her hair and throw it in the Ganges.

Cause and effect

A walk around the Mela area is an adventure in itself. Pilgrims will visit their favoured *ashram* (abode, sect) and have a *darshan* (view) of the sect Guru. They will listen to the sermons on morality, the value of a religious life, the meaning of *Ramacharitmanas*, Bhagavad-Gita, yoga and so on. They will see the epic dramas (*Ram Lila* and *Ras Lila*) organized by the various sects everywhere in the Mela. Many pilgrims also regard a visit to the Kumbh Mela as an opportunity for some pleasure. Exhibitions range from displays of deformed animals and human beings to modern trade fairs and fun fairs. Most pilgrims will witness elaborate Vedic forms of sacrifices performed in the camps of the more orthodox sects. They can observe several hundred religious specialists placed around the fire chanting continuously ancient Sanskrit mantras from the Vedas night and day for the whole period of the Kumbh Mela. At specific rhythmic intervals, ritual items are thrown into the fire - tons of it during the whole period.[6] The pilgrims are told that sacrifices are performed to effect certain specific ends - a mode of thinking which is further reinforced when observing the sadhus and their performances of asceticism.

If the pilgrims are present in the Mela on one of the three big days of bathing processions, they will be able to see thousands of sadhus, also females, some in ochre clothes, some in white, some naked, some riding on elephants and horses, and others again sitting on cars, all of them proceeding towards the Sangam, where the sadhus will take their bath in the holy river.[7] Many pilgrims can see the sadhus demonstrate the *sidhis*, the physical and mental powers which they claim to have obtained through yoga and ascetic disciplines. They might also see sadhus demonstrating their control over sexual energy. I have seen a sadhu pull a bus by tying a rope to his penis. I have heard of another sadhu who managed to lift a stone of 100 kgs. with his erect penis. Other sadhus indulge in extreme forms of asceticism, such as keeping an arm upright or always standing for a certain number of years. I found sadhus who had been standing on one leg for the past eight years and others who had been holding one arm upright for more than ten years. I also found sadhus who never speak (*mauni*). Other modes of asceticism, like the 'heat of the five fires', (see Manu 6.23) where the sadhu sits underneath the sun on the ground with burning cowdung around, are common to find in the Melas at Prayag Raj. This type of asceticism constitutes an important part of the initiation requirements for certain sects. It should be practised every day during the hours before and after midday from the spring festival in January to the festival of *Ganga Dashahara*, on the arrival of the monsoon in June. The heat of the sun and the burning cowdung is incredible, not least in the month of April, May and June.[8] One can also observe humorous sadhus. Coconut Baba was always chanting *bhajans* and *kirtan*s (religious songs, melodious repetitions of God's name) while running around with a coconut, glass and brass pot on his head. Because of the blessings of his Guru, the objects would always stay safely on his head, Coconut Baba said. Other sadhus, like Deoraha Baba, is believed to be extremely old. He claims to have disciples in the Himalayas who are more than 2000 years old. Deoraha Baba stated that since he has merged with the Almighty, he has no specific age.

In response to my question 'why, sadhus first answered *tapas* (lit. 'heat') and will-power.[9] They further stated that this tapas or will-power could be used to promote certain concrete ends, such as world peace. Most lay Hindus are familiar with the concept of tapas and the ascetic/yogic disciplines applied to produce it. They have, since childhood, heard the stories of the great sages who practised asceticism and produced tapas until they conquered even the Gods. One such legend is the story of the sage Bhagiratha who was standing on one leg with one arm upright for thousands of years until he managed to force the Gods to release the Ganges from heaven.

The demonstration of the Vedic sacrifices and the *sidhis* - the powers of the sadhus - contribute to the making and remaking of the 'cause and effect' interpretative scheme. This interpretative scheme informs pilgrims that actions like sacrifice and asceticism, if correctly performed, instigate a causal chain (*karmabandha*) which can effect the desired ends of its performers. The moral dimension of the 'cause and effect' interpretative scheme is taught to the pilgrims during the many sermons held by the reputed Gurus and also through the dramatizations of the epic scriptures. The pilgrims are informed that all people, sooner or later, must reap the consequences of their past actions, whether performed in this or in previous lives.

The marks of sin

The pilgrims are further reminded of the *karmalogical* constitution of reality when they observe the unending lines of beggars sitting along the roadside towards the bathing places, in front of the Hanuman temple and the fort of Akbar the emperor. The sights, the smells, the sounds, the sufferings, the colours, the songs of despair, the blind mens' hymns, in between snake charmers and begging ascetics, all these impressions of human destinies constitute a kind of *karmic phenomenology* - a display of the results of past actions. Pilgrims I asked testified to this interpretation: 'They are suffering the results of their past actions' was an answer they often gave me.[10]

Karma annihilation

Many pilgrims will have the chance to observe demonstrations of *samadhi* (the highest yogic state of mind and body control, a mystical state of bliss).[11] During such demonstrations, sadhus are buried some meters down in the ground and left (so they say) without food, water and air for long periods, for example one week. A demonstration of samadhi proves to the pilgrims that the sadhu has reduced his mental and bodily activities to a minimum. In samadhi, the adept is supposed to have complete mastery over his bodily functions like breathing and eating. He is believed to be beyond the world of dualities like hot/cold, hungry/satisfied, in-breathing/out-breathing, constantly dwelling in the supreme Atman/Brahman. A demonstration of samadhi proves that the sadhu has reached, or is very close to reaching Moksha. It also, along with the other extreme examples mentioned above, serves as a 'miracle' which demonstrates the truth of Hinduism and the efficacy of its many magic/religious techniques. Demonstrations of hard asceticism and samadhi remind the lay Hindu that men can become Gods or even more than Gods - the Absolute itself.

Moksha

Most pilgrims have heard about *Moksha*. But they are unclear about the deeper meaning of the term. They usually confuse Moksha with more common forms of soteriologies like paradise in heaven. A pilgrimage to Kumbh Mela can give them a more subtle understanding of Moksha - the highest value of Hinduism. They can listen to sermons on spiritual techniques like yoga and meditation given by the reputed Gurus of the different sects. Most of these sermons rely on the Yoga Sutra of Patanjali and the Vedanta standard. The pilgrims are informed that Moksha is not a matter of producing good karma (merit accumulation), but its opposite;

'karma annihilation'. The pilgrims are also informed about the three steps towards this ultimate goal of yoga:

The first step is about correct behaviour, correct thinking and the control of the senses (Gita 2.48, Yoga Sutra 2.30,32). The annihilation of the gross kind of karmas produced by ordinary moral actions is said to be the purpose behind these practices. The next step is about disciplines like bodily postures and breathing exercises. The annihilation of more subtle forms of karma to reach a detachment (*vairagya*, *pratyahara*) from external objects and allow the mind 'to follow its own nature', is said to be the purpose of such exercises. The last step is concerned with the practice of meditation in order to annihilate mental karma, the most subtle form of karma. When all kinds of karma production have stopped, the adept has indeed reached Moksha. The pilgrims will also be informed that yoga and meditation is a difficult way to religious liberation. They will be made to understand that the soteriology of Hinduism has a *variety* of ways and techniques to offer depending on the personal and spiritual qualities and abilities of the believers.

A more easy and common way is to reduce the production of new bad karma and to try to burn up the demerit - the accumulated bad karmas of the past. These simpler methods of progressive karma annihilation, such as the ritual bath, are easily observed in Prayag Raj. Pilgrims and specialists alike utter the following words when they take their bath:

Ganga maya mere pap haro - Take away my sins, mother Ganges.

Sin (*pap*) is another word for bad karma. Being cleaned by Mother Ganga is thus a form of karma annihilation. The entrance sign board to the centre of the Mela area is even more promising when it reads:

Ganga tava darshanath muktih - By seeing You, Ganges, one obtains liberation.

By seeing the holy river, even complete karma annihilation and Moksha is promised.

In many cases, the purpose behind the extreme forms of asceticism is also a form of progressive karma annihilation. In explaining their ascetic practices, some sadhus told me that they wanted to expiate sins, karma produced in earlier lives. As the Laws of Manu XI.54 states:

Penances, therefore must always be performed for the sake of purification, because those whose sins have not been expiated, are born again with disgraceful marks.

THE SOCIAL DISTRIBUTION OF THE LOGIC OF KARMA

I collected the following data during my fieldwork 1985-86 in Karchana village Eastern Uttar Pradesh. I made a survey to inquire into the distribution of the basic concepts of the Logic of Karma (cf. Jaer 1995). Most of the concepts surveyed were known by 92% to 100% of the persons asked. The difference between high castes and low castes was marginal.

Caste	Answers	Karma	Dharma	Atma	Samsara	Maya	Sh./Ash.	Sattvik	Rajasik	Tamasik	Moksha	Average
BRAHMINS	8 :	100%	100%	100%	100%	100%	100%	100%	100%	100%	100%	100%
KSHATRIYA	8 :	100%	100%	100%	100%	100%	100%	100%	100%	100%	100%	100%
VAISHYA	28 :	100%	100%	100%	71%	100%	100%	54%	46%	89%	86%	85%
service	:											
traders	7 :	100%	100%	100%	71%	100%	100%	71%	71%	100%	86%	90%
agriculturalists	21 :	100%	100%	100%	71%	100%	100%	48%	38%	86%	86%	83%
HIGH CASTES	44 :	100%	100%	100%	82%	100%	100%	70%	66%	93%	91%	90%
SHUDRA	14 :	100%	100%	100%	64%	100%	100%	64%	57%	79%	79%	84%
traders	7 :	100%	100%	100%	57%	100%	100%	43%	43%	71%	71%	79%
artisans/menials	7 :	100%	100%	100%	71%	100%	100%	86%	71%	86%	86%	90%
AVARNA	25 :	92%	100%	100%	80%	88%	88%	32%	36%	52%	60%	73%
labourers	25 :	92%	100%	100%	80%	88%	88%	32%	36%	52%	60%	73%
artisan/menials	:											
LOW CASTES	39:	95%	100%	100%	74%	92%	92%	44%	44%	62%	67%	77%

The conclusion to be drawn from this survey is quite clear; the knowledge of the concepts of the Logic of Karma is widely distributed in Karchana. It is more prevalent among the higher castes than among the lower, but the differences are marginal. The Logic of Karma is not in any way an esoteric doctrine, but a basic part of folk Hinduism.

Some examples of the lay man's knowledge

I asked various villagers how they understood some of the concepts above:

Shuddh/Ashuddh (pure/impure): A *Chamar* woman with six children stated that the work of cobblers, midwives (both belong to the Chamars), sweepers and washermen and the pig owned by the *Pasis* (pig raisers) were ashuddh. Everybody else, she stated, were equal. A Chamar man, the oldest in the community, stated that Brahmins are ashuddh. He explained his opinion as follows:

> Good actions (karma) are shuddh, bad actions ashuddh. The caste system is made by Brahmins. The caste system is bad. Hence, Brahmins are ashuddh. But (he hastened to add) *Pandit* work (the priestly work) is shuddh. If one cuts the skin, the blood is the same for higher castes as for lower castes.

Among the foodstuffs, many Chamars agree that items like meat, fish and eggs are ashuddh. But very few of them are vegetarians by conviction. They pay less attention to the ranking of foodstuffs as the Brahmin model suggests.

Guna (quality - substance): *Sattva* (pure), *rajas* (pure/impure) and *tamas* (impure) are often used by villagers more or less as synonyms of shuddh/ashuddh. A Brahmin informant described a sattvic life as follows:

> Everything should be done regularly, rhythmically - get up early, then look into you palms, then kiss and touch the earth, say good morning to Mother earth, then off to the latrine for making the body fresh. The holy thread must be wrapped around the ear. One should not speak to anyone. Then bath, worship, food and see what is your business. Then one should have a sattvic lunch: rice, lentils, *chapatti* (bread) and green vegetables, purified *ghee* (butter), milk and other milk products, without oil or spices. Sattvic life, every day the same, no change.

Rajasic persons were described by the same Brahmin as those who:

> save *Dharm*, Brahmins and cows. Rajasic persons should be well fed and well clothed and they should keep their promise. By caste, Thakurs are rajasic, but by actions, they are tamasic.

Karma: Villagers I spoke to differentiated karma from *kam*. All modern kinds of work for money were termed *kam*. But the work of the Brahmin priest was defined as karma and the money he receives for his services is said to be *dakshina* (compensation, gift for ritual services). Services rendered in the traditional way by other jajmani clients are also regarded as karma. If, for example, a barber arrives in his patron's house to perform his jajmani obligations, then he is performing karma. If, however, he is doing his modernized saloon business in the market, the barber is stated to do his kam. Likewise, the work of agricultural labourers, of bureaucrats and other workers, that is, the great majority of activities performed for the daily living by people in Karchana, are defined as kam.

Moksha (liberation): A Brahmin told me the following about Moksha:

> If we are doing here good actions, not giving troubles to others, doing good worship, not lying, then it can be possible we can get Moksha. Moksha means that you have not to come back to this world which is only *maya* - doing this thing and that thing,[12] buying this thing and that thing. In the other world you will only think about religious things. Thinking about religious things gives at least 1 *lakh* (100 000) more pleasure than thinking about worldly things. Moksha is very difficult. If you will make your aim from beginning to end, then you will get Moksha. Very few, perhaps 5%, get Moksha. The old Brahmin 'Mr. Misra' will get, but I am not sure because I am not able to see for myself. It is only my idea.

A Thakur had a similar version:

> *Moksha* is a very great thing, only possible in India. Moksha is that we are never to come back again to this world. In this world, nobody is happy, neither rich nor poor. Moksha; coming and going is finished. Moksha is somehow in another world, in heaven you can say. If a person has got Moksha, everything depends upon his choice. If he likes, he can come to this world as a visitor. Somehow, one person got Moksha here in this village: 'Mr. Singh', because he was killed in battle. I do not believe that 'Mr. Misra' will get Moksha. He has some knowledge, but no *sadhana* (religious discipline). May be he has 30% chance. In *Kali yug* (iron age) very few get Moksha. But Deoraha Baba will get Moksha. It is easier to get Moksha as a sadhu, but if a person really performs his duties as a householder, he can also get Moksha. When a person has got Moksha, he is satisfied in every way. No desire, no wants, no requirements. Moksha person feels 24 hours as we are doing just before discharge in fuck. People naturally try for Moksha. My own first desire is Moksha.

Conversations with lower castes regarding Moksha did not differ much from what we have heard here. They were less able to formulate their perceptions and they did, to a greater extent than the Brahmin and Thakur above, perceive Moksha as a kind of heaven. Heaven and hell are the main soteriological terms among the *Avarnas.*

I asked the villagers whether they believed in the law of karma - whether, as I phrased my question, they believed that a person is born in a high caste because of good actions in previous life and vice versa, whether a person was born in a low caste because of bad actions. 80% of the high castes and 75% of the low castes answered yes. The Shudras proved to be the strongest believers. 90% of them answered in the positive. The agricultural labourers (Avarnas) had the greatest number of non-believers. 34% of them answered that they did not believe in the law of karma.

Interpretative variations

It is but obvious that the villagers' interpretations of the concepts above vary: The Chamar woman, for example, conceived those castes ranked below the Chamars as ashuddh, and the others as equally shuddh. She thus made the hierarchical axes shuddh/ashuddh relevant with respect to those below her, while she rejected it with respect to those above. This would certainly not be the mode of application of shuddh/ashuddh among the higher castes.[13] Still, the Chamar woman exhibits a mode of thinking deeply infused with the Logic of Karma - the cultural logic which serves as the dominant ideology of Karchana lifeworld.

A CRITICAL PERSPECTIVE ON LOUIS DUMONT'S COMPARATIVE ANTHROPOLOGY

Dumont's theoretical position is derived from French structuralism (Dumont 1970:39) which is usually equated with Levi-Strauss.[14] One of the major sources which structuralism has drawn upon is the work of Durkheim who asserts the *priority* of the collective and universal over the individual and contingent; an emphasis on the relational at the expense of the element (Giddens 1979:18-19). Dumont inherits this position and states that there are two alternatives in contemporary sociology; Individualism, which he conceives as a superficial illusion, or Holism which he regards as the correct approach. Commenting on this unidimensional approach to social reality, Giddens concludes as follows;

...Durkheim's...stress upon the constraining nature of social facts leaves no place for the social actor as a conscious willing agent. (Giddens 1971:218)

And with respect to Levi-Strauss:

Levi-Strauss brackets history,..., in much the same way as he does the thinking and acting subject. (Giddens 1979:21)[15]

It is thus no surprise that the structuralism of Dumont should deny sociological relevance to 'individual' and 'action' in general (Dumont 1970:9) and karma (action) and kartri (individual agent) in the Hindu context (cf. Dumont 1960). Is Dumont's unidimensionalism a fertile theoretical entry point for the understanding of Hindu ideology?

The structural (Dharma) approach

Homo Hierarchicus (Dumont 1970) is a fascinating work not least because of Dumont's thought provoking comparative perspectives. The '*homo hierarchicus*' of Hindu society throws light upon the Western '*homo equalis*' which is indeed a very different cultural personality type. Thereby the context is given. On the one side is hierarchy, on the other equality. From this point of departure, Dumont arrives deductively at the following conclusions: For Hindu society, that 'on the level of life in the world, *the individual is not*' (Dumont 1960:42, my italics.). And for the modern West, that 'Ontologically, *society no longer exists*' (Dumont 1970a:9, my italics.). In spite of these propositions, Dumont still uses the 'individual' as the medium of translation and comparison between Hinduism and Capitalism. Two questions appear in this connection: a) What does Dumont mean by the 'individual'? And b) how does Dumont intend to locate the notion of the individual in the Hindu context?

Dumont distinguishes clearly between a concept of the individual as 'the empirical agent, present in the society' and a concept of the individual as 'the rational being and normative subject of institutions' (Dumont 1970:9). The latter definition is intimately linked to modern Western values of equality and liberty. Of this peculiar modern individual, he gives the following description: 'He is the measures of all things.... What is still called 'society' is the means, the life of each man is the end' (ibid.). He concludes that for sociological comparison between India and the West, only the individual in the second sense of the term linked to the values of equality and liberty, should be used.

Where in the Hindu context shall we be able to find an *idea* (and Dumont is first and foremost preoccupied with ideas and values) of the individual which resembles the definition given above? Following Dumont, we find that caste Hindus live as if unconscious of their own individuality. The caste Hindu is, so to say, dissolved in the collective consciousness. He has no substance, no reality in thought: 'To say that the world of caste is a world of relations is to say that the particular caste, the particular *man* have no *substance*: they exist empirically, but they have no reality in *thought*, no Being' (Dumont 1960:42, my italics). A caste Hindu, following Dumont, is merely a sum of relations and not a cultural personality comparable to the modern idea of the individual. Such a personality is, however, identified by Dumont outside caste society in what Dumont labels 'the individual-outside-the-world' - the renouncer (sadhu, sannyasi)) (1970:185). The renouncer is to be regarded as an individual since, following Dumont, Hinduism conceives the renouncer as a substance which appears real in thought.[16]

Undoubtedly, certain similarities exist between Dumont's picture of the renouncer and Marx's famous 'Robinson' metaphor of the modern individual. Robinson Crusoe lived on a deserted island with Friday, far outside the known world of those days. Following Marx's metaphor and the Robinsonadic way of thinking, the modern individual believes himself to be an independent and self-sufficient being, detached from the chain of social relations (Marx 1887:81). Dumont's identification of the renouncer as the individual of Hinduism is linked to this *seeming* fact that both the renouncer and the modern Western individual appear to be detached from the chain of social relations.

I cannot agree with Dumont on this issue. Dumont is confusing *different* levels of reality by comparing ideas and values with social relations. While the modern individual is seen explicitly in the context of his individualistic ideas and values, the renouncer is defined with reference to his structural position outside the world.

However, Dumont does ask himself how the renouncer may '...develop an independent way of thinking, an individualistic way of thinking? The answer is simply: that this occurs must simply be stated as a fact' (1970:185). Without documentation of any sort Dumont states in one place that 'The individual-outside-the-world has become to himself his own end as in the social theory of the West.' (Dumont 1970a:185). This description of the renouncer is fallacious. In opposition to the individualistic individual trying to increase his self and his property, often at the expense of society at large, the renouncer is a mystic, striving to decrease his self and his property towards the final extinction of individuality in the Absolute. It is indeed the individual as his own end which the renouncer should struggle to conquer.[17] It is difficult to find any description of the values or ideas of the renouncers which resembles those used by Dumont when he spells out the characteristics of the modern Western individual. Furthermore, Dumont does not present any data, either from written sources or from informants, which can help us to understand the ideas and values of the renouncer. This indeed is in contrast to other works of Dumont on the history of the 'individual' in the Western context (see Dumont 1965, 1971, 1977).

For convenience, let me sum up the main elements in Dumont's comparative approach. The idea of the modern individual, defined through the values of liberty and equality, is the medium of translation and comparison. In the Hindu context, the renouncer is identified as an individual comparable to the modern Western notion of the individual. And because the renouncer returns to the world of caste through begging, preaching and through the sect (Dumont 1970:185), a 'bridgehead' is established through which it is possible to translate and understand the world of caste. So far, these are Dumont's main arguments. Let me now proceed to present my own position in a close dialogue with Dumont.

The dual approach of action/structure (Karma/Dharma)

The individual must be defined in terms of being an agent and not as a value, as suggested by Dumont. Only then will it be possible to distinguish between two fundamental components in social analysis, viz., the collective and the individual. Furthermore, our definition of the individual as an agent is not only necessary for theoretical reasons, it is also suitable from the perspective of the Hindu tradition, where concepts such as 'individual', 'agency', 'action', 'personal identity', 'responsibility', etc., are important. Individuals so defined, do have different attitudes, values and ideas. They are *informed* by different ideologies.[18] Modern Western society is dominated by an individualistic and egalitarian ideology while traditional Hindu society is dominated by a holistic and hierarchical ideology. In his description of the structuring principles of these ideologies, Dumont states:

> Hindu society is organized around the concept of Dharma [the whole, the collective] in a way roughly similar to modern society around that of the individual. (Dumont 1971:140).

Dumont's *unidimensional* approach comes clearly to light in this quotation, where Hindu society is portrayed as organized solely around the concept of the whole (Dharma)[19] while modern society is organized around the concept of the individual. I have throughout this book maintained the necessity of a *dual* or better *dialectical* approach based on the concepts of action/structure and karma/Dharma. Let me again have a closer look at the karma/Dharma *configuration* of Hindu society.

Morality is a constitutive quality of both caste Hindus and modern man.[20] Caste Hindus discriminate between what they believe to be right or wrong. They experience punishment and reward in this world at the hands of their fellow beings and they expect punishment and reward in the life hereafter on account of their belief in universal retribution. This karmic ideology based on the two structuring principles karma and Dharma, is particularly powerful in the legitimation of caste society. Karmic ideology informs its believers that from earlier lives the soul is imprinted with a karmic residue - a moral account - which is the cause of the destiny of the lives of men. Everyone is conceived to be responsible for his own prescribed status. Birth in a specific caste group, be it high or low in the hierarchy, is not a random occurrence, but believed to be the outcome of one's karmic residue. Karmic ideology not only *justifies* a person's socio-existential conditions, but (like other ideologies) it also offers a cultural repertoire of answers to *existential* questions which may give hope and meaning to its believers. By monitoring his actions, thoughts and lifestyle in accordance with his svadharma, the individual will be able to create karmic 'capital' which will lead to a better destiny in a later life.

The patterns of actions, ideas and values held by the renouncer are also, in my opinion, more productively interpreted in a karmalogical perspective, i.e., a logic founded on the two structuring principles of karma and Dharma. The ideal renouncer strives towards a total solution of the quest for meaning. He seeks to eradicate the causality of actions and liberate himself from the wheel of existence.

The institution of the renouncer offers the most extensive solution to the karmic problem, involving, among other things, the withdrawal from the 'world' and from the liabilities of caste society. The renouncer seeks to live a life of asceticism and meditation, striving for final liberation. Both caste Hindus and renouncers conceive the quest for meaning within the context of a karmic ideology, which indeed is a *sine qua non* for the native rationalisations of the ideals and values of the renouncers.

If we aspire to compare the individualistic ideology of Capitalism with the holistic ideology of Hinduism, we should neither follow Dumont nor draw upon the concept of the individual as a medium of translation and comparison. Due to its importance in our modern theoretical tradition, as well as in the Hindu tradition, the concept of 'action' will prove a better starting point. The concept of action is linked to the concept of structure, as karma implies Dharma in the Hindu context. Action/structure as a theoretical framework, and karma/Dharma as the concrete structuring principles in the Hindu context, provide a better basis for an interpretation of Hindu society and its ideology.

It is noteworthy that Dumont, in his many works on Hindu ideology, scarcely mentions the concepts of karma and reincarnation. It is indeed challenging that Dumont, in a polemic with Weber, concludes that these beliefs only belong to the speculative tradition of Hinduism (Dumont 1960:448).[21] I disagree with Dumont. A majority of monographs from village India stress the importance of the belief in karma and reincarnation at the popular level. My own data from Karchana village demonstrate that many villagers are conceptually well acquainted with karma and reincarnation and that the great majority believe in them.[22] Indologists, historians of religion and others also stress the fundamental importance of these concepts in the textual tradition.[23] Dumont has overlooked the significance of karmic ideology because of his unidimensional model which does not maintain the distinction between individual/society and action/structure. As we have seen in this book, karmic ideology is indeed constituted through the relationship between karma and Dharma.

Another problem which follows from the unidimensional approach of Dumont and structuralism in general, is that this mode of thinking makes it theoretically difficult to distinguish between a collective system of ideas and the individuals and groups who are the social carriers of these ideas. The problems of socialization, internalization, acculturation, Sanskritization and Westernization etc. - diachronic processes - do not appear to be in the focus of interest. Dumont recognizes the question of acculturation between the Great and the little traditions. But he does not pursue them (Dumont 1971:141). Nor does he seem to acknowledge that interpretation - hermeneutical activity - is an integral part of social life itself. When Dumont states that Hindu society is organized around the concept of Dharma, he seems to overlook the fact that Hindu traditions have many philosophical and juridical schools which interpret Dharma differently. What Dharma is for South Indian Brahmins might be Adharma (not Dharma) for the northerners. Thus Dharma which is believed to be the eternal laws of God, is necessarily given a subjective, individual imprint (see Lingat 1973:170).

Dumont's theoretical model is heavily influenced by Durkheim, Mauss, Radcliffe-Brown[24] and Levi-Strauss (Galey 1982), who all stress the collective and objective at the expense of the individual and subjective. Like functionalists and structuralists generally, Dumont lacks a theory of the subject and of the relationship between action and structure.

Not withstanding the foregoing criticism, I would like to emphasize the importance of Dumont's works for an understanding of Hindu civilisation. I endorse Dumont's endeavors to unite the Indological and the anthropological approach to the study of Indian culture (Dumont & Pocock 1957). His idea of comparison between homo equalis and homo hierarchicus is most interesting.

NOTES ON THE ETHNO-SOCIOLOGY OF MCKIM MARRIOTT AND INDEN

The non-dualistic ethno-sociology of Marriott and Inden (Marriott 1976) proceeds from the indigenous assumption that the Hindus do not *separate* agent from action:

> ...those who transact as well as what and how they transact are thought to be inseparable 'code-substance' or 'substance-code.' (Marriott 1976:110)

or as formulated by Marriott in 1989:

> The 'means-end' and 'actor-action' dichotomies ....are overridden by
> Hindu notions of *karma*, according to which ends inhere in means
> and actors are products of actions...(Marriott 1989).

Following Marriott and Inden, the identification of agent and action and
means-end is an outcome of the systematic monism which they maintain
pervades Hindu thinking in general (Marriott & Inden 1977, Marriott
1976).

But the assumption of a pervasive monism ignores the dualistic systems
of Hinduism - the *Samkhya/Yoga* - which heavily influenced the Manu/
Gita. The ethno-sociological perspective also seems to confuse two orders
of reality. The inseparability of the agent from action and means from
ends is a *normative ideal* - a value - which the Hindus easily see as different
from the karmic/samsaric world built upon the reverse assumption than
the one advanced by Marriott: That is, as long as there is karma production,
as long as the karmic problem exists, the actor has *not reached identity* with
his actions nor means with ends. The statement, furthermore, that karma
means that 'actors are products of actions', is again only partly correct.
Karma has various connotations. Actors are the products of their past karma.
But if the actions performed in this life deviates from the person's *svadharma* said to be the appropriate action code for the person's *svabhava* -
the person's self-produced substance, his karmic ballast - then his present
karma will produce a karmic residue which will *influence* the person's future
substance (svabhava) and code (svadharma) and accordingly his future
actions.

Finally, the ethno-sociological monism of Marriott and Inden involves
conceptual problems. How do we maintain the meaning of the concept of
action in opposition to events if, as they say, agent and action are identical?
If the observable datum is a product of 'codes of actions, codes of conduct
(Dharma) naturally embodied in actors' (Marriott op.cit.:109) are we then
observing events or actions? As stated by Bauman in his article 'On the
philosophical status of Ethnomethodology' (1972): 'Thus, again,
ethnomethodology shares some of the most pernicious difficulties of early
existentialism ... , existentialism denied itself the right and ability to discern
the «right» choice from the «wrong»; ... ' (Bauman 1972: 17) Following
their monistic ethnosociology, Marriott and Inden do not distinguish
between norms, values, interpretative schemes, parameters and the agents
who are *informed* by these. They theoretically seem to deny the actors the
possibility of *interpreting* the codes. They seem to perceive codes more in
the information-technological sense and thereby leave the agents with no
possibility for choice nor any reflexive monitoring of actions. The out-

come is that Marriott and Inden, as Bauman suggests, seem to deny the actors the possibility of discerning right from wrong. But Hindus do indeed speak about good actions and bad actions. How can they do that if they also do not discriminate between agent and action, if the actors' behaviour were a direct product of the action-codes?

Another consequence of Marriott and Inden's ethnosociology is a lack of discrimination between action types. Marriott interprets Indian thinking as transactional (1976:109) For example, he regards the meditative karma type of the renouncer as belonging to the transactional sphere (Marriott 1976:132). What is missed by Marriott in this regard is that he has taken an *external* view. He has overlooked the inner logic (Potter 1980:205) - the subjective perspective - of the renouncer.

NOTES TO APPENDICES

1. I performed fieldwork in Prayag Raj during the Kumbh Mela of 1989. I am grateful for the financial support from the Nordic Institute of Asian studies towards this fieldwork. I have also visited the Kumbh Melas of Ujjain 1980 and Hardwar 1986 in addition to the Magh Mela of Prayag Raj 1980, 1985 and 1986. My data from participant observation in all these Melas provide the wider background for the presentation of Prayag Raj and the Kumbh Mela 1989. My fieldwork in 1985 - 86 in Karchana village 20 kms away from Prayag Raj is another important source of data on pilgrimage as seen from the perspective of the villagers there.

Seen from the trains running up and down between Delhi and Calcutta, Karchana does not seem to differ from the 'innumberable' other villages of the Ganges plains. But the villagers themselves, particularly those belonging to the dominant caste (Kshatriya), will boast that their village is something special. They will stress that their village was a land-holder, revenue collecting village rather famous in the area because of its brave forefathers. They will also point to the fact that their village is presently a village centre with a fast growing commercial arena and many public institutions like Development Block, schools, police station and *tahsil* (sub-district) headquarter. But the village, with its rigid and complex social hierarchy, its strong traditions and economic backwardness, is still a typical Eastern Uttar Pradesh village (Jaer 1995). Karchana is a multicaste village with a hierarchy of 29 jatis (subcastes) and a population of around 4000 persons. A majority of the community (72%) reported to receive the major part of their income (in cash and in kind) from agriculture.

2. *Sarada Devi* is one of the nine sister Goddesses of the Hindu pantheon and a very important Goddess in Karchana. Sarada Devi is the *kul Devi* (clan Goddess) of the Thakurs. See Gatwood 1985, *Devi and the Spouse Goddess - Women, Sexuality, and Marriage in India*, Manohar, New Delhi.

3. Bhardwaj's findings can be summarized briefly: As one moves along the continuum from a local to a pan-Hindu place of pilgrimage, pilgrims are increasingly drawn from the higher castes and have increasingly more transcendental reasons for going on pilgrimage. The observations I have made from the holy places mentioned above seem to fit Bhardwaj's findings quite well. On the 'Transcendental and Pragmatic Aspects of Religion' in general, see Mandelbaum 1966.

4. See Gold 1987, *The Lord as Guru*, Oxford University Press, New York.

5. I met some visitors to the Mela who stated that Mother Ganga was no longer there, that the river was merely a river, because the Goddess had returned to heaven. This was to be expected, they stated, because the river was destroyed by human pollution.

6. These sacrifices are survivals of the forms of karma (ritual action) recommended by the most ancient parts of the holy scriptures of the Hindus, i.e. the Vedas and the Brahmanas (1000 B.C.).

7. It is a matter of the greatest importance for the sadhu sects to reach the holy river for the sacred bath at the most auspicious time and place. The formal procession of ascetics at a Kumbh Mela was, and still is, an occasion for conflicts and even battles. There are reports, for example, from the Kumbh Mela at Hardwar in A.D. 1796, when two million people competed for the sacred bath. The reports have it that battles between various sects killed more than 5000 people. The issue of conflict was the order of priority of the different sects in the bathing processions (Ghurye 1964:111). Conflicts between sects were also reported during this Kumbh Mela at Prayag in 1989. Weapons were drawn, but the police managed to pacify the opposing groups before any serious accidents occurred.

8. *Tapas*, the creation of heat, is a cross-cultural phenomenon which can be observed among medicine men, shamans, fakirs and Yogis. On this issue, see Eliade 1973.

9. On *tapas* and Yoga, see Eliade 1973, *Yoga: Immortality and Freedom*, Bollingen Series, Princeton.

10. As the holy books state: 'Thus in consequence of a remnant of (the guilt of former) crimes, are born idiots, dumb, blind, deaf, and deformed men who are all despised by the virtuous.' (Manu 11.53) 'Thus they become men and women oozing with leprosy, born blind, infested with grievous maladies, and bearing the marks of sin.' (Garuda Purana 4.64)

11. On *samadhi*, see Eliade 1973 and also Patanjali's *Yoga Sutra*.

12. As it is stated in the *Maitri Upanishad* 2.7: '....(apparently)....a doer in the unreal -....'

13. It is uncommon among the higher castes where the attributional criteria of rank are more clear cut. When I told a Thakur that many lower castes ranked his own Thakur caste as no. 1 in the hierarchy, he just answered that they did not have sufficient knowledge. Naturally, the Brahmins are superior, he stated.

14. Levi-Strauss accepts the label *transcendental materialist* which Sartre put on him (Strauss 1966:246). The label 'transcendental materialism' undoubtedly indicates Levi-Strauss' preoccupation with the so called structures of the human mind (Strauss 1966:264). However, Dumont is not preoccupied with the structures of the human mind. Dumont, on his part, is concerned about societies as unique manifestations of the same universal structure (Dumont 1970:186, 232-34, 330). The key concepts constituting the universal structure of Dumont are the *whole* and *hierarchy*. Dumont emphasizes the point that for the Hindus, hierarchy is a conscious fact constituted through the opposition between the pure and the impure. In Capitalism, on the other hand, where hierarchy, according to Dumont, is suppressed to the *unconscious* level, it still by necessity manifests itself in pathological forms as racism, etc. (Dumont 1970:237).

15. Why did Giddens cite structuralism as a Kantianism without a transcendental subject (Giddens 1979:27)? In opposition to the *tabula rasa* of empiricism, we can certainly see a similarity between the cognitive structures of Kant and the structures of Levi-Strauss. But we can also see a similarity with the innate ideas of rationalism. The difference between Kant and structuralism is clear. Structuralism does not account for the relation between action and structure and the individual agent is not in focus at all. Thus the position of Kant has been labelled the *anthropocentric revolution* in the present work.

16. On the surface, Dumont's description of the renouncer and the caste Hindu may appear fascinating. But what seems to be striking on the surface often loses its power by closer

inspection. The common mode of the behaviour of renouncers is as much defined through group identity as that of caste Hindus, something which is testified in Hindu history by the recurring struggles between the sects (Ghurye 1964; Tripathi 1985). Furthermore, when we stress that the focus is ideas and values, the reality will agree even less with the descriptions of Dumont.

17. Elsewhere Dumont (1975) seems to be in doubt himself. It is only in relation to us that our '*individual*' and the renouncer have something in common. A comparison of ideas which can only be understood from one end is dubious.

18. Dumont defines 'ideology' simply as a system of ideas and values (Dumont 1970:4). To deepen the analytical potential of the concept, I restricted the usage of the concept of ideology to those ideas or values which conceal, reify or otherwise justify social structure.

19. Dumont defines Dharma solely in a holistic manner and overlooks the *svadharma* (individual Dharma) connotation of the term (cf. Kunst 1978).

20. It is symptomatic that positivist thinking in general, and Dumont must be counted as a positivist, does not pay attention to Man as a moral and responsible agent (Giddens 1976:95).

21. Following Weber; 'All Hindus accept two basic principles: the samsara belief in the transmigration of souls and the related karman doctrine of compensation. These alone are the truly "dogmatic" doctrines of all Hinduism, and in their very interrelatedness they represent the unique Hindu theodicy of the existing social, that is to say, caste system.' (Weber 1967:118)

22. In addition to the interpretative schemes of karmic ideology, we also find animistic representations combined with exorcism therapies, witchcraft, astrology, etc. To the villagers, there need be no conflict between these diverse schemes of interpretation.

23. On the significance of karma see Srinivas 1962, 1965, 1976; Lewis 1958; Mayer 1966; Babb 1975; Carstairs 1961; Campbell 1976; Karve 196., Berreman 1963; Khare 1970; Edgerton 1942; Naipaul 1979; Keyes and Daniel 1983. A rather interesting source for understanding the significance of karmic ideology is the controversies between Dr Ambedkar and Mahatma Gandhi (and the Congress party) (Ambedkar 1946:307).

24. Radcliffe-Brown's distinction between person and individual is quite symptomatic for the Durkheimian tradition. In social anthropology, according to Radcliffe-Brown, individuals do not exist: '...individuals are objects of study for physiologists and psychologists.' (1971:194)

BIBLIOGRAPHY

SOURCE MATERIAL OF SANSKRITIC HINDUISM

SRIMAD-BHAGAVAD-GITA
With Sanskrit text and English translation. By Swami Swarupananda. Twelfth Revised Edition. Advaita Ashrama, Calcutta, 1976.

SRIMAD BHAGAVADGITA
With Sanskrit text and English translation. By Jayadayal Goyandka. Third edition. Gita Press, Gorakhpur, 1978.

THE BHAGAVAD-GITA
With Sanskrit text and English translation. By R.C. Zaehner. Reprint, Oxford University Press, London 1979.

BRAHMA(VEDANTA)-SUTRAS
With text, word-for-word translation, English rendering, comments according to the commentary of Shankara. By Swami Vireswarananda. Fifth reprint. Advaita Ashrama, Calcutta, 1978.

GARUDA PURANA (SARODDHARA)
With Sanskrit text and English translation. By Ernest Wood and S.V. Subrahmanyam. Bharatiya Publishing House, Varanasi, 1979.

A SOURCEBOOK IN INDIAN PHILOSOPHY
Edited by Sarvepalli Radhakrishnan and Charles A. Moore. Fifth Princeton Paperback Printing. Princeton University Press, N.J., 1973

KAUTILYA'S ARTHASASTRA
Translated by Dr. R. Shamasastry. Sixth Edition. Mysore Printing and Publishing House, Mysore, 1960.

THE LAWS OF MANU
Translated by G. Buhler (Sacred Books of the East, vol. XXV.) Reprint, Motilal Banarsidass, Delhi, 1979.

MAHABHARATA
By C. Rajagopalachari. 21st Edition, Bharatiya Vidya Bhavan, Bombay, 1978.

RAMAYANA
By C. Rajagopalachari. 7th Edition. Bharatiya Vidya Bhavan, Bombay, 1971.

SAMKHYA KARIKA OF ISVARAKRISHNA
By C. Kuhan Raja. With Sanskrit text and English translation. Woolner Indological Series 4. V.V. Research Institute, Sadhu Ashram, Hoshiarpur, 1963.

SATAPHATA-BRAHMANA
Translated by J. Eggeling. (Sacred Books of the East, vol. 1-5). Reprint, Motilal

Banarsidass, Delhi, 1963.

SRIMAD BHAGAVATA MAHAPURANA
Translated by C.L. Goswami. 2 vols. The Gita Press, Gorakhpur, 1971.

THE THIRTEEN PRINCIPAL UPANISHADS
Translated by R.E. Hume. Reprint, Oxford University Press, London, 1975.

BRIHAD-ARANYAKA UPANISHAD
With the commentary of Shankara. With Sanskrit text and English translation. By
Swami Madhavananda. Fifth Edition. Advaita Ashrama, Calcutta, 1975.

EIGHT UPANISHADS
Volume one (Isa, Kena, Katha and Taittiriya). With the commentary of Shankara.
With Sanskrit text and English translation. By Swami Gambhirananda. Fourth
Edition. Advaita Ashrama, Calcutta, 1977.

EIGHT UPANISHADS
Volume two (Aitareya, Mundaka, Mandukya & Karika, and Prashna). With the
commentary of Shankara. With Sanskrit text and English translation. By Swami
Gambhirananda. Fourth Edition. Advaita Ashrama, Calcutta, 1978.

THE CALL OF THE VEDAS
With Sanskrit text and English translation. By A. C. Bose. Third edition. Bharatiya
Vidya Bhavan, Bombay, 1970.

A VEDIC READER FOR STUDENTS
With Sanskrit text and English translation. By A. A. MacDonell. Ninth Edition.
Oxford University Press, Delhi, 1976.

THE VISHNU PURANA:
A SYSTEM OF HINDU MYTHOLOGY AND TRADITION:
Translated by H.H. Wilson. London 1840. Reprint of 3rd ed., Punthi Pustak,
Calcutta, 1972.

PATANJALI'S YOGA SUTRAS
With the commentary of Vyasa and the gloss of Vachaspati Misra. With Sanskrit
text and English translation. By Rama Prasada. Second Edition. Oriental Reprint,
New Delhi, 1978.

BIBLIOGRAPHY

Abercombie, N. et al.:	1980. *The dominant Ideology Thesis*. Allen and Unwin, London.
Aguilar, H.:	1976. *The sacrifice in the Rigveda*. Bharatiya Vidya Prakashan, Delhi.
Alavi, H.:	1973. 'Peasant Classes and Primordial Loyalties', *Journal of Peasant Studies*, vol. 1.
Ambedkar, B.:	1946. *What Congress and Gandhi have done to the Untouchables*. Thacker and Company Limited, Bombay. 1948. *The Untouchables: who were they and how they became untouchables*. Amrit Book Company, New Delhi.
Asad, T.:	1972. 'Market Model, Class Structure and Consent: A Reconsideration of Swat Political Organisation', *Man*, vol. 7.
Babb, L.A.:	1975. *The Divine Hierarchy: Popular Hinduism in Central India*. Columbia University Press, New York.
Barber, B.:	1968. 'Social Mobility in Hindu India' in Silverberg, J. (ed.), *Social mobility in the caste system in India*. Mouton, The Hague.

Barnett, S., Fruzzetti, L., Ostor, A.: 1976. 'Hierarchy Purified: Notes on Dumont and his Critics', *J.O.A.S.*, vol. XXXV, no. 4, pp. 627-646.

Barth, F.:	1966. 'Anthropological Models and Social Reality', *The Royal Society Second Nuffield Lecture*, vol. 165. 1972. 'Et samfunn må forstås ut fra egne forutsetninger', *Forskningsnytt*, no. 4.
Barthes, R.:	1969. *Elements of Semiology*. Cape, London.
Basham, A.L.:	1977. *The Wonder that was India*. Fontana. 1981 *History and doctrines of the Ajivikas*. Motilal Banarsidass, Delhi.
Basu, J.:	1969. *India in the age of the Brahmanas*. Sanskrit Pustak Bhandar, Calcutta.
Baumer, B.:	1976. 'Empirical apperception of time' in *Cultures and time*. The Unesco Press, Paris.
Bauman, Z.:	1972. 'On the philosophical status of ethnomethodology', *Sociological Review*, vol. 21. pp. 5-23. 1973. *Culture as praxis*. Routledge & Kegan Paul, London.
Bailey, F.G.:	1977. *Stratagems and spoils*. Basil Blackwell, Oxford.
Beck, B.E.F.:	1969. 'Colour and heat in South Indian ritual', *Man*, vol. 4. 1972. *Peasant society in Konku: A study of right and left subcastes in South India*. University of British Columbia Press, Vancouver.
Beidler, W.:	1975. *The vision of self in early Vedanta*. Motilal Banarsidass, Delhi.

Bellah, R.N.:   1976. 'Religious Evolution' in Robertson, R. (ed.),
                       Sociology of Religion. Penguin, Harmondsworth.

Berger, P.L.:   1974. *The sacred canopy*, Anchor Books/Doubleday, New York.

Bernstein, R.J.:   1971. *Praxis and Action*. University of Pennsylvania Press,
                       Philadelphia.

Berremann, G.D.:   1963. *Hindus of the Himalayas*. University of California Press,
                       Berkeley.
                       1964. 'Brahmins and Shamans in Pahari Religion', *J.O.A.S.*, vol.
                       23, pp. 53-69.

Beteille, A.:   1965. 'Caste in a South Indian Village' in Beteille, A. (ed.) 1978,
                       Social Inequality. Penguin, Harmondsworth. Pp. 273-294.

Bhagat, M.G.:   1976. *Ancient Indian Asceticism*. Munshiram Manoharlal
                       Publishers Pvt. Ltd., New Delhi.

Bharati, A.:   1963. 'Pilgrimage In The Indian Tradition',
                       History of Religions, vol. 3, no. 1. Chicago.
                       1976. *The Tantric Tradition*. B.I. Publications, New Delhi.
                       1969. 'The Hindu Renaissance and its Apologetic Patterns'
                       J.O.A.S., vol. 24, pp. 267-287.

Bhardwaj, S.M.:   1973. *Hindu Places of Pilgrimage in India - A study in Cultural
                       Geography*.University of California Press, Berkeley.

Bhattacharya, K.:   1964. 'The Status of the Individual in Indian Philosophy',
                       Philosophy East and West, pp. 131-144.

Biardeau, M.:   1965. 'The ego principle in the Upanishad', *CIS*, no. 8, pp. 62-99.

Bloch, M.:   1977. 'The past and the present in the present', *Man* (N.S.), vol. 12.

Bose, A.C.:   1970. *The call of the Vedas*. Bharatiya Vidya Bhavan, Bombay.

Bougle, C.:   1958. 'The essence and reality of the caste system', *CIS*, no. II, pp.7-30.

Briggs, G.W.:   1982. *Gorakhnath and the Kanphata Yogis*. Motilal Banarsidass, Delhi.

Buhler, G.:   1979. See The Laws of Manu.

Campbell, J.G.:   1976. *Saints and householders. A study of Hindu ritual and myth among
                       the Kangra rajputs*. Kathmandu.

Cantile, A.:   1977. 'Aspects of Hindu Asceticism' in Lewis, I. (ed.), *Symbols and
                       Sentiments: cross cultural studies in symbolism*. Academic Press,
                       London, pp. 247-267.

Carstairs, G.M.:   1961. *The Twice-born. A Study of a Community of High-Caste Hindus*,
                       Indiana University Press, Bloomington.

Carus, P.:   1978. *The Gospel of Buddha*. National Book Trust, New Delhi.

Cohen, A.:   1969. 'Political Anthropology: The Analysis of the Symbolism of
                       Power Relations', *Man*, vol. 4.

Cohn, B.S.:   1969. 'The changing status of a depressed caste' in Marriot, McKim. (ed.), *Village India. Studies of the little community*. University of Chicago Press, Chicago and London, pp. 53-77.
1968. 'Notes on the history of the study of Indian society and culture', in Singer, M. and Cohn, B.S. (eds.), *Structure and change in Indian society*. Viking Fund Publications in Anthropology, no. 46, Aldine Chicago, pp. 3-28.

Cohn, B.S. and
Marriott, McKim: 1958. 'Networks and Centres in the Integration of Indian Civilization', *Journal of Social Research*, vol. I, no. 1, pp. 1-9.

Collingwood, R.G.:   1970. *The idea of history*. Oxford University Press, London.

Conze, E.:   1962. *Buddhist thought in India*, George Allen & Unwin Ltd.,London.

Damle, Y.B.:   1968. 'Reference group theory with regard to mobility in caste' in Silverberg, J. (ed.), *Social mobility in the caste system in India*. Mouton, The Hague, pp. 95-102.

Das, V.:   1977. *Structure and cognition. Aspects of Hindu Caste and Ritual*. Oxford University Press, Delhi.

Dasgupta, S.:   1957. *A history of Indian philosophy*. Cambridge University Press, Cambridge.

Davis, M.:   1976. 'A philosophy of Hindu rank from rural West Bengal', *J.O.A.S.*, vol. XXXVI, no. 1.

Derrett, J.D.M.:   1976. 'Rajadharma', *J.O.A.S.*, vol. XXXV, no. 4, pp. 597-609.
1978. 'The Concept of Duty in Ancient Indian Jurisprudence: The Problem of Ascertainment' in O'Flaherty, W.D. & Derrett, J.D.M. (eds.), *The Concept of Duty in South Asia*. Vikas, New Delhi, pp. 18-65.

Devaraja, N.K.:   1972. *An Introduction to Shankara's Theory of Knowledge*. Motilal Banarsidass, Delhi.

Deussen, P.:   1972. *The system of the Vedanta*. Motilal Banarsidass, Delhi.

Douglas, M.:   1980. *Purity and danger. An analysis of the concepts of pollution and taboo*. Routledge & Kegan Paul, London.

Dravid, R.R.:   1972. *The Problem of Universals in Indian Philosophy*. Motilal Banarsidass, Delhi.

Dumont, L.:   1971. 'A Structural Definition of a Deity of Tamil Nad: Aiyanar, the Lord' in *Religion, politics and History in India Collected Papers in Indian Sociology*. Mouton, The Hague, pp. 20-32.
1960. 'World Renunciation in Indian Religions', *CIS*, no. 5, pp. 20-43.
1978. 'Caste, Racism and "Stratification": Reflections of a Social Anthropologist' in Beteille, A. (ed.), *Social Inequality*. Penguin, Harmondsworth, pp. 337-361.
1971. 'The Conception of Kingship in Ancient India' in *Religion, politics* op.cit.
1965. 'The Functional Equivalent of the Individual in Caste Society', *CIS*, no. 8, pp. 85-99.
1965. 'The Modern Conception of the Individual: Notes on Its Genesis', *CIS*, no. 8, pp. 13-61.

174 CAPITAL AND KARMA

1970. *Homo Hierachicus. The Caste System and Its Implications*. The University of Chicago Press, Chicago.
1966. 'A Fundamental Problem in the Sociology of Caste', *CIS*, no. 9, pp. 17-37.
1967. 'Caste: A Phenomenon of Social Structure or an Aspect of Indian Culture?', in Rueck, A. de, and Knight, J. (eds.), *Caste and Race: Comparative Approaches*. J. and A. Churchill, London, pp. 28-38.
1971. 'The Individual as an Impediment to Sociological Comparison and Indian History', in *Religion, politics* op.cit.
1975. 'On the Comparative Understanding of Non-Modern Civilisations', *Daedalus*, CIV, pp. 153-172.
1982. *Way of Life. King, Householder, Renouncer*. Vikas Publishing House, New Delhi.

Dumont, L. and
Pocock, D.F.:
1957. 'For a Sociology of India', *CIS*, no. 1, pp. 7-22.
1957. 'Village studies', *CIS*, no. 1, pp. 23-41.
1957. 'On the different aspects or levels in Hinduism', *CIS*, no. 1, pp. 40-55.
1959. 'Pure and impure', *CIS*, no. 3, pp. 9-40.
1960. 'For a Sociology of India: A Rejoinder to Dr. Bailey', *CIS*, no. 4, pp. 82-89.

Durkheim, E.:
1976. *The elementary forms of the religious life*. George Allen & Unwin, London.

Edgerton, F.:
1942. 'Dominant ideas in the formation of Indian culture', *Journal of the American Oriental Society*, vol. 62, pp. 151-156.
1944. *The Bhagavad-Gita translated and interpreted by Edgerton*. Series, Harward Oriental, vol. 38. 39. Cambridge, pp. 55-80.

Eliade, M.:
1971. *The Myth of the Eternal Return or Cosmos and History*. Princeton University Press, Princeton, N.J.
1969. *YOGA Immortality and Freedom*. Princeton University Press, Princeton, N.J.
1957. 'Time and Eternity in Indian Thought', *Papers from the Eranos yearbook*, N.Y. pp. 173-200.
1974. *Patterns in Comparative Religion*. Meridian, N.Y.
1976. *Det hellige og det profane*. Gyldendahl Norsk Forlag, Oslo.
1977. 'Mythologies of Death: An Introduction', in Reynolds, F.E. and Waugh, E.H. (eds.), *Religious encounters with death: insights from the history and anthropology of religion*. Pennsylvania State University Press, University Park, Pa, pp. 13-23.

Evans-Pritchard, E.E.:
1980. *Witchcraft Oracles and Magic among the Azande*. Oxford University Press,London.

Farquhar, J.N.:
1925. *The Fighting Ascetics of India*.
Bulletin of John Rylands Library, vol.9.

Filliozat,:
1969. *The Classical Doctrine of Indian Medicine: its origin and its Greek parallels*. Delhi.

Fiske, A.:
1972. 'Scheduled Caste Buddhist Organizations', in Mahar, A. (ed.), *The Untouchables in Contemporary India*. University of Arizona Press, Arizona, pp. 113-142.

Fox, R.G:
1969. 'Varna Schemes and Ideological Integration in Indian Society',

Comparative studies in Society and History, vol. 11, pp. 27-45.

Fürer-Haimendorf, C. V.: 1953. 'The After-Life in Indian Tribal Belief', *Journal of the Royal Anthropological Institute*, vol. 83, pp. 37-49.
1963. 'Freedom and conformity in tribal, Hindu and Buddhist societies of India and Nepal', in Bidney, D. (ed.), *The concept of freedom in anthropology*. Mouton, The Hague, pp. 152-169.

Gadamer, H.G.: 1962. 'On the problem of Self understanding', in Linge, D.E. (ed.), *Philosophical Hermeneutics*. University of California Press, Berkeley 1977, pp. 44-58.
1962. 'The Philosophical Foundations of the Twentieth Century', in Linge op.cit, pp. 107-129.
1966. 'The Universality of the Hermeneutical Problem', in Linge op.cit., pp. 3-17.
1966. 'Man and Language', in Linge op.cit. pp. 59-69.
1967. 'On the Scope and Function of Hermeneutical Reflection', in Linge op.cit., pp. 18-43.
1969. 'The Science of the Life-World', in Linge op.cit. pp. 182-197.

Gandhi, M.K.: 1926. *The Bhagavadgita*. Orient Paperbacks, New Delhi.

Gatwood, L.E.: 1985. *Devi and the Spouse Goddess - Women, Sexuality, and Marriage in India*. Manohar Publications, New Delhi.

Geertz, C.: 1973. *The Interpretation of Cultures*. Basic Books, New York.

Gellner, E.: 1979. 'Concepts and society', in Wilson, B.R. (ed.), *Rationality*. Basil Blackwell, Oxford, pp. 18-49.
1975. 'The New Idealism - Cause and Meaning in the Social Sciences', in Giddens, A. (ed.), *Positivism and Sociology*. Heinemann, London, pp. 129-156.

Glasenapp, H.v.: 1942. *The Doctrine of Karman in Jain Philosophy*. Bombay.

Gold, D.: 1987. *The Lord as Guru*. Oxford University Press, New York.

Ghurye, G.S.: 1950. *Caste and Class in India*. Popular Book Depot, Bombay.
1953. *Indian Sadhus*. Popular Prakashan Bombay.

Giddens, A.: 1971. 'The "Individual" in the Writings of Emile Durkheim', *Archives Europeennes de Sociologie*, vol. 12, pp. 210-228.
1976. *New Rules of Sociological Method*. Hutchinson & Co., London
1979. *Central Problems in Social Theory. Action, Structure and Contradiction in Social Analysis*. The Macmillan Press Ltd., London.

Godelier, M.: 1975. 'Antropologi och ekonomi', in Godelier, M., *Bas och överbyggnad*. Bokförlaget Pan Nordstedts, Stockholm.

Gombrich, R.F.: 1975. 'Buddhist Karma and Social Control', *Comparative Studies in Society and History*. Mouton, The Hague, vol. 17, pp. 212-220.

Gonda, J.: 1965. *Change and continuity in Indian Philosophy*. London.

Goody, J. & Watt, J.: 1968. 'The consequences of Literacy', in Goody, J. (ed.), *Literacy in Traditional Societies*. Cambridge University Press, Cambridge.

Gough, E.K.: 1972. 'The Social Structure of a Tanjore Village', in Marriott, M.

(ed.), *Village India*. op.cit. pp. 36-52.
1971. 'Caste in a Tanjore Village', in Leach, E.R. (ed.), *Aspects of Caste in South India, Ceylon and North-West Pakistan*. Cambridge University Press, Cambridge, pp. 11-60.

Gurevich, A.J.:
1976. 'Time as a problem of cultural history', in *Cultures and Time*. The Unesco Press, Paris, pp. 229-245.

Halbfass, W.:
1980. 'Karma. Apurva, and "Natural" Causes: Observations on the Growth and Limits of the Theory of Samsara', in O'Flaherty, W.D. (ed.), *Karma and Rebirth in Classical Indian Traditions*. University of California Press, Berkeley, pp. 268-302.

Harper, E.B.:
1964. 'Ritual Pollution as an Integrator of Caste and Religion', *J.O.A.S.*, vol. 23.

Harris, M.:
1978. *Cows, Pigs, Wars, and Witches. The Riddles of Culture*. Random House, New York.
1980. *Cultural Materialism: The Struggle for a Science of Culture*. Random House, New York.

Harshananda, S.:
1979. *All about Hindu Temples*. Ramakrishna Institute of Moral and Spiritual Education, Mysore.

Havell, E.B.:
1948. *The History of Arian Rule in India*. London.

Heesterman, J.C.:
1964. 'Brahmin, Ritual and Renouncer', *Wiener Zeitschrift für die Kunde Süd und Ost Asiens*, vol. 8, pp. 1-31.
1978. 'Veda and Dharma', in O'Flaherty, W.D. & Derret, D. (eds.), *The concept of duty in South Asia*. Vikas, New Delhi, pp. 80-95.

Hegel, G.W.F.:
1971. *Phenomenology of Mind*. London.
1930. *Grundlinien Der Philosophi Des Rechts*. Leipzig.

Herman, A.L.:
1976. *The Problem of Evil and Indian Thought*. Motilal Banarsidass, Delhi.

Hocart, A.M.:
1950. *Caste, A Comparative Study*. London.

Hopkins, E.W.:
1902. *The Great Epic of India*. New York.

Hopkins, T.J.:
1971. *The Hindu Religious Tradition*. Dickenson Publishing Company, California.

Horton, R.:
1979. 'African Traditional Thought and Western Science', in Wilson, B.R. (ed.), *Rationality*. Basil Blackwell, Oxford, pp. 131-171.

Hume, D.:
1975. *A Treatise of Human Nature*. Oxford.

Hubert, H. & Mauss, M.:
1964. *Sacrifice - its nature and function*. University of Chicago Press, Chicago.

Iyer, K.A.S.:
1969. *Bhartrihari. A study of the Vakyapadiya in the light of the Ancient Commentaries*. Deccan College, Poona.

Jaer, Ø.:
1984. 'Et Arbeidsbegrep for sammenlignende kulturforskning', *Dugnad*, vol. 10., pp. 69-78, Oslo.
1987. 'The Ideological constitution of the Individual', *CIS* (N.S.),

vol. 21, no. 2, Sage Publications, New Delhi.
1995. *Karchana. Lifeworld-Ethnography of an Indian Village.*
Scandinavian University Press, Oslo.

Jarvie, I.C. and Agassi, J.: (1970) 1979. 'The Problem of the Rationality of Magic', in Wilson,
B.R. (ed.), *Rationality.* Basil Blackwell, Oxford, pp. 172-193.

Jeanniere, A.:   1977. 'The pathogenic structures of time in modern societies', in
                         Time and the Philosophies. The Unesco Press, Paris, pp. 107-123.

Jonas, H.:   1963. *The gnostic religion: The message of the alien God and the
                         beginnings of Christianity.* Beacon Press, Boston.

Kant, I.:   1915. *Kritik der prachtischen Vernunft.* Leipzig.
                         1922. *Metaphysik der Sitten.* Leipzig.
                         1925. *Grundlegung zur Metaphysik der Sitten.* Frankfurt.
                         1942. *Critique of pure reason.* London.

Kaplan, D. and
Manners, R.A.:   1972. *Culture Theory.* Prentice Hall, Englewood Cliffs, New Jersey.

Karve, I.:   1961. *Hindu Society - An Interpretation.* Deccan College, Poona.

Keesing, R.M.:   1976. *Cultural Anthropology. A Contemporary Perspective.* Holt,
                         Rineheart and Winston, New York.

Keith, A.B.:   1921. *Karmamimamsa.* London.
                         1925. *The Religion and Philosophy of the Veda and Upanishads.* Vol. 2.
                         Cambridge Massachusetts.

Keyes, C.F. and
Daniel, E.V.:   1983. *Karma - An anthropological Inquiry,*
                         University of California Press, Berkeley.

Khare, R.S.:   1970. *The Changing Brahmans. Associations and Elites among the
                         Kanya-Kubjas of North India.* Chicago University Press, Chicago.

Klausen, A.M.:   1968. *Kerala Fishermen and the Indo-Norwegian Pilot Project.*
                         Universitetsforlaget, Oslo.

Knipe, D.M.:   1977. 'Sapindikarana: The Hindu Rite of Entry into Heaven', in
                         Reynolds, F.E. and Waugh, E.H. (eds.), *Religious Encounters With
                         Death.* Pennsylvania State University Press, Pennsylvania, pp. 111-125.

Kolenda, P.:   1978. *Caste in Contemporary India: Beyond Organic Solidarity.*
                         Benjamin Cummings, Menlo Park, California.

Kopytoff, I.:   1969. 'Ancestors as elders in Africa', in Hammond, P.B. (ed.),
                         Cultural and Social Anthropology: selected readings. Macmillan, New York.

Kosambi, D.D.:   1956. *An Introduction to the Study of Indian History.* Popular Book
                         Depot, Bombay.
                         1965. *The Culture and Civilization of Ancient India.* London.

Kunst, A.:   1978. 'Use and Misuse of Dharma', in O'Flaherty, W.D. & Derrett,
                         J.D.M. (eds.), *The Concept of Duty in South Asia.* Vikas, New Delhi,
                         pp. 3-17.

Larson, G.J.:   1980. 'Karma as a "Sociology of Knowledge" or "Social Psychology" of Process/Praxis', in O'Flaherty, W.D. (ed.), *Karma and Rebirth in Classical Indian Tradition*. University of California Press, Berkeley, pp. 303-316.

Leach, E.:   1961. *Rethinking Anthropology*. Athlone Press, London.
1968. 'Ritual', *International Encyclopedia of the Social Science*, New York.
1971. 'What Should We Mean by Caste', in Leach, E. (ed.), *Aspects of Caste in South India, Ceylon and North-West Pakistan*, Cambridge University Press, Cambridge, pp. 1-10.
1977. *Political Systems of Highland Burma*. The Athlone Press, University of London, London.
1982. *Social Anthropology*. Fontana Paperbacks, Fontana.

LeClair, E.E.:   1968. 'Economic Theory and Economic Anthropology', in LeClair, E.E. and Schneider H.K. (eds.), *Economic Anthropology*. Holt, Rinehart and Winston Inc., New York.

Levi-Strauss, C.:   1966. *The Savage Mind*. The University of Chicago Press, Chicago.
1977. *Structural Anthropology*. Penguin Books Ltd., Harmondsworth.

Lewis, O.:   1958. *Village Life in Northern India*. Vintage books, Illinois.

Lingat, R.:   1963. 'Time and the Dharma'. *CIS*, no. 6.
1973. *The Classical Law of India*. University of California Press, Berkeley.

Littleton, C.:   1966. *The new comparative mythology. An Anthropological assessment of the theories of Georges Dumezil*. California.

Livergood, N.D.:   1967. *Activity in Marx's Philosophy*. Mouton, The Hague.

Lodrick, D.O.:   1981. *Sacred Cows, Sacred Places. Origins and survivals of Animal Homes in India*. University of California Press, Berkeley.

Lukacs, G.:   1971. *History and Class Consciousness*. Merlin, London.

Lukes, S.:   1970. 'Some problems about rationality', in Wilson, B.R. (ed.), *Rationality*. Basil Blackwell, Oxford, pp. 194-213.
1973. *Individualism*. Basil Blackwell, Oxford.
1977. *Power, Radical view*. Macmillan, London.

Lynch, O.M.:   1969. *The Politics of Untouchability*. Colombia University Press, New York.
1977. 'Method and Theory in the Sociology of Louis Dumont: A Reply', in Kenneth David (ed.), *The New Wind. Changing identities in South Asia*. Mouton, The Hague, pp. 239-262.

MacDonald, K.S.:   1979. *The Brahmanas of the Vedas*. Bharatiya Book Corporation, Delhi.

Madan, T.N.:   1962. 'Is the Brahmanic Gotra a grouping of Kin?', *Southwestern Journal of Anthropology*, pp. 59-77.
1985. 'Concerning the Categories Subha and Suddha in Hindu Culture. An explorative Essay', *Journal of Developing societies*, vol. 1., pp. 11-29.

Mahapatra, L.K.:   1978. 'Gods, Kings and the Caste System in India', in Misra, B. and Preston, J. (eds.), *Community, Self and Identity*. Mouton, The Hague, pp. 7-24.

Mahar, M. (ed.):   1972. *The Untouchables in Contemporary India*. University of Arizona Press, Arizona.

Mainkar, T.G.:   1969. *A comparative study of the commentaries of the Bhagavadgita*. Motilal Banarsidass, Delhi.

Maitra, S.K.:   1963. *The Ethics of the Hindus*. University of Calcutta, Calcutta.

Malinowski, B.:   1948. *Magic, Science and Religion and other essays: selected and with an introduction by Robert Redfield*. Boston.

Mandelbaum, D.:   1966. 'Transcendental and Pragmatic Aspects of Religion', *American Anthropologist*, vol. 68.

Maquet, J.J.:   1961. *The Premise of Inequality in Ruanda*. Oxford University Press, London.

Marriott, M.:   1979. 'Little Communities in an Indigenous Civilization', in Marriot, M. (ed.), *Village India: Studies in the Little Community*. The University of Chicago Press, Chicago, pp. 171-222.
1971. 'The Feast of Love', in Singer, M. (ed.), *Krishna: Myths, Rites, and Attitudes*. The University of Chicago Press, Chicago, pp. 200-213.
1976. 'Hindu Transactions: Diversity Without Dualism', in Kapferer, B. (ed.), *Transaction And Meaning*. Philadelhia, pp. 109-142.
1968. 'Multiple Reference in Indian Caste System', in Silverberg, J. (ed.), *Social Mobility in the Caste System in India*. Mouton, The Hague, pp. 103-114.
1968. 'Caste Ranking and Food Transactions: A Matrix Analysis', in Singer, M. and Cohn, B.S. (eds.), *Structure and Change in Indian Society*. Aldine, Chicago, pp. 133-172.
1989. 'Constructing an Indian ethnosociology', *CIS* (N.S.), vol. 23, no.1, pp.1-41.

Marriott, M. and
Inden, R.B.:   1977. 'Toward an Ethnosociology of South Asian Caste Systems', in David, K. (ed.), *The new Wind. Changing identities in South Asia*. Mouton, The Hague, Paris, pp. 227-236.

Marx, K.:   1975. *Economic and Philosophical Manuscripts*. Early Writings MARX. Penguin Books, Harmondsworth, pp. 279-400.
1975. *Theses on Feuerbach*. Early Writings op. cit., pp. 421-424.
1973. *Grundrisse*. Penguin Books, Harmondsworth.
1970. *Contribution to the critique of political economy*. New York.
1969. *Resultate des unmittelbaren Produktionsprozesses*. Frankfurt a.M.
1887. *Capital, vol. 1.*, Progress Publishers, Moscov.
1956. *Capital, vol. 2.*, Progress Publishers, Moscov.
1959. *Capital, vol. 3.*, Progress Publishers Moscow.

Marx, K. and Engels, F.   1970. *The German Ideology*. (ed.) Arthur C.J., Lawrence & Wishart, London.

Mauss, M.:   1964. see Hubert & Mauss op.cit.
1972. *A General Theory of Magic*. Routledge & Kegan Paul, London.
1974. *The Gift*. Routledge & Kegan Paul, London.

Mayer, A.C.:   1966. *Caste & Kinship in Central India*. University of California Press,

Berkeley.

McKormack, W.:   1963. 'Lingyats as a Sect', *Royal Anthropological Institute Journal*, vol. 93, pp. 59-71.

McHale, J.:   1979. 'Time and the future sense', in *Time and the Sciences*. The Unesco Press, Paris, Pp. 85-101.

Miller, E.J.:   1954. 'Caste and territory', *American Anthropologist*, vol. LVI, 3, pp. 410-420.

Mishra, R.S.:   1971. *Studies in Philosophy and Religion*. Bharatiya Vidya Prakashan, Varanasi.

Mokerjee, S.:   1980. *The Buddhist Philosophy of Universal Flux*. Motilal Banarsidass, Delhi.

Moore, C.A. (ed.):   1968. *The Status of the Individual in East and West*. University of Hawaii Press, Honolulu.

Muir, J.:   1874-1890. *Original Sanskrit Texts on the Origin and History of the People of India, their Religion and their Institutions*. 5 vols. London.

Müller, F.M.:   1860. *A History of Ancient Sanskrit Literature so far as it illustrates the primitive Religion of the Hindus*. London.

Nadel, S.F.:   1970. 'Malinowski on Magic and Religion', in Firth, R. (ed.), *Man & Culture*. Routledge & Kegan Paul, London, pp. 189-208.

Naipaul, V.S.:   1979. *India: A Wounded Civilization*. Penguin, Harmondsworth.

Na-Rangsi, S.:   1976. *The Buddhist Concepts of Karma and Rebirth*. Mahamakut Buddhist University, Bangkok.

Obeyesekere, G.:   1980. 'The Rebirth Eschatology and Its Transformations: A Contribution to the Sociology of Early Buddhism', in O'Flaherty, W. (ed.), *Karma and Rebirth in Classical Indian Traditions*. University of California Press, Berkeley.
      1981. *Medusa's Hair: an essay on personal symbols and religious experience*. Chicago University Press, Chicago.

O'Flaherty, W.D.:   1973. *Asceticism and eroticism in the mythology of Siva*. Oxford University Press, London.
      1980. 'Karma and Rebirth in the Vedas and Puranas', in O'Flaherty, W.D. (ed.), *Karma and Rebirth in Classical Indian Traditions*. University of California Press, Berkeley, pp. 3-37.
      1980. *The Origins of Evil in Hindu Mythology*. University of California Press, Berkeley.

Orenstein, H.:   1968. 'Toward a Grammar of Defilement in Hindu Sacred Law', in Singer, M. and Cohn, B.S. (eds.), *Structure and Change in Indian Society*. Aldine, Chicago, pp. 115-132.

Pandey, R.B.:   1969. *Varanasi the heart of Hinduism*. Orient Publishers, Varanasi.
      1969. *Hindu Samskaras*. Motilal Banarsidass, Delhi.

Panikkar, R.:   1972. 'The law of karman and the historical dimension of man', *Philosophy East and West*, vol. XXII, no. 1, pp. 25-43.
      1974. 'Toward a typology of time and temporality in the ancient

Indian tradition', *Philosophy East and West*, vol. 24, no. 2, pp. 161-164.
1976. 'Time and history in the tradition of India: Kala and karma',
in *Cultures and time*. The Unesco Press, Paris, pp. 63-89.

Pappu, S.S.R.P. (ed.)   1987. *The Dimensions of Karma*. Chanakya Publications, Delhi.

Pelto, P.J. and Pelto, G.H.: 1970. *Anthropological Research*. Cambridge University Press,
Cambridge.

Pocock, D.F.:   1962. 'Notes on Jajmani relationship'. *CIS*, vol. VI, pp. 78-95.
1967. 'The Anthropology of Time-Reckoning', in Middleton, J.
(ed.), *Myth and Cosmos. Readings in Mythology and Symbolism*.
University of Texas Press, New York, pp. 301-314.
1972. *Kanbi and Patidar. A study of the Patidar community of Gujarat*.
Clarendon Press, Oxford.

Poggi, G.:   1972. *Images of Society: Essays on the sociological theories of Tocqueville,
Marx, and Durkheim*. Oxford University Press, London.

Polyani, K.:   1957. 'The Economy as Instituted Process', in Polyani, K.,
Arensberg, S., Pearson, H. (eds.), *Trade and Market in the Early
Empires*. The Free Press, New York.

Potter, H.K.:   1964. 'The Naturalistic Principle of Karma', *Philosophy East and
West*, no. XIV, pp. 39-49.
1976. *Presuppositions of India's Philosophies*. Connecticut.
1980. 'The Karma Theory and Its Interpretation in Some Indian
Philosophical Systems', in O'Flaherty, W.D. (ed.), *Karma and rebirth
op.cit.* , pp. 241-209.

Preston, J.J.:   1980. 'Sacred Centres and Symbolic Networks in South Asia'. *The
Mankind Quarterly*, vol. XX, no. 3-4, pp. 259-293.

Radcliffe-Brown, A.R.: 1971. *Structure and Function in Primitive Society*. Routledge & Kegan
Paul, London.
1958. 'Method in Anthropology', in Srinivas, M.N. (ed.), *Selected
Essays*. Chicago, p. 177.

Radhakrishnan, S.:   1971. *Indian Philosophy*. 2 vols. Muirhead Library on Philosophy.
George Allen & Unwin, London.
1980. *The Hindu View of Life*. Unwin Paperbacks, London.
1977. *Eastern Religion and Western Thought*. Oxford University Press,
Delhi.

Radhakrishnan, S.,
Moore, C.A. (eds.)   1973. *A sourcebook in Indian Philosophy*. Princeton University Press,
Princeton, New Jersey.

Raja, C.K.:   1963. *Poet-Philosophers of the Rigveda*. Ganesh & Co. (Madras)
Private Ltd., Madras.
1963. *The Samkhya Karika of Ishvarakrishna*. V.V. Research Institute,
Sadhu Ashram, Hoshiarpur.

Rajagopalacharya, C.   1959. *Hinduism doctrine and way of life*. Bharatiya Vidya Bhavan, Bombay.

Ramanujan, A.K.:   1973. *Speaking of Siva*. Penguin Books. Harmondsworth.

Redfield, R.:   1963. *The little community and Peasant society and culture*. Chicago

University Press, Chicago.

Reyna, R.: 1962. *The Concept of Maya from the Vedas to the 20th Century*. Asia Publishing House, Bombay.

Richards, J.F.,
Nicholas, R.W.: 1976. 'Symposium: The Contributions of Louis Dumont' *J.O.A.S.*, vol. XXXV, no. 4, pp. 579-580.

Rocher, L.: 1980. 'Karma and Rebirth in the Dharmasastras', in O'Flaherty, W.D. (ed.), *Karma and Rebirth op.cit.*, pp. 61-89.

Rowe, W.L.: 1968. 'The New Cauhans: A Caste Mobility Movement in North India', in Silverberg, J. (ed.), *Social Mobility in the Caste System in India*. Mouton, The Hague, pp. 66-77.

Rubin, I.I. 1972. *Essays on Marx's Theory of Value*. Black & Red, Detroit.

Sahlins, M.: 1976. *Stone Age Economics*. Tavistock Publications, London.
1976. *Culture and Practical Reason*. University of Chicago Press, Chicago.

Sartre, J.P.: 1975. *Being and Nothingness*. Washington Square Press, New York.

Saussure, F.de: 1959. *Course in General Linguistics*. Philosophical Library, London.

Schanz, H.J.: 1977. *Til rekonstruktionen af kritikken af den politiske økonomis omfanglogiske status*. Modtrykk, Aarhus.
1977. *Antikritik - reflektioner over kritikken af kapitallogikken*. Modtrykk, Aarhus.

Schmidt, A.: 1971. *The Concept of Nature in Marx*. NLB, London.

Schutz, A.: 1976. *The Phenomenology of the Social World*. Heinemann Educational Books Ltd., London.

Sharma, B.R.: 1972. *The Concept of Atman in the Principal Upanishads*. Dinesh Publications, New Delhi.

Sharma, I.C.: 1965. *Ethical Philosophies of India*. George Allen & Unwin, London.

Singer, M.: 1955. 'The Cultural Pattern of Indian Civilization', *J.O.A.S.*, vol. XV, pp.23-36.
1964. 'The Social Organization of Indian Civilization', *Diogenes*, pp. 84-119.
1971. 'The Radha-Krishna Bhajanas of Madras City', in Singer, M. (ed.), *Krishna: Myths, Rites, and Attitudes*. University of Chicago Press, Chicago, pp. 90-138.
1972. *When a Great Tradition modernises*. Pall Mall, London.

Singer, P.: 1970. *Sadhus and Charisma*. Bombay.

Smart, B.: 1976. *Sociology, phenomenology and Marxian analysis: a critical discussion of the theory and practice of a science of society*. Routledge & Kegan Paul, London.
1982. 'Foucault, Sociology and the problem of Human Agency', *Theory and Society*, vol. 11, pp. 121-141.

Spiro, M.E.:

1971. *Buddhism and Society. A Great Tradition and Its Burmese Vicissitudes*. Allen & Unwin, London.

Srinivas, M.N.:

1965. *Religion and Society among the Coorgs of South India*. Asia P ublishing House, London.
1972. 'The social system of a Mysore Village', in Marriot, M. (ed.), *Village India*. Chicago University Press, Chicago, pp. 1-35.
1959. 'The Dominant Caste in Rampura', *American Anthropologist*, vol. 61, pp. 1-16.
1960. 'The Social Structure of a Mysore Village', in Srinivas, M.N. (ed.), *India's Villages*. Asia Publishing House, Bombay.
1962. *Caste in modern India and other essays*. Media Promoters & Publishers, London.
1980. *INDIA: Social Structure*. Hindustan Publishing Corporation, Delhi.
1976. *The Remembered Village*. Oxford University Press, Delhi.

Staal, F.:

1975. *Exploring Mysticism*. University of California Press, Berkeley.
1963. 'Sanskrit and Sanskritization', *J.O.A.S.*, vol. 22, pp. 261-275.
1969. 'Sanskrit Philosophy of Language', in Sebeok, T.A. (ed.), *Linguistics in South Asia*, vol. 5, Mouton, The Hague, pp. 499-531.

Stcherbatsky, T.:

1976. *The Soul Theory of The Buddhists*. Bharatiya Vidya Prakashan, Delhi.

Steiner, G.:

1977. *After Babel. Aspects of Language and Translation*. Oxford University Press, Oxford.

Stephen, D.J.:

1979. *Studies in Early Indian Thought*. Delhi.

Stevenson, H.N.C.:

1954. 'Status Evaluation in the Hindu Caste System'. *Journal of the Royal Anthropological Institute*, London, pp. 43-65.

Stevenson, I.:

1974. *Twenty Cases Suggestive of Reincarnation*. University Press of Virginia, Charlottesville.

Stevenson, S.:

1929. *The rites of the twice born*. London.

Tendulkar, D.G.:

1961. *Mahatma. Life of Mohandas Karamchand Gandhi*. Delhi.

Thorner, D.:

1966. 'Marx on India and the Asiatic mode of production', *CIS*, vol. 9, pp. 33-69.

Tilak, D.G.:

1935. *Gita Rahasya*. Poona.

Touraine, A.:

1975. 'Towards a Sociology of Action', in Giddens, A. (ed.), *Positivism and Sociology*. Heinemann, London, pp. 75-100.

Turner, B.S.:

1974. 'The concept of social "stationariness": utilitarianism and marxism', *Science and Society*, vol. 38, pp. 3-18.

Vallee Poussin, L.:

1979. *The way to Nirvana*. New York.

Van Buitenen, J.A.B.:

1971. 'On the archaism of the Bhagavata Purana, in Singer, M. (ed.), *Krishna: Myths, Rites, and Attitudes*. University of Chicago Press, Chicago, pp. 23-40.
1974. *Ramanuja on the Bhagavadgita*. Delhi.

Van der Leeuw, G.:   1925. *Einfuhrung in die Phänomenologie der Religion*. Ernst Reinhardt,
                         München.

Varma, V.P.:   1963. 'The Origins and Sociology of the Early Buddhist Philosophy
                         of Moral Determinism', *Philosophy East and West*, vol. 13, pp. 25-47.

Vasu, R.B.S.C.:   1978. 'Introduction', in *Patanjali's Yoga Sutras*. Munshiram
                         Manoharlal Publishers PVT. Ltd., New Delhi.

Venkateswaran, T.K.:   1971. 'Radha-Krishna Bhajanas of South India: A
                         Phenomenological, Theoretical, and Philosophical Study', in
                         Singer, M. (ed.), *Krishna: Myths, Rites, and Attitudes*. Chicago
                         University Press, Chicago, pp. 139-172.

Vireswarananda, S.:   1978. *Brahma-Sutras*. Advaita Ashrama, Calcutta.

Wadley, S.:   1977. 'Power in Hindu Ideology and Practice', in Kenneth, D. (ed.),
                         The new Wind. Changing identities in South Asia. Mouton, The
                         Hague, Paris, pp. 133-157.

Walli, K.:   1977. *Theory of Karman in Indian Thought*. Bharata Manisha,
                         Varanasi.

Walsh, G.:   1976. 'Introduction', in Schutz, A., *The Phenomenology of the Social
                         World*. Heinemann Educational Books, London.

Weber, M.:   1964. *The Theory of Social and Economic Organization*. The Free Press,
                         New York.
                         1967. *The Religion of India*. The Free Press, New York.
                         1964. *The Sociology of Religion*. Beacon Press, Boston.
                         1976. *The Protestant Etic and the Spirit of Capitalism*. George Allen &
                         Unwin, London.
                         1975. 'Subjectivity and Determinism', in Giddens, A. (ed.), *Positivism
                         and Sociology*. Heinemann, London, pp. 23-31.

Whorf, B.L.:   1976. *Language Thought & Reality*. The M.I.T. Press, Massachusetts.

Wilson, B.R.:   1979. 'A Sociologist's Introduction', in Wilson, B.R. (ed.),
                         Rationality. Basil Blackwell, Oxford.

Winch, P.:   1977. *The Idea of a Social Science and its Relation to Philosophy*.
                         Routledge & Kegan Paul, London.

Wiser, W.H.:   1958. *The Hindu Jajmani System: a Socio-Economic System Interrelating
                         Members of a Hindu Village Community in Services*. Lucknow
                         Publishing House, Lucknow.

Witt-Hansen, J.: 1977.   'The Futurologist', in *Time and the Philosophies*. The Unesco Press,
                         Paris, pp. 243-256.

Wrong, D.:   1961. 'The oversocialized conception of the individual', *American
                         Sociological Review*, vol. 26, pp. 183-192.
Yogananda, P.:   1977. *Autobiography of a Yogi*. Bombay.

Zaehner, R.C.:   1979. *The Bhagavad-Gita*. Oxford University Press, London.

Zelliot, E.:   1972. 'Gandhi and Ambedkar - A study in Leadership', in Mahar, M.
                         (ed.), *The Untouchables in Contemporary India*. The University of

Arizona Press, Tucson, pp. 69-96.

Zimmer, H.:   1974. *Myths and Symbols in Indian Art and Civilization*. Princeton University Press, Princeton.

INDEX